Gambling with the Future

THE EVOLUTION OF ABORIGINAL GAMING IN CANADA

Yale D. Belanger

PURICH
PUBLISHING
LIMITED
SASKATOON, SK. CANADA

Purich Publishing Ltd.
Box 23032, Market Mall Post Office, Saskatoon, SK, Canada, S7J 5H3
Phone: (306) 373-5311 Fax: (306) 373-5315 Email: purich@sasktel.net
Website: www.purichpublishing.com

Library and Archives Canada Cataloguing in Publication

Belanger, Yale Deron, 1968-
Gambling with the future : the evolution of aboriginal gaming in Canada / Yale D. Belanger.

(Purich's aboriginal issues series)
Includes bibliographical references and index.
ISBN 1-895830-28-1

1. Indians of North America — Gambling — Canada. 2. Gambling on Indian reservations — Canada. 3. Gambling — Government policy — Canada. 4. Indian business enterprises — Canada.
I. Title. II. Series.

E98.G18B45 2006   338.4'779508997071   C2006-905219-0

Cover design by Duncan Campbell.
Editing, design, layout, and map by Donald Ward.
Index by Ursula Acton.
Printed in Canada by Houghton Boston Printers & Lithographers.

Publishers' Note: Most legal case citations are to CanLII (www.canlii.org), a not-for-profit organization initiated by the Federation of Law Societies of Canada, which provides free access to legal resources.

URLs for websites contained in this book are accurate to the time of writing, to the best of the author's knowledge.

The publishers gratefully acknowledge the assistance of the Cultural Industries Development Fund (Saskatchewan Department of Culture, Youth and Recreation) in the production of this book.

To Tammie-Jai
with love

CONTENTS

ACKNOWLEDGEMENTS

Writing this book has not been an individual effort, as the sole authorship might imply. In fact, the support I received from a number of people during the past three years was integral to the completion of this project.

Purich Publishing has treated me well. In particular, to Don Purich and Karen Bolstad: thanks for taking my (unsolicited) telephone call back in October 2003 when I suggested you take a chance on an unproven scholar and subsequently for sticking with me as I researched this book, completed my dissertation, all the while changing universities in the process. Finally, your critical commentary and optimism enabled the completion of this project while also forcing me to become a more disciplined scholar.

The excellent work of research assistant Yuri Beaulieu greatly expedited the completion of this book. This is the second project I have worked on with Yuri and he has proven himself both a capable researcher and critical thinker, the latter of which I found invaluable during various stages of this project. University of Lethbridge and Alberta Gaming Research Institute (AGRI) librarian Rhys Stevens reviewed an early draft of the manuscript, offering much-needed suggestions that ultimately resulted in an improved product. His demonstrated diligence in sending me online gaming reports and library resource acquisition updates must also be applauded.

I must thank David Newhouse for both introducing me to the field of Aboriginal gaming and providing me with the opportunity to guest edit the *Journal of Aboriginal Economic Development's* (JAED) special issue in 2002 on the subject. Dr. Robert Williams expanded my understanding of where Aboriginal gaming fits into the larger spectrum of gambling research generally while taking the time to respond to my many queries and offering advice and encouragement. I have benefited from quality time spent with Dr. Leroy Little Bear discussing the subtleties of Native law and the evolution of Aboriginal gaming law. Thanks to Dr. Joe Garcea for graciously sharing his research.

This is the first book of mine that Donald Ward has handled as editor, and his careful reading and insightful commentary concerning some of the more dubious sections of my work led to improved clarity. To be sure, the final product differs appreciably from the manuscript I initially submitted, and I commend Don for rendering my academic ramblings more accessible to a wider readership. For the help that Don gave me, I am indebted.

This study could not have been completed without the financial assistance provided by the Alberta Gaming Research Institute (*Small Research Grant Award #S7*); or the permission of the National Archives of Canada (NAC) to research in and quote from their archives.

Finally, special thanks to Tammie-Jai, who has remained incredibly supportive of my work while enduring my preoccupation with First Nations gaming and Native political issues. She has been a source of inspiration and her encouragement and support enabled the completion of this work. It is this dedication and love that make the darkest hours of any academic project appear trivial and infinitely surmountable. I am grateful to have her in my life.

ABBREVIATIONS USED IN THE TEXT

AFN	Assembly of First Nations
AGC	Alberta Gaming Commission
AGLC	Alberta Gaming and Liquor Commission
ALC	Atlantic Lottery Corporation
AMC	Assembly of Manitoba Chiefs
BCE	Before Current Era
BIA	Bureau of Indian Affairs (US)
CAGE	Citizens Against Gambling Expansion
CAGES	Coalition Against Gambling Expansion in Saskatoon
CANDO	Council for the Advancement of Native Development Officers
CAW	Canadian Auto Workers
CDC	Community Development Council
COA	Casino Operating Agreement
CNR	Canadian National Railway
CPR	Canadian Pacific Rail
CUPE	Canadian Union of Public Employees
DIA	Department of Indian Affairs
DIAND	Department of Indian Affairs and Northern Development
FBI	Federal Bureau of Investigation (US)
FNCP	First Nations Casino Project
FNGC	First Nation Gaming Commission
FSI	Federation of Saskatchewan Indians
FSIN	Federation of Saskatchewan Indian Nations
GFA	Gaming Framework Agreement
GTA	Greater Toronto Area
IAA	Indian Association of Alberta
IAB	Indian Affairs Branch
ICNI	Inuit Committee on National Issues
IEDF	Indian Economic Development Fund
IGRA	*Indian Gaming Regulatory Act* (US)
INAC	Indian and Northern Affairs Canada
IRS	Internal Revenue Service (US)
KGC	Kahnawake Gaming Commission
KKTC	Ktunaxa/Kinbasket Tribal Council
LERN	Living Effectively in Rama Now
MCCR	Ministry of Consumer and Commercial Relations
MGCC	Manitoba Gaming Control Commission
MIA	Manitoba Indian Association
MIT	Mohawk Internet Technologies
MLA	Member of the Legislative Assembly

MLC	Manitoba Lotteries Commission
MP	Member of Parliament
NBBC	Native Brotherhood of British Columbia
NAIG	North American Indian Games
NCC	Native Council of Canada
NDP	New Democratic Party
NEDP	Native Economic Development Program
NIB	National Indian Brotherhood
NIGA	National Indian Gaming Association (US)
NIGC	National Indian Gaming Commission (US)
NLRB	National Labor Relations Board (US)
NSGC	Nova Scotia Gaming Corporation
OCN	Opaskwayak Cree Nation
OLC	Ontario Lotteries Corporation
OLGC	Ontario Lottery and Gaming Corporation
OMAA	Ontario Métis Aboriginal Association
OPP	Ontario Provincial Police
PBDC	Paskwayak Business Development Corporation
PSAC	Public Service Alliance of Canada
RCAP	Royal Commission on Aboriginal Peoples
RCMP	Royal Canadian Mounted Police
RDEK	Regional District of East Kootenay
REC	Racing Entertainment Centre
RFP	Request for Proposal
RM	Rural Municipality
RNWMP	Royal North West Mounted Police
RWDSU	Retail, Wholesale and Department Store Union
SARS	Severe Acute Respiratory Syndrome
SCI	Starnet Communications International Inc.
SIGA	Saskatchewan Indian Gaming Authority
SIGL	Saskatchewan Indian Gaming Licensing
SJC	Special Joint Parliamentary Committee
SLGA	Saskatchewan Liquor and Gaming Authority
SPPC	Saskatoon Prairieland Park Corporation
STC	Saskatoon Tribal Council
TGC	Tribal Gaming Commission (US)
TLE	Treaty Land Entitlement
UOI	Union of Ontario Indians
USI	Union of Saskatchewan Indians
VLT	Video Lottery Terminal

Canadian Aboriginal Casinos

1. St. Eugene Mission Resort, Cranbrook
2. Enoch Casino Resort, Enoch First Nation
3. Gold Eagle Casino, North Battleford
4. Northern Lights Casino, Prince Albert
5. Painted Hand Casino, Yorkton
6. Bear Claw Casino, Carlyle
7. Aseneskak Casino, Opaskwayak Cree Nation
8. South Beach Casino, Brokenhead First Nation
9. Golden Eagle Casino, Kenora
10. Casino Rama, Mnjikaning First Nation
11. Blue Heron Charity Casino, Scugog Island   (Casino locations are approximate.)

The Aseneskak Casino, The Pas

A Search for Clarity

On 1 March 1996, the Gold Eagle Casino opened in North Battleford, Saskatchewan. Less than a week later, the Northern Lights Casino opened in Prince Albert. These were the first casinos in Canada to be owned and controlled by First Nations. They were soon followed by others. In July, the Mnjikaning opened its government-sponsored Casino Rama to a receptive Ontario public. It was followed by two more in Saskatchewan: the Bear Claw Casino on the White Bear reserve opened in November, followed by the Painted Hand Casino in Yorkton in December. During this active eight-month period in 1996, the public got its first glimpse into the evolution of First Nations gaming in Canada. In a few years it had expanded from a scattering of bingo parlours on reserves to five high-stakes casinos in two provinces, generating hundreds of millions of dollars during their first year of operations. Despite what appeared to be a rapid emergence of "Indian casinos" nationally, however, the creation of these establishments was not without political and economic resistance.

The phenomenon can be traced to a government-sanctioned, community-based lottery operated by the Opaskwayak Cree Nation (OCN) in Manitoba, beginning in 1984. The Canadian government's historic inability to foster economic development on reserves played a key role in the OCN's decision to pursue gaming, a fact that other First Nation leaders would subsequently emphasize. Combined with the success stories filtering into Canada describing how once-destitute US Indian tribes were now economically viable following the establishment of reservation casinos, gaming appeared to be an economic panacea. First Nations leaders were careful to take the moral high road, arguing that gaming was more than a means of generating quick money to satiate local needs; it was the economic seed that, if properly managed, could fuel local economies from which healthier communities could spring. The resulting jobs would help retain local youth, who would no longer have to seek employment outside their communities. Reliance on government programs would decrease, and political stability would result.

Gaming as self-sufficiency: that was the theme promoted by First Nations leaders who were intent on channelling gaming revenues into community infrastructure, establishing community police and fire departments while advancing health and social programming — in essence, providing First Nations with everything the Canadian government had promised in treaties and policy initiatives but was unable to bring about. From a First Nations perspective, gaming could potentially produce economic stability, thereby engendering political stability and the agency required to compete with neighbouring non-Native communities. Testimonials from First Nations leaders in the early 1990s confirm this belief. In 1993, an Osoyoos band councillor envisaged a proposed $60-million casino resort creating "at least 200 jobs."[1] A planned $40-million resort at Nanaimo anticipated $50 million in annual revenues and 1,500 jobs,[2] and it was expected that a $75-million complex at Kahnawake would produce upwards of 3,000 jobs and $50 million profit during its first year of operations.[3]

The final report of the Royal Commission on Aboriginal Peoples (RCAP), released in 1996, echoed First Nations' fears concerning sluggish economic progress. Its authors urgently recommended government support for community-based initiatives aimed at rebuilding economies "that have been severely disrupted over time, marginalized, and largely stripped of their land and natural resource base," and that "under current conditions and approaches to economic development, we could see little prospect for a better future."[4] The authors prophetically warned, "a more self-reliant economic base for Aboriginal communities and nations will require significant, even radical departures from business as usual."[5]

This book explores the evolution of the First Nations gaming industry in Canada while attempting to shed light on why many First Nations continue to champion gaming as the economic development instrument needed to stimulate reserve economies. The purpose is to examine why First Nations chose gaming, and to show the positive and negative aspects of the experience across Canada. In light of the paucity of literature examining First Nations gaming in Canada, this book seeks to give access to a complex history embracing multiple cultures and political agendas, and to offer a context for those interested in how and why the industry has developed as it has. The industry is fluid in nature, and so this book also underscores the ideological basis of First Nations gaming, its key role in helping to restore a handful of reserve economies, and how it has become a central talking point in the Aboriginal self-government debate.

The economic potential of gaming is what excited First Nation leaders who were seeking to reinvigorate local economies, which by the 1980s were significantly depressed. Historically, First Nations economies relied on a mixture of fishing, hunting, gathering, trapping, and trade. Some chose to accumulate wealth; others did not. These differences notwithstanding, contact with Europeans altered First Nations economies, which became increasingly interdependent with growing settler economies. Despite impressive levels of co-operation and trade, European and British thinkers considered First Nations economies to be substandard. The 17th-century British philosopher John Locke placed them at an early stage of cultural development, which he predicted would transform with greater interaction with settler society:

> A system of European commerce based on the motive to acquire more than one needs, satisfied by surplus production for profit on the market, is economically superior to the American Indian system of hunting and gathering, based on fixed needs and subsistence production, in three crucial respects: it uses the land more productively, it produces a greater quality of conveniences, and it produces far greater opportunities to work and labour by expanding the division of labour.[6]

The settler economy soon came to dominate, and by the 18th century First Nations land bases and resource stocks had been severely eroded.[7] The trend continued into the 1870s when the first numbered treaties were signed. The Canadian government viewed these treaties as land surrenders for cash payments; they provided for the allocation of reserve lands for First Nations' use and benefit, as well as assistance in agriculture, education, and health services. The federal government implemented the *Indian Act* in 1876, imposing Canadian-style governing processes on all aspects of First Nations life. Significantly, the *Act* resulted in the implementation of the band-style municipal governance model which remains in place today. This model limited local powers, hindering First Nations leaders who were seeking to foster economic development. Little changed during the following century; by 1969 the levels of poverty, illness, and social dysfunction on many reserves confirmed that local economic development was at a standstill.

In the late 1970s, Aboriginal leaders initiated an aggressive lobbying effort to re-establish self-government. Within a decade, gaming was also being promoted by a handful of First Nations politicians as the apparatus needed to finance self-government. Considering the escalating costs of Indian Affairs in Canada, it would seem logical that gaming should have been considered, among other strategies, an appropriate solution to many pressing economic issues. But as political scientist W. Dale Mason states in *Indian Gaming*, the roots of First Nations policy development both in the United States and Canada lie "deep in the conflicting worldviews of two peoples: one reared in the European tradition of liberal democratic society; the other, in tribal-based communal societies."[8] This suggests that, when two interpretations of events are polarized, establishing a relevant and mutually acceptable outcome is an onerous task. Researchers working on First Nations issues in Canada can attest to the fact that federal officials have wrestled, albeit minimally, with First Nations policy creation and legislation, but the fundamental conflict Mason highlights has, over time, been refined into a process whereby liberal democratic principles concerned mainly with the rights of individuals within capitalistic societies have come to guide First Nations policy development. The system is far from egalitarian, however, as the government's continued adherence to its myopic vision of First Nations as being in need of societal integration influences all policy and legislative directives aimed at fulfilling the ultimate goal of Indian assimilation.

Despite these difficulties, First Nations leaders continue to promote their self-government agenda and, with it, increased control over gaming. The reason is straightforward: paramount to governing oneself is an established economic foundation to fund the day-to-day process of government. At present, however, the primary source of reliable funding available to First Nations communities is federal and provincial government transfer payments. While these will remain, in one form or another, subsequent to the establishment of self-governance, legitimate self-governance requires financial autonomy. The all-important question, then, is how to finance the system; this is, once again, the primary reason many First Nations leaders are advocating high-stakes gaming. Fuelling this aim are the statistics from the expanding US tribal gaming industry, which confirm in certain cases the tremendous gains to be had by opening reservation casinos, entrenching further in the collective First Nations psyche the attitude that gaming has the potential to be the economic panacea that community leaders' dreams are made of.

Arguably, gaming represents a new twist on an old theme: simply, First Nations leaders seeking economic development and utilizing such opportunities for the benefit of their communities. What gaming advocates initially promoted was nation building — specifically, how to establish the conditions that would, in due course, result in sustained, self-determined, social and economic development while simultaneously creating replicable economic models for other First Nations. Nation building also encompasses the development of "parallel social, economic, cultural, and political institutions run by and for the benefit of" their constituents.[9] Yet successful self-governance requires a continual and consistent funding base.[10] As we shall see, the nation-building agenda has, in turn, stimulated the gaming debate, with First Nations leaders accepting the need to establish strategic direction, create efficient and stable institutions and local policies, and ensure the separation of politics from business management.[11]

Stimulating the debate further is Ottawa's position that a First Nation's right to self-government will be recognized only after it has met the federal criteria necessary to a stable reserve economy. In its Financial Arrangements section, the Inherent Rights Policy of 1995 is clear:

All participants in self-government negotiations must recognize that self-government arrangements will have to be affordable and consistent with the overall social and economic policies and priorities of governments, while at the same time taking into account the specific needs of Aboriginal peoples. In this regard, the fiscal and budgetary capacity of the federal, provincial, territorial and Aboriginal governments or institutions will be a primary determinant of the financing of self-government.[12]

The reason has to do with the fact that reserve-based economic ventures have rarely succeeded, and continue to "play a minor or insignificant role as a source of personal incomes and general revenue for all but a handful of bands/tribes."[13] As First Nations advance their self-governance claims, several revenue-generating endeavours can be anticipated, including resource-sharing agreements, the sharing of tax bases generated from sales and income taxes and gaming revenues, and specific compensation settlements and land transfers, all of which can contribute to a First Nation's government's independent revenue base. Yet self-governance is a double-edged sword, especially when it comes to casino operations. Casinos bring with them a host of social issues and the consequent need to develop community-based programs to deal with them. First Nations leaders are also facing increased opposition to casino development from mainstream Canadian society.

To date, several First Nations communities have gained access to gambling revenues through agreements with provincial authorities. First Nation gambling ventures are regulated in one of three ways: 1) a community applies for a licence as any other charitable organization would; 2) a community negotiates an agreement with the host province to operate a casino, which may be on or off reserve, depending on the province; or 3) a license to conduct gambling events is obtained from a provincially-approved licensing body. First Nations gaming in Saskatchewan, for example, is overseen by the Saskatchewan Indian Gaming Authority (SIGA).[14] These three means of regulation have resulted in eight First Nations-controlled casinos in BC, Saskatchewan, Manitoba, and Ontario. In addition, various First Nations are party to agreements like the Nova Scotia model, which permits Mi'kmaq control over reserve-based video lottery terminals (VLTs). Within two years, there will be at least one new First Nation casino in Alberta (with several applications pending) and two more in Saskatchewan.

Each province may establish its own regulatory environment. In Saskatchewan, four of the six full-time casinos are located on reserves, and First Nations account for more than 70 per cent of the jobs in a work force now numbering more than 1,100. The provinces of Alberta and Manitoba have a gaming policy permitting First Nations casinos, while the Ontario model has the Mnjikaning First Nation acting as host community for Casino Rama, from which revenues are distributed to the 132 provincial First Nations. In Nova Scotia, New Brunswick, Manitoba, and Quebec, agreements are in place permitting First Nations to operate VLTs on reserves, to hold high-stakes bingos, and to sell lottery tickets. Similar agreements do not exist in Newfoundland/Labrador or Prince Edward Island. In BC, the First Nations-controlled enterprise near Cranbrook was one of three casinos — the other two were non-Native — approved in the late 1990s prior to a provincial moratorium on casino expansion.[15]

The reaction to reserve casinos from both politicians and the general public has been mixed. The fact that First Nations gaming in Canada has failed to meet anticipated returns, despite the fact that most casinos are operating in the black, complicates any academic assessment of the industry. The negative reaction from certain mainstream politicians and members of the public may be attributable to gaming's potential to exacerbate social problems. It may also have to do with the idea that casinos seem to be bucking a tradition that has its roots in hand games, complex counting competitions, and well-known events such as lacrosse and derivations of field hockey. To some, high-stakes casinos represent a transition to modernity and the necessity of participating in the Canadian economic process, which, in turn, eschews traditional practice. According to this logic, the alteration of tradition brings a loss of authenticity and purity, prompting some to label the new approach as inauthentic or deviant.[16] But this argument is spurious. First Nations have invariably demonstrated the ability to adapt as required; gaming is simply a modern variation of a traditional practice that has been contextually altered for success. Available evidence demonstrates that tribal casinos in the US are economically advantageous to both the reservation and the state.

Gaming and Economic Development

By the mid-1990s, US tribal gaming had become a legitimate sector within the larger tourist industry.[17] Such was the case in New Mexico, where a 1996 study showed that Indian gaming resulted in a net gain of 15,013 jobs and $250 million in income, along with $24.8 million in state tax revenue directly attributable to gaming.[18] Of the $262.3 million in net earnings, $195.4 million was a result of resident spending while $66.9 million was attributable to tourist spending.[19] By 1999, the overall impact of the Indian casino on the New Mexico economy included 41,173 new jobs, $898.8 million in wages and salaries, and $168.5 million to the state general fund.[20] During this same period in Wisconsin, where Indian casinos had become successful, it is estimated that removing betting limits, increasing hours of operation, and permitting a greater variety of table games would double the number of jobs created, increase income, and swell state sales tax revenue by $50 million annually.[21]

In Minnesota, a 1994 study showed that the per-resident income of workers in the local hospitality and amusement industries was positively affected by the introduction of an Indian casino, although the author was unable to conclude that the casino had a similarly positive impact on surrounding, county-wide personal per capita income.[22] One year later, it was found that the communities nearest to Indian casinos experienced greater growth and, in certain cases, reversed losses in new business development.[23] Indian gaming created both direct and indirect employment without forcing the state to draw on tax revenues.[24] Eight years later, following the introduction of Indian casinos, three of four rural counties sampled in Mississippi, Indiana, Missouri, and Iowa experienced increased employment and income.[25] In Louisiana, too, Indian casinos had a positive impact on both the tribes and the surrounding communities.[26]

Bureau of Indian Affairs statistics indicate that the introduction of Indian gaming in the US has led to increased reservation populations and employment, while reducing poverty. Similarly, non-Indian communities near reservations that have casinos have benefited through increased employment.[27] A national study conducted in 2000 by the Harvard Project on American Indian Economic Development found that Indian casinos were responsible for the realization of significant socio-economic benefits for surrounding communities. In no cases were negative economic impacts observed.[28] The Harvard Project also reported that, "in all but two categories, census-measured socio-economic improvement is greater for gaming reservations than for non-gaming reservations," while admitting that "the progress evident among non-gaming tribes in the 1990s suggests that it is not so much gaming that is driving the socioeconomic changes evident across Indian America as it is a broader policy of Indian self-government."[29] Nevertheless, "the census data make it clear that, on average, Indians on both gaming and non-gaming reservations have a long way to go to with respect to addressing the accumulation of long-enduring socio-economic deficits in Indian Country."[30]

This is not to suggest that gaming is always a win-win situation. There are many social and political issues that must be considered when pursuing a casino project. But again, the paucity of literature examining tribal casinos in the US and the general absence of Canadian data make it difficult to determine the significance of such issues. A national US study conducted in the late 1990s found that the introduction of casino gambling in general resulted in an increase in personal bankruptcy filings, although these numbers corresponded with a general rise in bankruptcies during the mid-1990s which could not be explained by casino gambling.[31] Some authors have taken aim at the Canadian government, describing its regulatory stance as paternalistic and failing to take into account the fact that many people see gambling as a source of entertainment.[32] In terms of a casino's impact on community infrastructure, increases in local traffic undoubtedly affect not only the host community but neighbouring communities as well. A recent study showed that road segments in San Diego needed improvement following the opening of an Indian casino and the resultant increase in traffic. However, there are, as yet, no specific studies that would allow academics and community leaders to elaborate on these issues.[33]

Other issues, such as the introduction of new wealth, has at times resulted in factionalism within American Indian communities and a handful of Canadian ones, undermining economic and cultural revitalization efforts.[34] A peripheral effect of this phenomenon is emergent community divisions that result in political disagreements that range from frustration to violence. The most visible example occurred at Akwesasne through late 1989 and early 1990, where the issue of casino gambling sparked confrontations between Mohawks that ultimately left two men dead.[35] Sioux Harvey's study of how the Pequot and Navajo each approached internal gaming issues indicates that culture plays a critical role in whether a tribal community is prepared to deal with the exigencies of gaming. In the end, the Pequots embraced gaming while the Navajo decided against it, despite the potential economic benefits.[36]

Gaming and Social Pathologies

Canadian statistics show that, since 1992, there has been a 2½ per cent increase in the number of people gambling, with casinos and VLTs listed as the preferred activity. These two activities alone accounted for almost 60 per cent of government revenue from gambling in 2000.[37] This is an impressive figure, and it is the primary reason why Aboriginal communities looking to improve their economies are attracted to casinos. The literature on gaming is problematic, owing to its focus on problem and pathological gaming to the detriment of the economic, social, and political dynamics associated with First Nations gaming. There are no Canadian economic impact studies that examine any of the eight First Nations casinos. Admittedly, while First Nations leaders regularly see gaming as a nation-building issue, problem and pathological gaming are often de-emphasized, as are the associated consequences for individuals, families, and their communities. But this is something First Nations leaders are increasingly aware of, and the issues continue to influence the evolution of First Nations gaming.

Challenging our understanding of these issues is the relative newness of the industry in both Canada and the US and the dearth of research assessing its impact. The majority of studies investigating First Nations problem gaming in Canada were conducted in the 1990s, with Alberta researchers leading the way in prevalence and incidence studies concerning First Nations people.[38] Existing studies imply that First Nations gamblers are as much as three times more likely to develop gambling problems than non-First Nations gamblers — 18 per cent versus six per cent — and that "First Nations communities in Canada likely will be at greater risk, as many of their communities experience high rates of substance abuse and have lower than average levels of income and education."[39] Despite these studies, it is still questionable as to whether First Nations people are statistically more likely to become problem gamblers.

At this period in the history of First Nations gaming, when there are more gamblers than non-gamblers, it is incumbent upon researchers to consider all the potential difficulties that may arise when pursuing gaming.[40] Gambling currently accounts for approximately 10 percent of total leisure expenditures, making it one of the fastest-growing sectors of the economy.[41] It is also estimated that problem gambling among Canadian adults ranges from 1.2 to 1.9 per cent, although results from across Canada indicate that incidents of problem/pathological gambling vary from province to province. A 1995 study concluded that 19 per cent of Ontarians were problem or potentially pathological gamblers, while one per cent was classified as likely pathological gamblers.[42] Similarly, a 1995 Manitoba study showed that 78 per cent of respondents had gambled in the past year, and that, of the total sample, eight per cent were classified as at risk for problems and three per cent were classified as problem gamblers.[43]

The growth of the industry in Canada tends to distort our perceptions about the rise of First Nations problem and pathological gambling. Educated by the media, we come to accept that the majority of the millions of dollars being generated originate from non-First Nations gamblers, and that where First Nations people are gambling, the money is recycled back to the individual in the form of job creation resulting from improved economic conditions or through reserve-based social programs aimed at problem gamblers. Simultaneously, the literature implies that First Nations problem and pathological gaming is a limited phenomenon recent to Canada. Beyond the basic profile of the problem gambler as an unmarried man below the age of 30, there is no clear pattern that suggests problem gambling among First Nations people is significantly higher than it is among the general population.[44]

A number of studies investigating US tribal gaming, on the other hand, suggest that Indians are three times more likely to become problem gamblers. The number of American studies drastically outnumbers those produced in Canada, and we must rely on US data in our attempts to anticipate trends. Anticipating the growth of First Nations gaming, researcher David Hewitt created a study focusing on First Nations problem gambling in Alberta in 1994. A snowball sample of 156 self-identified heavy gamblers aged 15 to 82 was assembled, consisting of 79 per cent status Indians. Fifty-six per cent of the participants were reserve residents while 20 per cent lived in rural areas. Entitled *The Spirit of Bingoland*, Hewitt's team discovered that approximately 95 per cent of respondents experienced at least one significant problem with gambling while regularly reporting economic and social problems.[45]

The problem gamblers identified in the study faced a variety of social issues, including family problems, low income levels, and family and friends with similar problems. Most notably, the study suggested that gambling problems among youth are significant, and that treatment programs are urgently needed.[46] Hewitt conducted a second study the following year that involved a total of 961 First Nations students from 28 Alberta schools to determine gambling prevalence among Alberta First Nations youth in grades 5 to 12. The goal was to illustrate the social, cultural, and personal factors related to gambling and problem gambling. Hewitt showed that 89 per cent had gambled in the past year. He estimated that 28 per cent were problem gamblers, and that another 21 per cent were at risk of developing a problem.[47]

Additional data are needed to evaluate the efficacy of current policies promoting First Nations casinos. In Edmonton, for example, a study found that 76.7 per cent of men and 63.8 per cent of women had gambled more than once, indicating that gambling is a widespread behaviour. The peak age of onset was 25 to 29 years. Pathological gamblers were more likely to have made suicide attempts (13.3 per cent), to have been convicted of offences (26.7 per cent), to be spouse and child abusers (23.3 per cent and 16.7 per cent, respectively) and to have spent long periods unemployed (40 per cent). In addition, eight per cent had trouble at home or work because of gambling, and 60 per cent borrowed or stole to support their activities.[48]

How will the introduction of the Enoch casino west of Edmonton influence these statistics? And how will the introduction of First Nations casinos affect the illegal gambling operations in major urban centres in western Canada? We know that patrons of illegal gambling are predominantly male, and that they range in occupation from professional to blue collar. We know also that expanded legal gambling has had a dampening influence on illegal gambling. Similarly, licensing and regulatory procedures have had a positive impact on corruption in legal gambling, which does not appear to have been infiltrated by organized crime. Moreover, certain types of gambling venues, such as casinos and racetracks, attract certain types of crimes.[49] How will the introduction of additional First Nations casinos affect these trends?

Bringing Clarity

A detailed assessment of decision-making within the Canadian bureaucracy and First Nations communities offers insights into the ways in which the structure of the First Nations-Canada political relationship has over time influenced the development of the First Nations gaming industry. Those nations involved in gaming have reacted in various ways, ranging from co-operation to defiance as provincial and federal jurisdictions sought to retain regulatory authority. This renders impossible the construction of a homogeneous First Nations gaming experience. The goal of this book, then, is to highlight the trends and the similarity of experience. As is the case with all relationships, First Nations-provincial government relationships related to gaming are constantly changing. The long-term ramifications are unknown, and must be analyzed as part of the evolving First Nation experience. This involves a retrospective analysis of where things went wrong economically and how First Nations faced these challenges, resulting in a number of communities gravitating to casinos to improve socio-economic conditions.

Chapters one to seven are arranged chronologically. Chapters one through three introduce the history of Indian gaming in North America in the pre- and post-contact period. In an era dominated by a Protestant theology in which gambling was seen as an ill-advised use of time and energy, First Nations gaming practices came under fire with the arrival of the first colonists and missionaries who were unwilling or unable to accept gaming's economic, theological, political, secular, and cultural roles in First Nations culture. The immediate attack on First Nations gaming practices was largely ineffective, and eventually gave way to the larger, nation-building issues that came to dominate the mid-19th century colonial agenda. The attack on gaming continued through *Indian Act* provisions aimed at eradicating Aboriginal traditions, which, when combined with Ottawa's integration of restrictive British gambling laws, turned what had been a rich gaming tradition into an illegal activity. First Nations gaming interests fell within this matrix of laws, policies, and political relationships, effectively restricting reserve economic development. With the emergence of self-government discussions in the 1980s, First Nations leaders faced with poor reserve economic conditions began to gravitate toward gaming as a cure for their ills.

Chapters four through seven deal with the contemporary history of First Nations gaming, assessing the impact of the US tribal gaming industry on the evolution of its Canadian equivalent, the receptiveness of both First Nations and mainstream Canadian society to gaming, and the dynamics involved with establishing the First Nations gaming industry. Acknowledging that the growth of First Nations gaming brought new challenges, questions, and political pressures to bear, chapters eight to nine explore the political dynamics First Nations leaders continue to face within the industry. The concluding chapter attempts to identify current trends in First Nations gaming, the goal being to identify areas for research if academics are to determine the positive and negative outcomes of gaming. Ultimately, the book's intent is to break down the conceptual, economic, and political barriers hindering the successful growth of the First Nations gaming industry.

The term "First Nation" is used as the primary descriptor for Aboriginal peoples in Canada. The term "Indian," as used in legislation or policy, appears in discussions concerning such legislation or policy and as it refers to issues as they occurred in relation to Indian populations in the United States. Owing to the time period, a multitude of definitions is used to describe First Nations people in Canada. For example, when discussing specific North American Indigenous nations, Cree, Blackfoot, and Ojibwa, to name a few, will be used. Finally, names of communities and bands in this book are those that were in use during the periods under study. The term "Native" is employed as it appears in official correspondence, when describing post-1969 political events, and when discussing the Native perspective of events.

The First Nations gaming industry in Canada is in its infancy, and many of the ramifications of adopting gaming as an economic development tool are as yet unknown. Concerns related to First Nations have become increasingly amplified at a time when many communities are seeking either to expand their operations or to enter the marketplace. In light of the revenues to be had, the question of whether gaming is an appropriate strategy is difficult to answer, and one that can only be examined by each First Nation studying the industry. The intent of this book is to bring clarity to a discussion that threatens to become incomprehensible to outside interests.

CHAPTER ONE

The Historical Perspective

In 1997, researcher Margo Little posed an important question in her Master's thesis, *The Moral Dilemma of High Stakes Gambling in Native Communities*: "Has gambling been an integral part of the distinct society of Natives?"[1] It is a question all academics engaged in the study of First Nations gaming need to consider, as it forces us to examine the historical record to establish gaming and wagering practices and the role they played in First Nations culture prior to and following British and European contact. It suggests, further, that the current trend did not emerge from a vacuum, but that First Nations' desire to use casinos as an economic development tool represents little more than a contemporary twist on an old method of doing things.

Arguably, traditional gaming practices were designed as much for entertainment as they were "group experiences, focusing upon skills necessary to sustain the collective interests of a community," whereas "casino gambling activities are entirely focused upon individuals gaining private property, at the expense of other individuals."[2] Until we are able to appreciate fully the antecedents of First Nations gaming and its significance to the historical culture, however, it is impossible to engage in any meaningful analysis of the role gaming plays in contemporary First Nations society. It is necessary to evaluate how European and British social forces affected these practices, how Canadian Indian policy took aim at and ultimately forced many of these historic practices underground, and how prevailing economic trends have forced First Nations leaders to further alter and expand traditional gaming practices if they were to challenge the socio-economic conditions being experienced on reserves across Canada. The current debate is being framed largely by those who warn of gaming's negative consequences, but even in the face of concerted opposition, First Nations leaders remain loyal to an enterprise they anticipate can benefit their communities, regardless of the short-term social and economic costs.

Gaming as Universal Norm

"Of the universality of gambling there is no doubt," wrote the British historian John Ashton, "and it seems to be inherent in human nature."[3] The earliest reference to gambling as a pastime can be traced back 5,000 years to ancient Egyptian murals that depict board games such as draughts, and tomb paintings that show a nobleman in afterlife playing a game of hounds and jackals.[4] The Egyptians played a variety of games, as evidenced by the possessions of Queen Hatasu (BCE 1600), which included "her draught board, and twenty pieces, ten of light coloured wood, nine of dark wood, and one of ivory — all having a lion's head."[5] Other games were also played, and betting was a regular occurrence; gambling for sheep and antelope was common. The anthropologist Kathryn Gabriel cites evidence that a "Sumerian board game was found in a royal cemetery dated to circa 2600 BCE. Antelope ankle bones, presumed to have been used as dice, are often found in prehistoric tombs and burial caves found around the world."[6] Chinese and Indian games of skill, including chess, illustrate the complexity of the games played in antiquity.

The Greeks and Romans participated in dice games, and soldiers from both cultures used spinning chariot wheels by which to wager — the forerunner of roulette. The Romans also used lotteries to facilitate the division of property among relatives, and as a game of chance for financial gain. This form of gaming became popular in England and Western Europe in the 16th century, as did horse racing, although the latter can be traced further back, with Homer, Ovid, Herodatus and Xenaphon being counted among the earliest turf writers. Card playing emerged in 12th century China, reaching Europe via Spain in the late 14th century; these games were later imported into the Americas by Christopher Columbus. By the early 1600s, horse racing in England was common, with the thoroughbred industry evolving from the horse breeding interests of Henry VIII.[7] Clearly, gaming and betting on games of chance transcends spatial and temporal boundaries.

As various researchers were studying western gaming practices, a handful of academics in the late 19th century began for the first time to examine the phenomenon among First Nations. Most of these writers were anthropologists driven by the popular notion that the North American Indian race was on the verge of extinction, and many visited First Nations communities in an effort to salvage as much data as they could chronicling the "Indians' final days." First Nations games and wagering practices soon became a sub-field of study, resulting in the publication of archaeological papers and ethnographies illustrating First Nations' gaming activities, which were shown to be highly sophisticated, varying by region, age group, gender, season, and purpose.[8] These academics slowly came to accept the proposition that the First Nations of the Americas possessed a rich gaming history as well as a wide variety of games and wagering practices. The current interest in First Nations gaming, then, is not new, but represents a reawakening of academic curiosity that dates back to the late 19th and early 20th centuries.

Academics and popular writers generally accept that pre-contact North American gaming was an important facet of most First Nations societies. In an attempt to better reflect its role, to provide nuances to colonial-First Nations relationships while helping to explain the contemporary First Nations fascination with high-stakes gaming, writers have recently begun to tap the rich written record of the Jesuits, recorded in the *Jesuit Relations*, the correspondence and travelogues of French and British officials, settlers' diaries, and First Nations oral histories. Combined with archaeological evidence from Canada to Panama, this has added to our knowledge of historic First Nations gaming practices. Yet we remain limited in our understanding of these practices, and the apparently rapid evolution of First Nations gaming remains a mystery to many.

Our contemporary academic understanding of historic First Nations gaming practices can, in large part, be traced to the work of Frank Cushing of the Bureau of American Ethnology in Washington, DC, and his colleague, Stewart Culin, who served as Director of the University of Pennsylvania's Museum of Archaeology and Palaeontology, and later as Curator of Ethnology at the Institute in Arts and Sciences of the Brooklyn Museum in New York City, 1890-1920.[9] Both men were deeply interested in Indian games, and their field research reflects their efforts to record as much information as possible before it was lost. Cushing began his research in the 1880s, and travelled throughout the United States, documenting Indian games. Unfortunately, he passed away in 1900, before publishing his findings. Culin picked up where Cushing had left off, and, in 1907, published a massive monograph entitled *Games of the North American Indian*. The 846-page inventory represented 14 years of research and still represents the most comprehensive account to date of Indian games and wagering practices.

Altogether, Culin identified 36 games among the 229 North American tribes he observed. He balked at the notion that games were "trivial in nature and of no particular significance," and in the end his contributions to the field were hailed by W. H. Holmes, Chief of the US Bureau of Ethnology, as demonstrating that games were not only "an integral part of human culture," but that they were "engaged in by both men and women, apparently as a pastime and played persistently." Culin's conclusion that "games of all classes are found to be intimately connected with religious beliefs and practices" was provocative, and, according to Holmes, improved our collective "understanding of the technology of games and of their distribution." Holmes cited Culin as contributing "in a remarkable manner" to our "appreciation of native modes of thought and of the motives and impulses that underlie the conduct of primitive peoples generally." [10]

Despite Holmes's naïve and culturally insensitive commentary, his assessment was nevertheless accurate: Culin had confirmed gaming and gambling to be an integral component of North American First Nations culture. They were both a pastime and an entertainment, and they also had divinatory and magical functions, the latter "performed in order to discover the probable outcome of human effort, representing a desire to secure the guidance of the natural powers by which humanity was assumed to be dominated."[11] It would be more than eight decades before Kathryn Gabriel's study, *Gambler Way,* expanded on Culin's fundamental themes.

Historic Gaming Practices in Canada

Stewart Culin confirmed the pre-contact existence of First Nations games in modern-day Saskatchewan, Manitoba, British Columbia, Quebec, New Brunswick, and Nova Scotia. He examined a number of gaming activities, ranging from straw games to bowl games to more complicated games of chance that involved complex counting systems. Detailed descriptions of betting habits were not included, but Culin did identify the importance of wagering for certain games and described the excitement generated as they grew in intensity. Oral histories and archeological investigations confirm his findings. The remains of gaming equipment have been found throughout Canada, and include disks made of wood, pottery, bone, horn, seashells, fruit pits, and nutshells, as well as wooden sticks and items carved from deer bones, reeds, and animal teeth.[12]

These late 19th and early 20th century academic studies provide a starting point, but there remains a dearth of literature concerning First Nations gaming practices in Canada. It is possible, however, to piece together an understanding of First Nations gaming by using the existing record to determine its importance and the role wagering played in Aboriginal societies. The *Jesuit Relations,* particularly Jean de Brébeuf's commentary on Indian games, is insightful, as are the journals and field notes of fellow missionaries John Long, Nicolas Perrot, François Xavier de Charlevoix, and Paul Le Jeune. Despite the detailed nature of their observations, however, they cannot be taken at face value, for they represent European norms and attitudes. As a result, First Nations gaming was generally presented as an idolatrous pastime in which lazy individuals hoped to improve their living conditions through games of chance that usually ended with the participants losing their possessions. The later historian Francis Jennings suggested that the "Catholic imperative for converting and including the heathen compelled Catholics to learn something about them in order to do the holy work effectively," even if "the Protestant principle of elitism worked out in practice of exclusionism and indifference."[13] Read closely, British and European observations can still convey a sense of the importance of gaming to First Nations people.

The first Europeans to witness Aboriginal games and wagering practices firsthand were the French Récollets and Jesuits. Early correspondence from both groups discussed First Nations wagering on games of chance, concluding that they were indicative of an uncivilized people. Ignoring the complexity of the games themselves, these early missionaries represented the First Nations of this nation as people in need of assistance on their path to civilization. This led to repeated attempts to force them to abandon gaming.[14] Some writers, such as Jerome Lallemant, were able to see beyond their Eurocentric biases to conclude that "this new world has the same nature as the old; it has the same virtues and vices just like Europe."[15] The Récollet Zenobins Membre was also keenly aware that, among First Nations, "much [is] given to play, like all the Indians in America, that I am able to know."[16] His confrère Gabriel Sagard recorded, however, that during his stay among the Huron, they passed their time "gambling, sleeping, singing, dancing, smoking or going to feasts."[17] In western Canada, the Reverend J. W. Wilson wrote that, among the Siksika (Blackfoot) of Alberta, "their chief amusements are horse racing and gambling."[18] This did not deter missionaries from trying to convert them to Christianity, but convincing them to abandon gaming was not easily accomplished. "We give them Instruction or Catechism in our cabin," wrote the Jesuit Paul Le Jeune, "for we have as yet no other suitable Church. This often was the most we can do: for their feasts, dances, and games so occupy them that we cannot get them together as we would like."[19] Similar pronouncements are regularly found in the written record.

For others, gaming and wagering soon became a point of social and academic fascination. Le Jeune, in particular, became more and more intrigued with First Nations gaming, noting in 1633 that, "Sometimes, in order to show that they have courage, a Savage will bind his bare arm to that of another; then putting between the two arms, upon the flesh, a piece of lighted tinder, they leave it until it is entirely consumed, burning themselves to the bone. The man who withdraws his arm and shakes off the fire is considered lacking in courage."[20] He also indicated that "these Savages are great gamblers," and he was surprised to find groups travelling great distances to gamble. This did not hinder him from writing about the amoral nature of First Nations gaming, especially after witnessing what he considered to be severe gambling losses experienced by a newly converted member of the Huron Nation in 1640. Seeking affirmation of his position, he quoted a local leader's objection to gaming and how his people "do nothing but gamble in our cabins." Reacting to these concerns, Le Jeune admonished the participants to "come and confess, and be careful not to hide any of your sins."[21]

Games of chance such as the straw game or the bowl game were written about frequently, although they did not generate the same level of excitement among British and European observers as lacrosse did. Lacrosse was a focal point among the chroniclers of First Nations games as early as the late 16th century. Perhaps this interest was a result of the game's perceived popularity among all First Nations, or it could have resulted from the level of excitement it generated among the spectators. It could also have been owing to its similarity to English team games; observers could relate to it, and it was therefore easier to write about. Lacrosse was estimated to have emerged in the early 15th century, and the games were a public spectacle that could last upwards of three days, with hundreds of players scattered across a field half a mile in width. The Cherokee, Iroquois, Ojibwa, and Choctaw all played lacrosse, and the game often pitted communities against one another, resulting in hefty wagers.[22]

In 1667, the French government agent Nicolas Perrot provided a detailed description of a lacrosse match at Sault Ste. Marie. Lacrosse, he claimed, was the favourite ball game among the First Nations of the region, dating back to at least 1636, and he described in detail the rules and nature of the game. The most telling aspect of his writing was his portrayal of villages wagering with neighbouring communities and the resulting spectator craze as both teams engaged in battle.[23] This description resonates with historian Kenneth Cohen's conclusion that lacrosse was more than a game; it was a diplomatic tool employed to facilitate cross-cultural interaction, both between First Nations and with European and British newcomers.[24]

Gaming of this type was a social event that enabled various bands and larger tribes to interact in a non-hostile environment, permitting the renewal of social, political, and economic relationships. "High revelry" was invariably the result. These events, which could be considered the precursor to the modern-day powwow, whereby individuals from various bands and tribes interact socially and competitively with one another, "were occasions of feasting and gift giving, accompanied by singing, dancing, gambling and contests of skill." As Le Jeune noted, "This year we have seen a solemn game or challenge between two nations, who had a fierce contest." Those "who bet or wagered were seated on either side, watching their players, each favouring his own side with many gestures and many cries, according to their enthusiasm and their interest," resulting in the two nations losing "a quantity of porcelain, and other things which had been staked."[25]

The lack of understanding demonstrated by Europeans and the British concerning the purpose of gaming, its inherent complexities, and its socio-economic role in Aboriginal society are important themes in the literature. The "cultural dimensions of gambling" were "largely ignored," or appear in the literature "as anecdote."[26] Culin's conclusion that "games of pure calculation, such as chess, are entirely absent" is contradicted by the fact that Europeans and Britons alike were confronted with complex games that were largely incomprehensible to the missionaries and early settlers, all of whom had been reared in comparably simple dice and card games.[27] The Jesuit Superior Paul Ragueneau acknowledged the complexity of First Nations games in his dispatches to France, "But, in this almost unexampled poverty, there are nevertheless among them both poor and rich, noble and plebeian; and they have their ornaments, — especially the women, — for the public feasts and ceremonies of games, dances, and feasts, which have little more than the name in common with those of Europe."[28] In their efforts to understand and describe different gaming formats, European and British observers began to categorize games into those of chance and those of skill. Whether by choice or necessity, many of the early writers chose to describe the games in simple terms, and those who did attempt to describe the complexities of certain games wound up admitting that the games were beyond their comprehension. An excellent example is the straw game, which was played with straws or reeds that were uniform in breadth and length. Andrew McFarland David explained:

> In its simplest form, the game consisted, in separating the heap of straws into two parts, one of which each player took, and he whose pile contained the odd number of straws was the winner. Before the division was made the straws were subjected to manipulation, somewhat after the manner of shuffling cards. They were then placed upon a deer-skin or upon whatever other article was selected as the surface on which to play. The player who was able to make the division into two heaps, with many contortions of the body and throwing about of the arms, and with constant utterances to propitiate his good luck, would make a division of the straws with a pointed bone or some similar instrument, himself taking one of the divisions while his adversary took the other. They would then rapidly separate the straws into parcels numbering ten each and determine from the fractional remainders, who had the odd number.[29]

The French, according to the Jesuit Pierre Boucher, were unable to comprehend the game. Some years later, Charlevoix was forced to concede his inability to understand the straw game's rules, describing it "as much of art as of chance in the game and that the Indians are great cheats at it."[30] Did Charlevoix actually witness cheating, or did he use the word to mask his failure to grasp the complexities of a game he described as "purely of the mind and of calculation, in which he who best knows how to add and subtract, to multiply and divide with these straws will surely win"?[31] Missionaries across North America made similar observations about other games, but the complexities of First Nation games did little to convince them of the inaccuracy of their of preconceived notions of "Indians being primitive and ignorant savages."[32]

Clearly, some Europeans were surprised by the ingenuity and complexity of certain games, but few presented First Nations as anything more than primitive. This becomes understandable when one considers that European and British philosophies about gambling saw the practice as ill-advised and a waste of time.

The Puritan ideal of succeeding through hard work was antithetical to the gambler's hope of obtaining a livelihood by participating in games of chance. The gambler was, by definition, lazy and unable to accept societal norms.

Yet the similarity of games among various tribes indicates that they were designed for more than gambling; they also promoted cultural interaction. The Cree, Mississauga, Nipissing, and Ottawa tribes all demonstrated enthusiasm for a contest called the moccasin game. In two separate articles written by anthropologists Alanson Skinner (1915) and Albert Reagan and F. W. Waugh (1919), the Cree of Saskatchewan and the Ojibwa of Fort Bois, Minnesota, were shown to play a variety of similar bowl games, and, in one instance, played the game known as "snow snake" in the same manner.[33]

To observers not conversant with Aboriginal epistemologies, descriptions of gaming and gambling were often confined to the rules and wagering practices. But First Nations gaming extended far beyond these conventions. Gaming in First Nations communities was an important religious rite; it was also used for divination purposes, as evidenced by tales of gambling exploits interwoven into the oral tradition.[34] Games were an important means of wealth distribution as well. In the card games of the Tlinglit in north-western British Columbia, an individual's gambling losses were re-circulated throughout the community.[35] Gaming has also been associated with healing and funerary customs in several First Nations cultures, while Culin describes how, in some cultures, games were held at the request of a sick person in the hopes of becoming well.[36] He also documented how, among the South Dakota Wahpeton and Sisseton, games were used to distribute a dead individual's belongings throughout the community, to the benefit of many.[37]

In 1637, following a missionary's lengthy speech chastising his audience's foolish beliefs and superstitions, the man "fell sick, though not seriously; and for two or three consecutive days the game of dish was played in his cabin, — probably by order of the doctor, or in consequence of some dream. This is one of the excellent remedies they have."[38] Later that year, the Jesuit François Le Mercier claimed a "little hunchback had declared that the whole country was sick; and he had prescribed a remedy, namely, a game of crosse, for its recovery." The request had been forwarded to all the local villages, and "the Captains had set about having it executed, and the young people had not spared their arms."[39] Later that year, a game of lacrosse took place on 16 May following a powerful spiritual leader's warning that the weather, and the fate of the upcoming growing season, depended on a successful game. Three days later, following an unsuccessful game, "nearly half a foot of snow fell and the following night it froze very hard."[40]

In 1670, upwards of 300 people attended what the Jesuit Claude Dablon described as a Huron ceremony near Quebec. The son of a leading headman recently deceased invited various local tribes "to attend the games and spectacles which he wished to hold in his father's honour."[41] A decade later another Jesuit, Jacques Bigot, stationed at Sillery, Quebec, noted:

> Some persons having held games in honour of the Moon, for the recovery of a Young man's health, — notwithstanding all the opposition of The Fathers, and of the more fervent Christians, — nearly all died shortly afterward. This opened the eyes of the others, and made Them Understand that there is a God who wreaks vengeance for the Insults offered to him.[42]

Gaming was frequently mentioned in relation to religious and spiritual forces that missionaries and settlers often associated with magic. Not unlike the modern gambler's faith in good luck charms and otherworldly powers, many First Nation societies believed that gaming could act as a conduit to greater understanding and better luck, and some carried pouches containing good luck charms.[43] The anthropologist John Ewers reported in the 1950s that, prior to Blackfoot horse races, precautions "were taken to prevent a horse medicine man from coming near the race horses for fear that he might use his secret power to make one of the horses tire or falter in the stretch."[44]

Much the same can be said for the relationship between gaming and what Kathryn Gabriel described, inaccurately, as Indian mythology. Oral history was the primary method to catalogue events and social norms and mores, and within this body of knowledge rest stories detailing the significance of gaming to each tribal society. The term "mythology" does little to capture the significance of games to tribal history and social philosophies. Nevertheless, Gabriel did observe that gaming was an important *motif* in oral histories, as did Margo Little, who noted that historic gaming practices "reveal gambling as part of the Native quest for spiritual guidance," adding that gaming was "often a reflection of the tribe's attempt to connect with the positive or good forces in the universe."[45] Culin, Gabriel, and Little all identified the interwoven nature of gambling imagery with creation stories, myths, legends, and songs, representing a varied cross-section of different tribes. From an epistemological perspective, in which constant flux informs gambling practices, participating in games of chance "recreates and relives the establishment of cosmos and meaning out of chaos."[46]

Where gaming is mentioned in the historical record, it is often juxtaposed with missionary pronouncements concerning, and settler amazement at, its frequency and intensity. Thus, while Gabriel Lalemont could write in the *Jesuit Relations* that "Savages, although passionately fond of gambling, show themselves superior to our Europeans. They hardly ever evince either joy in winning or sadness in losing, playing with most remarkable tranquility,"[47] there were also horror stories in which impassioned gambling had led to murder, leading de Brébeuf to proclaim that gambling had never led to a positive outcome. He also wrote that the people he witnessed gambling later informed him personally, "that it is the sole cause of assaults and murders."[48] In 1636 he recorded: "On the 14th of April, the son of Chief Aenons, after having lost at the game of straws a Beaver robe and a collar of four hundred Porcelain beads, had such a fear of meeting his relatives that, not daring to enter the Cabin, he became desperate, and hanged himself to a tree."[49]

Two centuries later, the Jesuit Edward Winslow claimed to have witnessed a gambling-related murder among the Massassiot: "It happened that two of their men fell out as they were in game (for they use gaming as much as any where, and will play away all, even their skin from their backs, yea their wives' skins also, though it may be they are many miles distant from them, as myself have seen,) and growing to great heat, the one killed the other."[50]

Where gaming occurred, so too did wagering. Items wagered could include clothing, horses, weapons, or game pieces. Like gaming, wagering was also used for a variety of reasons beyond simple gambling. It facilitated the movement of goods between different groups, and was a means of exchanging goods without resorting to raiding and open warfare. Large-scale gaming occurred regularly and involved several communities. Lacrosse and the straw and dish games were usually large-scale events involving numerous tribes and exorbitant wagering. As Perrot described it, "This game of straw is ordinarily held in the cabin of the chiefs, which are large, and are, so to speak, the Academy of the Savages."[51] The Iroquois played the game "snow snake" that involved a number of individuals and wagering on the part of large crowds.[52] Among west coast groups such as the Klamath and Flathead, ball games, guessing games, and hand games were played with as few as two players, although they were intended for a large number of participants.[53] Some games involved just a few players, but First Nations gaming generally tended to be community-oriented.

Despite stories to the contrary, gaming, even in large gatherings where feelings ran high, rarely became violent. The Jesuit Paul Du Ru wrote that, among the Chitimacha in particular, "It is astonishing how calmly they gamble. Apparently winning or losing is alike to them, I have enjoyed watching them to notice how impossible it would be to judge the course of the play by their expression, particularly in the games that call for little movement."[54] Similarly, the Récollet missionary Chrestien Le Clercq claimed that participating in gambling activities was more a "diversion, and to enjoy themselves with their friends," adding that Indians he worked with were "very faithful in paying whatever they have lost in the game, without quarrelling or expressing the least word of impatience."[55]

The contrasting perceptions of First Nations gambling speak less about the reality of the situation than about European agendas concerning the need to "civilize the savage." To confirm the inability of Canada's Aboriginal population to control their emotions, and even kill over games of chance, was to impress on one's superiors the need to continue with missionary work. It was an effective means of maintaining one's employment.

Viewed through the European lens, First Nations gaming was often considered the cause of aggressive behaviour. The lack of control displayed by Indians when placing bets became a prevalent theme. Words such as "squander" and "frivolous" were frequently used when describing betting patterns. Culin himself pointed out several occasions in which betting ended with one or more community members losing all their personal possessions. He claimed that, among the Assiniboine of North Dakota, it was common for an individual to "lose everything — horses, dogs, cooking utensils, lodge, wife, even to his wearing apparel, and be obliged to beg an old skin from someone to cover himself."[56] In other cases, European observers criticized individuals for their failure to acknowledge the value of the goods they were wagering, leading one to protest: "They wager a new gun against an old gun which is not worth anything, as readily as if it were good, and they give as a reason that if they are going to win they will win as well against a bad article as against a good one, and that they would rather bet against something than not bet at all."[57]

Such observations fail to integrate First Nations beliefs about the minimal importance of personal possessions, and once again reflect the worldview of the observer. If an individual lost the majority or even all of his possessions, it would not result in extreme personal hardship for that individual, whereas tales from the United Kingdom and Europe speak of families left destitute following high-stakes card games. The concept of wagering and loss as it applied to Europeans and the British did not parallel First Nations gaming and wagering practices. In many First Nations communities, an individual's wealth was frequently measured by the lack of possessions. This is not to suggest that hierarchies, social rank, and prestige were nonexistent; however, in such a setting, a person who lost everything to gambling would still be taken care of, for a community was not healthy unless each of its member was also healthy. Gambling losses were invariably offset by community generosity.

Academic investigators generally left unexamined those games that did not mirror European games of chance. The straw game and the bowl game were considered gaming owing to their similarity to European dice games, whereas toboggan, snowshoe, and canoe races were classified as sports. But First Nations gaming was inclusive; it involved wrestling, jousting, archery, spear throwing, and foot races, to name a few. According to oral histories, sports were a game type that community members could wager on, enabling cross-cultural contact with other groups who wished to participate.

Chroniclers of First Nations games also fail to mention the importance of archery in their field notes and monographs. Bow and arrow technology originated among the Inuit, eventually making its way to southern North America through the Fraser Valley of British Columbia.[58] The bow, used for hunting, warfare, and ceremonies, was an important tool in many societies. To help maintain one's skills, competitive games were developed to test the shooter's accuracy from varying distances. Young boys played a variety of games that improved their overall skills, while adults participated in games for entertainment that often involved healthy wagers. Equestrian events and other games were essential to maintain skills, while providing entertainment as well. In northern Canada, anthropologists tended to overlook the traditional games of the Dene and the Inuit because of their perceived simplicity. At the end of the day, then, we are left with an incomplete catalogue of First Nations games, since many did not fit into the overall cultural dynamic of the observers who were cataloguing them.

Gaming as Vice

The Puritans and religious groups such as the Jesuits arrived in North America intent on civilizing *"les sauvages"* by converting them to Christianity. This resulted in the creation of laws and policies aimed at helping settlers dispossess the original inhabitants of the land, who were considered ill-equipped or not ready to properly use the territories they inhabited. Policies were developed to aid this process, and First Nations found themselves targeted by colonial legislators and missionaries who were determined to civilize them.

The Puritans' early 17th century emigration from England was an attempt to start anew, to escape a society that was in decay. Unfortunately for First Nations, most of the first settlers happened to be anti-gaming zealots. The Puritan ideal of gaming as a vice was, like the image of the Indian as savage, imported to North America and soon became rooted in colonial legislation aimed at retarding gambling in the colonies. According to anthropologist Roy Harvey Pearce, the Puritan knew that he had to be a civilizer, and he saw gaming as an activity that could be exploited to justify draconian measures aimed at altering First Nations' socio-cultural practices. As the colonies became power bases, the Puritans' ability to employ their ideology to civilize the savage grew in a process the historian Robert Berkhofer has labeled "the Indian as justification and rationale."[59] The Puritan drive to abolish gaming hearkened back to the 14th century when the first laws against gaming were introduced in Britain. Gaming statutes were developed during the Hundred Years War (1337-1453), when England was under the threat of attack from France and all male citizens were called upon to be ready to defend the realm. Archers, in particular, were to practice their longbow skills rather than squander their time playing dice games.[60] The longbow was the pre-eminent military weapon of the day, deadly at both long range and at close quarters,[61] and it was critical that archers maintained a regular practice schedule to preserve their skills. Notwithstanding the constant threat of attack, days engaged in battle were few and far between, and many archers took to playing dice to escape boredom.[62]

The English historian John Ashton described this period as one in which gamblers and gamers were considered amoral, yet "dicing went on, unimpaired in popularity."[63] Fearing that his army was in disarray, Richard II (1377-1399) made it a crime punishable by death for any archer to be caught gambling at dice when he was supposed to be improving his longbow skills.[64] A century and a half later, Henry VIII (1509-1547) reaffirmed Richard's statute for similar reasons. The English obsession with dice games continued unabated, "in spite of legal fulminations, until Elizabeth's time, when we probably hear more of it, owing to the greater dissemination of literature in that reign."[65] According to English common law, gambling was not illegal, although Britain's Parliament did pass legislation to curb corruption. As the psychologist Alex Blaszczynski wrote, "The Statutes of Richard II (1388), Edward IV (1477) and Henry VIII (1541) were aimed at discouraging gaming in favour of the maintenance of public order, promoting archery and military practice." He added that, "authorities were concerned that gaming impoverished soldiers, preventing them from purchasing weapons and resulting in many 'heinous murders, robberies and felonies'."[66]

This period in Britain has been described as one in which "people were using their wives and homes as collateral" to play games "that were almost universally fixed by means of dice that were loaded with weights, or shaved off on one side to increase the odds of producing winning or losing combinations of numbers."[67] Gambling houses came to be viewed as social irritants that promoted corruption. In response to public concern, in 1657 the British Parliament passed additional legislation permitting the recovery of gambling debts that had resulted from fraud and other practices, of which the ruling classes were frequently victim.[68] But the statute that criminalized dicing is the point from which the perception of "gaming as a vice" developed, and to which all later statutes can be traced.[69]

In North America, First Nations gaming practices came under attack. Interestingly, the First Nations being studied by clerics showed little interest in the European and British card and dice games that were now infiltrating their communities. It would be several centuries, in fact, before they began to express any interest in them at all. This did not deter missionaries — and, to a lesser extent, colonial officials — from trying to prevent First Nations from gaming of any kind, for gambling was considered incompatible with the goal of elevating First Nations to the level of civilized human societies. Barthélemy Vimont, superior general of the Jesuit mission in Canada, for instance, encouraged a 30-year-old Huron man, Eustache Koukinapou, to abandon gaming, for there was "but one thing that is your tyrant, and that is gambling; it is your passion and your evil spirit. You must give it up entirely if you wish to be a good Christian."[70]

Vimont further admonished Koukinapou that, by "putting your foot in the Church to be made a child of God," he must "resolve firmly to leave the game," warning him further that, as "soon as you perceive that your heart wishes to be wicked, do not allow it to be excited by play. Abandon everything; it is better to lose all than to offend God."[71] Similar efforts by Perrot resulted in the invention of "another Game, — a worldly one, — for destroying all the superstitions of our Savages, and giving them some excellent themes for conversation."[72] Le Mercier described it as "composed of emblems, representing the sacraments, the virtues, the commandments, the principal sins, etc."[73] Entitled *From Point to Point*, it represented "the point of birth to the point of Eternity."[74] Perrot intended to have the game engraved with "directions for playing it given at the bottom of the card on which it will be printed." Le Mercier was impressed at how quickly the Iroquois picked it up, although little mention was made of the game following these initial writings.[75]

The attack on gaming could be seen as one facet of the larger European- and British-led assault on First Nations culture which was aimed at converting First Nations to Christianity. As the French influence waned in North America and missionaries and government officials spent less time interacting with Aboriginal leaders, the British Crown stepped in to accept the role of First Nations guardian. In 1755, the Imperial Indian Department was established to continue the work of civilizing the Indian, this time through policy rather than missionary activities.[76] Aboriginal rights were curtailed as the Crown made its first wholesale attempt to assimilate First Nations into the growing colonial society.[77] By the early 1800s, officials were of the view that the civilizing of First Nations could only be accomplished if individuals rejected tradition and adopted the norms of colonial society.[78]

Canadian Policy

By the turn of the 19th century, First Nations leaders were accustomed to colonial legislation. Laws such as the Royal Proclamation of 1763 had been designed to limit the encroachment of settlers into First Nations' territories, but by the 1830s, the civilization agenda had been formally adopted by the colonial government, and laws and policies aimed at assimilation were developed. Responsibility for First Nations was transferred from the military to the civilian Department of Indian Affairs, resulting in a bureaucracy whose purpose was to guide the cultural integration of Indians into the colonial mainstream.[79] First Nations were increasingly viewed as obstacles to Western expansion. Following Confederation in 1867, the new federal government embarked on an aggressive social program aimed at assimilating the original inhabitants of the land; the policy was considered to be a progressive political approach to cultural differences.[80] The *Indian Act* of 1876 was created to implement assimilation,[81] and beginning in the 1880s, residential schools were established to instruct First Nations children in Canadian cultural norms.[82] The reserve system was established to segregate First

Nations from Canadian society while paradoxically promoting their incorporation into that very society.[83]

The intent of the *Indian Act* was to dismantle historic First Nations political, economic, and social processes, while simultaneously augmenting federal control over them. Indian agents placed on newly established reserves were responsible for enforcing the *Indian Act*, if necessary by withholding treaty entitlements such as food, clothing, housing, and education.[84] The reserve system was established, and municipal-style band councils replaced hereditary councils, thereby enabling First Nations to participate in the Canadian political culture. The band council was, however, "intended to serve as a pliable instrument that would advance the general aims of federal tutelage and support the day-to-day objectives of field officers."[85] The provisions of the *Indian Act* were aimed at encouraging First Nations to alter — and in many cases abandon — the social and cultural practices that had been the foundation of their culture for millennia. The government targeted religious and social practices because "officials and missionaries contended that certain indigenous religious practices were immoral and seriously undermined the assimilative objectives of Canadian Indian Policy."[86]

The Potlatch and the Sundance were outlawed in 1885 and 1894, respectively, as were the games associated with each event. The transformation of First Nations religious ideology and practice was considered essential if the assimilation of First Nations into Canadian society was to succeed. Most games were outlawed, as was any form of wagering. No longer could games be used as a mechanism of wealth distribution. Nor could they be used as a means of promoting inter-tribal contact, predicting future events, asking for spiritual guidance, or even as simple entertainment to promote tribal unity. By this time, historic gaming practices were considered both illegal and immoral.

By the early 20th century, Canada's policy of assimilation resulted in the alteration of First Nations' economic, political, and religious processes. Municipal-style band councils guided by younger men had in most cases become permanent fixtures, replacing hereditary councils. The imposition of Euro-Canadian religions challenged traditional religious beliefs, including the spiritual role of gaming. The government further secured its foothold through a number of failed economic initiatives, such as peasant farming on the prairies, which were designed to hasten First Nations assimilation but had the effect of rendering many First Nations impoverished and reliant on the government for their very survival. One unforeseen consequence of Canada's aggressive assimilative policies was the infiltration of the capitalist mentality into Aboriginal communities. This ideology became prominent, often resulting in an individual's desire to obtain and retain personal possessions, which was antithetical to First Nations gaming where it still existed.

Also by the early 20th century, government officials were showing less concern with gaming. Where it was possible, First Nations leaders developed strategies that enabled the continuation of gaming and gambling. Historian Allison Fuss Mellis has revealed how many Plains Indian cultures, including the Lakota, Crow, and Northern Cheyenne, adapted their equestrian tradition to correspond with US government-sanctioned rodeo events. In Canada, participating in rodeos permitted First Nations individuals to travel to different communities, reaffirming political alliances while renewing familial relationships. This had the effect of circumventing federal acculturation programs while simultaneously strengthening many of what Mellis described as core Indian values: reverence for horses, family, generosity, community, and competition.[87]

Many First Nations traditions went underground, including the Potlatch. A central institution in the social and political life of most plateau and west coast nations, the Potlatch was used both to transfer and confirm property rights while enabling the redistribution of community wealth. Outlawed because it offended capitalist-minded politicians opposed to the giving away of personal possessions, the Potlatch was eventually performed only during Christian holidays, such as Christmas, when gift-giving was an acceptable practice. Games also went underground, where they endured out of sight of the Indian agent.[88]

By the 1960s, First Nations were gaming and wagering more openly, thanks in part to the groundwork laid by a handful of Native political organizations such as the Indian Association of Alberta, the North American Indian Brotherhood, the Union of Saskatchewan Indians, and the Union of Ontario Indians. These organizations lobbied Ottawa for increased political standing, which led, in turn, to a resurgence of traditional Aboriginal values.[89] The revival of powwows and similar competitive gatherings occurred during this period. The North American Indian Games (NAIG) emerged in the late 1960s, as did the American Indian Athletic Association. Powwows became increasingly popular, followed by the creation of the Arctic Winter Games in 1970. The Indigenous Games of the Artic was also created as a social event, emphasizing older Alaskan games such as the scissors broad jump, the kneel jump, the arm pull, the head pull, the toe kick, and the Indian stick pull, to name a few.[90]

Conclusion

First Nations gaming in Canada is an historically documented fact, demonstrating among most Aboriginal communities a continuity of cultural engagement. Early in the colonial occupation of North America, settlers, government officials, and missionaries took aim at what they considered to be pagan practices, including gaming. Despite the limited and culturally biased presentation of First Nations gaming practices, we have been given a glimpse into that world where games of chance were at once secular and religious. First Nations games were easily as complex as European games; they could involve the entire community or as few as two individuals. But the First Nations of this nation did not differentiate between sport and games of chance: that was a European convention that arbitrarily placed the bowl game, the snow snake, archery, equestrian events, and lacrosse into separate categories. Despite the combined secular and theological assault on First Nations gaming, however, the importance of games and wagering to Indigenous cultures did not die out. It resisted the policies that promoted First Nations assimilation into Canadian society, despite the *Indian Act* of 1876 which effectively outlawed First Nations games and wagering. During the late 19th and early 20th centuries, the games went underground, and were played away from the eyes of prying federal Indian agents until a cultural resurgence in the 1960s brought First Nations games once again into the open.

CHAPTER TWO

The Evolution of Canadian Gaming Legislation

At the start of the 20th century, federal legislation had largely curtailed First Nations gaming interests in Canada. By century's end, however, First Nations were significantly involved in the nation's gaming industry — specifically, operating casinos.

Like all other casinos in Canada, First Nations gaming establishments must conform to provincial gaming legislation, which, in turn, dictates how they are to function, including the percentage of the take on games of chance and slot machines, and criteria related to labour unions. That these enterprises should be subject to provincial legislation has been widely challenged by First Nations leaders, who argue that reserve gaming operations are shielded from provincial laws by virtue of section 91(24) of the *British North America Act* of 1867, which recognizes Canada's sole responsibility for "Indians and lands reserved for Indians." As such, state-sanctioned gaming is acceptable, but to operate outside the legislative strictures is to defy provincial jurisdiction and risk *Criminal Code* charges. Despite the ongoing debate, it is important to understand federal and provincial gaming legislation, for these laws dictate to First Nations how their entrepreneurial vision is to unfold.

Today the provinces are responsible for regulating high-stakes gaming — the result of a 1985 provincial-Canada agreement whereby federal officials agreed to transfer jurisdiction for lotteries and other forms of gaming to the provinces. The changes to the *Code* prohibited all forms of lotteries, bingos, and other games of chance unless licensed by the province. As legal scholar Bradford Morse has written, "Although the criminalization of many forms of gambling was not particularly new, the delegation to provincial governments of all regulatory matters represented a significant departure from the past."[1] After Confederation in 1867, Canada assumed responsibility over gaming and developed legislation for its regulation. Post-Confederation gaming legislation was then derived from colonial laws imported from Britain and Europe by anti-gaming zealots in the 17th century. Many of those laws have been changed as circumstance dictated, but the roots of current gaming legislation can be traced back to the idea that gaming is a vice that must be regulated by the state.

Despite the significant growth of the Canadian gaming industry, criminologist Colin Campbell and sociologist Garry Smith have each registered their concern at the lack of scholarly attention paid to the history of legalized gambling in Canada.[2] Their discussion is aimed at how public discourse about gaming has changed over time and how these changes have been built into federal gaming legislation, but the prevalent view of gaming as an immoral activity — which, in turn, has informed policy makers and legislators — continues to influence our understanding of the origins of society's resistance to gaming. In the case of First Nations, this point is particularly salient, especially when we examine popular attitudes about First Nations gaming establishments. What follows is a brief history of the evolution of Canadian gaming legislation, aimed at providing a legal context for later discussions concerning the emergence of First Nations gaming in Canada.

Post-Confederation Gaming Legislation

Following Confederation in 1867, the Parliament imported British gambling legislation that ultimately resulted in federal restrictions on all forms of gaming for the next quarter-century.[3] Politicians took particular aim at lotteries, which were considered synonymous with corruption. The history of European lotteries can be traced to 1434 when a public lottery was held in Sluis, Holland to raise revenues to strengthen the town's defences.[4] Financiers eventually used lotteries to raise funds for North American colonization while encouraging economic development and territorial expansion. The English monarchy, for instance, granted the Virginia Company of London permission to establish a lottery to raise money for colonial operations. While lotteries "had been a device employed by the Crown in England since the early 16th century to raise funds for public works," and "continued to be lawful so long as they were authorized by parliament,"[5] they were eventually abolished following complaints that the Crown was losing both money and control over colonial expansion.[6] The loss of revenue eventually led to the Virginia Company's dissolution, although at one point all thirteen colonies of the original United States employed lottery schemes and encouraged their citizens to play as a civic responsibility.[7] Benjamin Franklin once supervised a Pennsylvania lottery to raise money to buy guns. In 1744, the colony of Massachusetts used a lottery to raise money to defend the Atlantic coast against French incursions. Following the start of the War of Independence, a lottery was initiated to help finance the struggle against the British, who had made lotteries illegal in 1769.[8]

Lotteries were not as popular in Canada, although they did occur in areas occupied by the French for the benefit of the Catholic Church.[9] They were subject to regulation in Upper and Lower Canada and eventually outlawed in 1856, although pressure from the Church resulted in Canada East amending the laws to permit lotteries for charitable purposes as long as cash prizes were not offered.[10] Nevertheless, in the United States, after "scandal and fraud in the lottery system was revealed in the 19th century, states began to outlaw the use of lotteries."[11] Canada soon followed suit.

In 1886, Parliament amalgamated existing English statutes regarding lotteries and games of chance into a general Act.[12] This did not deter groups across Canada from trying to use lotteries to raise funds. Montreal resident Sir Robert Herbert, representing the English Land and Colonization Company of the Province of Quebec, concocted one of the more grandiose schemes of the period. Working with Ontario brewer Henry Calcutt and James Alexander of Guelph, Herbert was intent on settling "the fertile lands of the magnificent province of Quebec."[13] An application was submitted to the federal Minister of Justice requesting that the government authorize the Royal Colonization Lottery scheduled for 16 December, when "fifty-thousand pounds worth of real estate and other valuable property will be distributed."[14] In all, Herbert and his colleagues claimed that, of the £50,000 in prizes, they would give away 100 homestead farms, 50 lots, and nine larger prizes of real estate valued at £22,000.[15] In those instances where a winner did not want to accept land as a prize, lottery officials promised that they were "prepared to find a purchaser for the land within 60 days from the day of the drawing at a discount of five per cent should the winners prefer cash."[16]

It would appear that the application was not processed, and officials outside the Justice Ministry were not informed of the lottery. All the same, Herbert and his colleagues forged ahead, contracting with the Montreal Advertising Company to promote the event in both Canada and the United Kingdom.[17] By September, however, a number of federal politicians had been alerted to the scheme through correspondence from the Office of the High Commissioner for Canada in London.[18] The manager of the Bank of Montreal wrote the federal Minister of Justice, informing him that they were not the bankers for the lottery, as claimed in the official advertising.[19] By early November, the Secretary of State in Ottawa was informed that the lottery application had been denied, "on account of the objections which it presents."[20] In the end, the Royal Colonization Lottery never took place. The Minister of Justice wrote to the Lieutenant-Governor of Quebec, reminding him that lottery schemes were illegal while suggesting curative action to prevent the lottery from taking place.[21] He also alerted the Postmaster General of Canada, who immediately forwarded instructions to the Postmaster of Montreal "to restrain delivery of correspondence addressed to the Royal Colonization Lottery."[22]

By 1892 the *Criminal Code of Canada* had been enacted, absorbing English statutes concerning lotteries. Based on a codification of English common law, the *Code* reflected the 1802 English *Gaming Act*, the preamble to which stressed the need to protect "servants, children, and unwary persons."[23] It permitted raffles "in a restricted setting of a charity or religious bazaar if permission had been granted by a municipality, the article being given away was not valued at more than $50, and it had been first been offered for public sale."[24] The new *Code's* gaming provisions reflected the attempt by colonial legislators to establish independent gambling legislation in Canada, and it was little more than a facsimile of the British-influenced *Gaming Act* of 1802, demonstrating an inability on the part of Canadian legislators to rely on anything other than precedent to guide them. Strict adherence to the *Gaming Act* reflected what had, by Confederation, become the societal internalization of Victorian beliefs concerning morals, economics, and social organization in Canada: the notion that gambling challenged the sanctity of work and self-discipline, threatened family stability, diverted revenues from legitimate businesses, and inevitably resulted in crime, bankruptcy, unemployment, and suicide.[25] *Criminal Code* amendments prohibited governments and individuals alike from keeping a common gaming house, conducting lotteries, cheating at play, or gambling in public conveyances.[26]

Restrictions on gambling were gradually eased, however, and in 1896 the *Code* was for the first time amended to permit betting between individuals on horse racing. Amendments in 1900 allowed small raffles — not to exceed $50 in prize money — while sanctioning limited forms of gambling that fell into two categories: games of chance offered at agricultural fairs and exhibitions, and government-chartered racetracks. Local associations, accordingly, began to organize events at fairs and exhibitions to raise money for educational activities. The Canadian Parliament during this period also began awarding gaming privileges to private, incorporated turf clubs, which historian Suzanne Morton has described as "a powerful, real, and self-styled gentry in Canada that continued well into the 20th century."[27] In 1906, the *Criminal Code* gambling provisions were once again amended, only this time the term "lottery scheme" was included — a not insignificant phrase that was interpreted to include all games of chance, including bingo, roulette, and blackjack.[28]

Ironically, these amendments occurred during an era of increasing opposition to gaming Canada-wide. By the early 1900s, groups such as the Moral and Social Reform Council of Canada had generated a fervent moral opposition to gambling, and in 1909 H. H. Miller, MP, brought a Private Member's Bill before the House of Commons seeking to limit the growing business of betting on horse racing. Intent on eliminating gambling on and off the track, the Bill provoked extensive deliberations in the House. It passed second reading on 3 December 1909, and it was suggested that a Select Committee be established for further investigation. Following a public debate before a Special Committee of the House of Commons in early 1910, the Miller Bill was eventually amended. Owing in part to the undeniable fact that many Canadians were not opposed to gambling, the government sanctioned pari-mutuel betting on horse races, a system whereby gamblers who had backed the first three places split the bets made by the losers, with a percentage of the total presented to the track. The Bill had an unintended consequence: while it made betting on horse races legal, it granted horse racing a legal monopoly that lasted for seven decades. The government legalized temporary games of chance the same year, provided the revenues were used for charitable or religious purposes. As Campbell and Smith observed, "horse racing clearly enjoyed support from an influential coterie of successful businessmen who owned, bred and raced horses who recognized the economic benefits accruing to their sport through the vehicle of racetrack gambling."[29]

Following Canada's entrance into World War I, opposition to gaming once again flourished, although this time it was focused not on the immorality of gambling but on the assertion that it was "counter-productive to Canada's commitment to the War effort."[30] Responding to anti-gaming lobbyists, Prime Minister Robert Borden's Progressive Conservative government passed an Order-in-Council that came into effect on 1 August 1917, declaring that, "in view of the conditions created by the present war and the desirability of encouraging in every way possible thrift and economy . . . and of taking steps to prevent as far as possible extravagant and unnecessary expenditure, that the exception in favour of horse racing . . . should be rescinded during the continuance of the present war and immediately thereafter."[31] Borden later appointed a one-person Royal Commission — Dr. J. G. Rutherford — to investigate horse racing in Canada. Following a trip across Canada to hold public hearings, Rutherford recommended not only the resumption of horse racing but the introduction of pari-mutuel betting machines. The Order-in-Council was rescinded and the *Criminal Code* was amended to reflect the Royal Commission's recommendations.

The early 1920s were characterized by the easing of gaming provisions, to the chagrin of moralists who maintained their lobbying efforts. Parliament responded in 1926 by strengthening the ban on dice games, owing to an influx of professional con men to Montreal;[32] the ban remained in place until 1998. It was during this period that Ottawa began to distance itself from enforcing *Criminal Code* gambling provisions, permitting local authorities to assume jurisdiction. Ironically, this made it difficult for local authorities to regulate gaming, as it remained a federal responsibility. In a paper detailing the polarizing effect poker playing had on the citizens of early 20th century Lethbridge, Alberta, historian Chris Hosgood examined how "gambling cut to the heart of social, moral, religious and cultural tensions," describing how local officials, including the chief of police, were unable to deal with gaming activities owing to their inability to charge gamblers with violations of local by-laws; responsibility for regulating gambling lay with the federal government.[33] The issue of jurisdiction was hotly debated, the people of Lethbridge complaining that federal officials failed to employ the *Criminal Code* to halt corrupt activities, despite the fact that responsibility for law enforcement lay with the federal government.[34]

Two other episodes in southern Alberta are informative. The first occurred in December 1912 following the Lethbridge Police's arrest of 15 men for violating a city by-law prohibiting gambling. The men were found guilty, but their convictions were quashed on appeal. The message, according to Hosgood, was that "gamblers would have to be charged under the *Criminal Code*."[35] In October 1913, a gambling operation in nearby Granum was shut down by the Royal North West Mounted Police, and eight men were charged with playing or looking in on a common gaming house. Six of the men were eventually convicted, and, despite claims of police incompetence that resulted in as many as 12 men escaping the raid, regional gambling was temporarily halted. The raid was based on reports that the gamblers were being deceived and losing large sums of money. The Deputy General of Alberta, in a letter to an irate moral reformer in 1912, explained that "the Provincial Government is powerless to take action against persons who gamble unless there is something in the nature of a rake-off by the persons in control of the premises." He went on to state that the "fact that people meet and play with each other for money, without anyone other than themselves losing or making money, does not constitute an offense under the *Code*," and further claimed that "until the law is amended, the Provincial authorities are helpless." All charges were eventually dropped, owing to a lack of evidence indicating that a rake-off had in fact been occurring. This was no doubt disappointing to local officials and the RNWMP, who claimed that, "despite months of reconnaissance, weeks of planning, the hiring of an informant, a decision to by-pass local law enforcement officers who might compromise the operation, and a dramatic late night raid, jurisdictional conflict and legal uncertainty compromised and embarrassed police attempts to control gambling."[36] There are additional examples from across Canada demonstrating local, provincial, and federal attempts to end gambling and how the *Criminal Code* often hindered them in their efforts.

By 1925, pro-gambling lobby efforts, specifically by members of agricultural fairs and exhibitions, resulted in a *Criminal Code* amendment enabling operators to offer games of chance at agricultural fairgrounds during annual fairs. Agricultural Minister W. R. Motherwell, who had been attempting to rescind post-World War I legislation making raffles and games of chance illegal on midways,[37] acknowledged that many provinces found gambling at fairs an essential element in financing educational and agricultural activities. Motherwell later spoke of the need to reinstate games of chance at a time of increasing resistance to legalized gambling. The Province of Alberta led the fight to see gambling provisions expanded to formally exempt fraternal organizations. Supported mainly by the Elks, officials claimed that their petition campaign had, as of 1930, netted the support of 60 Members of Parliament. Minister of Justice Ernest Lapointe, however, declined to act, and even refused to propose the idea to Parliament.[38]

This type of gambling was, according to Campbell and Smith, presented during the 1930s as "contributing to the viability of the fairs" which, in turn, contributed to improving "regional economic growth and prosperity."[39] Not all types of gaming were gaining in popularity, however. Federal officials reacted negatively to the introduction of the Irish Sweepstakes to Canada during the Depression, though prohibitionists were upset that the law making it illegal to purchase or possess tickets rarely deterred those seeking to play the Sweepstakes.[40] This helped fuel opposition in Parliament to the lottery, which in the shifting gambling discourse of the day was now being portrayed as "a *disease* that held potential to *addict* individuals." Lotteries, according to one MP, could lead to more "extensive legalized gambling, and gambling is a disease once you get the germ is pretty hard to shake."[41] At the same time, political and public discussion began to refer to gaming as more than simply racetrack gambling, and lotteries were for the first time potentially being considered as a source of much-needed revenues to assist the federal and provincial governments with social programs during the Depression. In Vancouver in 1932, for example, a plebiscite was held to determine voter support for a proposed provincial sweepstakes, and 72 per cent of voters supported the proposal.[42]

The Depression's impact in Canada led Liberal MP C. G. Power to sponsor a Private Member's Bill in 1933 that would enable provincial Attorneys General to authorize sweepstakes.[43] As with the Miller Bill of 1910, gaming opponents expressed concern over what they deemed to be the immoral nature of gambling. When put to a vote in April 1933, the Bill was defeated 76 to 15. The debate did not end there, however, for "a bill identical to the one defeated in 1933 was introduced and passed in the Senate in 1934."[44] Again, opposition to the Bill was significant. Opponents cited the difficulty of obtaining convictions from illegal gambling, although there was no evidence to support such assertions. Nevertheless, Prime Minister R. B. Bennett's personal opposition to the bill led to its dying on the order paper six months after it was tabled.[45] Three further attempts to reintroduce lottery legislation were soundly defeated during the next three years. While new laws aimed at better defining gambling were regularly defeated, *Criminal Code* amendments were ratified to appease gambling proponents; in 1938 the *Code* was again amended to permit gambling at incorporated social clubs and at places used "occasionally" by charitable or religious organizations.

The Move Toward Lotteries

During the next 15 years, various changes occurred in Canada's gambling laws. The gaming furor had not abated, but various jurisdictions pursued lotteries at different times. In 1948, for example, the Attorney General of Manitoba laid charges in response to a complaint about a Winnipeg lottery, although the proceeds were used chiefly for charitable purposes and public service activities. The charges were later dismissed when the courts determined that the activity was not illegal according to the *Criminal Code*. The matter was later referred to the Deputy Minister of Justice, F. P. Varcoe, who also expressed the opinion that the lottery could not be considered illegal. In the interim, the Postmaster General became involved and refused to deliver mail addressed to the lottery operators, citing the *Post Office Act*, which made it illegal to manage lotteries through the mail. Varcoe supported the Postmaster General, indicating that the latter's powers "were broad enough to refuse access to the mails even to organizations and activities declared legal by the courts." Cabinet was later informed that "officials of the Post Office had expressed the opinion that any change in this present practice of refusing mailing privileges to those engaged in lotteries, regardless of their legality, would result in the development of numerous undesirable practices in this connection." Although the Cabinet agreed to return all seized mail to the lottery operators, it also concluded that "the Postmaster General should reserve full freedom of action in the exercise of his discretionary powers so that he might refuse mail services in the event that" the mails are used "for purposes of this sort."[46]

In 1949, for the first time since its inception, the *Criminal Code of Canada* underwent a review by a Royal Commission. The goal was to "revise ambiguities, adopt uniform language, eliminate inconsistencies, rearrange provisions and Parts, simplify and make the *Code* exhaustive."[47] Owing to the controversial nature of gaming, however, the commission refused to address gambling laws. A Joint Parliamentary Committee was struck in 1954 to examine the issue, and the hearings were open to the public. The committee considered the expansion of legalized gambling, but instead chose to maintain the status quo.[48] Although committee members acknowledged the growing support for lotteries across the country, if operated for charitable and benevolent purposes, they ultimately recommended that no state lotteries be established in Canada — simultaneously initiating a period in which the federal government had sole authority over gambling legislation while limiting public participation in the process.[49]

Despite the committee's recommendations, Cabinet had begun to consider amending the *Criminal Code* to make lotteries legal. In February 1959, Minister of Justice E. Davie Fulton suggested to Cabinet that he "be authorized to proceed with the preparation of new provisions regarding lotteries and gambling," and that "further study be given to these matters with a view to submitting possible amendments in 1960." Quebec had by this time created a bill authorizing provincial lotteries to raise funds for hospitals and universities, and provincial officials were seeking federal approval prior to putting the legislation into effect. Cabinet approved the Quebec initiative, but eight months later withdrew its support, arguing "that no government would get any advantage by trying to settle the lotteries question, and none of the provinces, except Quebec, wished to be saddled with the responsibility." It was agreed "not to introduce at the forthcoming session amendments to the *Criminal Code* to authorize lotteries."[50] The decision halted Quebec's attempts to establish a provincial lottery.

The next year, the Department of Justice once again initiated debate on the issue, this time by preparing a draft amendment to the appropriate *Criminal Code* sections. It was anticipated that the proposed amendments "would give the provinces authority, within defined limits, to determine what kinds of lotteries were permissible within each province."[51] The lotteries would be confined to provincial boundaries, so that one province could not canvass in another. Once again Cabinet considered the proposal, and while most ministers agreed that "the substance of the proposed scheme would represent an improvement in the rather archaic provisions of the *Criminal Code* on lotteries and gambling," many were also concerned that "such action would provoke public controversy, and the intention of the government would be misinterpreted in some quarters."[52] Supporters of the amendment argued that most Canadians would favour "the relaxation of laws on lotteries and gambling, and that the government would win kudos by taking an initiative on this subject."[53] Despite a prolonged debate, the Cabinet once again refused to pursue changes to federal gambling legislation.

Pressure from Quebec remained strong, however, forcing federal officials once again to revisit the issue in January 1963. Responding to Quebec Premier Jean Lesage's demands for *Criminal Code* amendments to permit Quebec to conduct lotteries, Cabinet replied that, notwithstanding support for the proposal in Quebec, many federal ministers were unwilling to sanction provincial lotteries.[54] When it was suggested that the "federal government might be widely criticized . . . if it appeared to be blocking the holding of lotteries," a meeting of provincial Attorneys General was proposed so that "a plan might be worked out for amendment of the *Criminal Code* to permit lotteries subject to appropriate financial limits and to special forms of supervision, and to licensing by provincial or municipal authorities."[55] Recommending a transfer of responsibility from federal to provincial jurisdictions and the creation of a licensing process was unprecedented. This time Cabinet agreed that lotteries for public revenue purposes should be permitted, though it informed Lesage that it would not propose *Criminal Code* amendments during the current session of Parliament.[56]

In April 1963, Lester B. Pearson led the Liberal Party to victory over John G. Diefenbaker's Progressive Conservatives, and by the end of the year the new government had suggested that "the *Criminal Code of Canada* be amended so as to permit the operation of an annual lottery by provincial governments, with suitable restrictions on the sale of tickets other than the province of origin." In particular, "the present provisions of the *Criminal Code* relating to gaming and lotteries were in need of revision." There was "general agreement that, if lotteries were to be legalized, such provisions should apply equally in all provinces."[57] Cabinet authorized Minister of Justice Lionel Chevrier to prepare a Bill to amend the *Criminal Code* with a particular view of "permitting the operation of lotteries by provincial governments."[58] This would not be the last word on amending the *Criminal Code*, however; between 1963 and 1967, six different Bills with similar objectives were introduced.[59]

The timing was right for gambling proponents, for it appeared that support for lotteries was more widespread than anticipated. For years, Quebec had lobbied the federal government for the right to hold a provincial lottery. As of 1963, Canadian eyes turned south, to the New Hampshire Legislature, where State Representative Larry Pickett had for a decade been promoting state sweepstakes as a viable means of raising revenue. On 30 April 1963, New Hampshire Governor John King finally signed the state sweepstakes Bill. Less than a year later, on 10 March 1964, a special ballot was held, in which 198 of the state's 211 voting communities supported the sale of sweepstakes tickets. Two days later tickets for the New Hampshire Sweepstakes went on sale.[60] By 1967, the State of New York had established a lottery, followed by New Jersey in 1970, initiating a trend that would result in the creation of twelve state lotteries by 1974. In the meantime, the Canadian House of Commons continued to be guided by the 1954 Joint Committee's recommendations concerning charitable and religious organizations.

Federal Gambling Legislation: 1969–1985

It was apparent by 1967 that gaming as a vice was gradually losing political currency in Canada. In that year, Justice Minister Pierre Trudeau announced that he would introduce an omnibus bill promoting extensive revisions to the *Criminal Code*. The Bill anticipated allowing "state lotteries at the option of the federal or provincial governments." The proposed legislation clearly indicated that "the term 'lottery scheme' as it was used in the *Code* was not to be restricted to true lotteries, but encompassed any 'game,' that is, any game of chance or mixed chance and skill." The Bill ultimately died on the order paper, but this did not deter Trudeau's successor, John Turner, from reintroducing similar legislation in 1969. Turner acknowledged that the "attitude towards lotteries in Canada varies in various parts of the country," and his legislation would recognize that fact.[61] Turner's Bill proposed a "local option," whereby regions that did not desire state-sponsored gaming would be permitted to establish appropriate legislation, while regions that found gaming acceptable could also devise appropriate legislation permitting its implementation. Despite opposition from the New Democratic Party — NDP leader David Lewis charged that raising operational revenue through lotteries would permit those with the most to avoid contributing more to the federal treasury — the Liberal government's omnibus bill was passed into law in May 1969, thereby enabling either the federal government or a provincial government to conduct a broad range of lottery schemes.[62]

Since there was, according to the Justice Department's Hal Pruden, "no authority for the federal government to license others to conduct a lottery," the legislation was marketed "on the basis that the funds raised would be used for public 'good causes' because the lottery scheme revenues would go to governments or to charitable or religious organizations."[63] By 1970, Quebec had established its own lottery. Manitoba followed, creating a Centennial Sweepstakes in which $70,000 was paid to the winner, and Alberta soon instituted two similar, though smaller, sweepstakes. *The Manitoba Lotteries Act* was passed in 1971, followed by the creation of the Manitoba Lotteries Commission, which was responsible for managing government lotteries, and the Manitoba Lotteries Licensing Board, which was responsible for licensing religious and charitable organizations.[64] By 1974, the provinces of Manitoba, Saskatchewan, Alberta, and British Columbia had established the Western Canada Lottery Foundation.[65] British Columbia and Ontario briefly resisted demands to establish provincial lotteries, but BC eventually passed its own *Lottery Act*, and by 1975 the Ontario Lottery Corporation had been established.[66] Gaming revenues could not be channeled into existing programs and expenses, but they could be assigned to new areas of spending. Quick to follow its own lead, the federal government introduced Lotto-Canada to help offset the expected deficit of the 1976 summer Olympics in Montreal.[67]

Canada's First Ministers' reacted negatively to the federal scheme, arguing that it placed Ottawa in direct competition with the provincial lotteries, violating the spirit of the 1969 gaming legislation.[68] Gaming became a hot political issue once again during the 1979 federal election, with the Progressive Conservatives promising "to dismantle Lotto-Canada and to abandon operation of lotteries."[69] Following the PC victory, Prime Minister Joe Clark formulated an agreement with the provinces whereby Ottawa agreed to transfer jurisdiction over lottery schemes to the provinces in exchange for an annual payment of $25 million adjusted for inflation.[70] Clark's government soon lost a non-confidence vote, however, and the Liberals returned to power in 1980. Lotto-Canada was immediately restored and the government announced that it was going to introduce sports pools, going so far as to amend the *Criminal Code*.[71] Again the provincial premiers reacted negatively, arguing that the amendments contradicted the 1979 transfer of jurisdiction agreement. Federal officials charged that the provinces were engaged in pool betting operations under the guise of lotteries.

Unable to resolve the issue, the parties resorted to litigation, and in 1985 an agreement between the federal government and the provinces was reached.[72] Ottawa agreed to place a bill before Parliament officially repealing federal authority to conduct lottery schemes and pool betting operations. The provinces, in return, would provide a $100-million payment for the 1988 Calgary Olympics in addition to maintaining the annual payments according to the 1979 agreement. In December 1985, *Criminal Code* amendments prepared by the Department of Justice, the Interprovincial Lottery Corporation, and the provinces formally removed federal authority over lottery schemes and pool betting operations. The Bill clarified that a province "could conduct a lottery scheme on or through a computer, video device or slot machine, but could not license others to do so. Prior to this bill, there would have been some who believed that a province could, in theory, license others to conduct lottery schemes using these mechanisms."[73]

Casino gambling in Canada expanded to a full-time enterprise in December 1989 when the Manitoba provincial government opened Canada's first permanent year-round casino, the Crystal Casino, at the Hotel Fort Garry in Winnipeg. By 1994, Club Regent and McPhillips Street Station had been added to the provincial enterprise, and Video Lottery Terminals (VLT) were introduced. It is reported that casino operations brought in $250 million in revenue for the province that year.[74]

The Provinces Start Gambling: 1967–present

As Colin Campbell observed, "the 1969 amendment to the *Criminal Code* marked the transformation of policy regarding various forms of gambling from federal prohibition to provincial regulation."[75] The provinces, however, would focus less on lotteries and more on casino-style games of chance. In western Canada, in particular, those involved in charitable gaming gravitated toward casino-style games such as blackjack and roulette. In 1967, the annual Klondike Days fair opened a week-long casino at the Edmonton Exhibition Grounds, resulting in the "concept of gambling for both entertainment purposes and for generating revenues."[76] By the early 1970s, other Alberta cities such as Lethbridge, Red Deer, Medicine Hat, and Calgary were profiting from the exhibition exemptions by running casino-style gambling operations during annual agricultural exhibitions. Yet the question of the legality of these temporary casinos remained, and until 1974 the only casino gambling technically permitted in Western Canada was at agricultural fairs — although by 1975 the Alberta Attorney General's office was granting casino licenses to charitable organizations. This resulted in a liberal interpretation of the *Criminal Code* whereby organizations were eventually sanctioned to manage lottery schemes with provincial approval.[77]

Following what has been described as "a rapid proliferation of organizations seeking to conduct fundraising activities within Alberta," the province introduced a licensing system in 1976, recognizing casinos as "an alternative fundraising activity by eligible community organizations, which were required to be accountable for the use of proceeds and the conduct and management of casino gambling."[78] It also marked a significant ideological shift as government officials began to consider gaming for its revenue-generating potential rather than simply as a form of entertainment. Provincial gaming policy continued to evolve, and by 1979 lotteries were under provincial jurisdiction. In 1980 Alberta's first permanent, privately operated charitable casino opened in Calgary, followed in 1981 by a second operation in Edmonton. A provincially funded lottery study was commissioned in 1985 to determine Albertans' views on the disbursement of unused lottery revenue.

Perhaps the most significant change in the 1985 amendments to the *Criminal Code* was that which permitted the provinces to operate mechanical gaming devices. The Alberta Lottery Fund was established in 1989, followed by the first test run of VLTs at summer fairs in Edmonton and Calgary. The experiments were deemed a success, and in 1992 the provincial VLT program was introduced. The demand for VLTs expanded rapidly, and the number of casinos increased as well. By 1994 there were three permanent casinos located in Calgary and Edmonton, increasing to 11 the following year, with three that operated only on weekends.[79] With casinos cashing in on the VLT craze came a corresponding transformation of small-scale operations to larger, more sophisticated ones. This was a direct result of legislation that permitted the doubling of casino slot machines, serving liquor on the gaming floor, and permitting casinos to open on Sundays.[80] Fearing unsustainable industry growth and at the same time trying to appease lobby groups demanding government accountability concerning the social impact of gaming, Alberta in 1999 placed a moratorium on provincial casino construction. Following a 20-month review of licensing policies, the final report contained 61 recommendations which resulted in new provincial gaming policies intended to "reflect this government's continued commitment to maintaining the unique charitable gaming model of this province."[81] On 1 March 2002, officials lifted the moratorium, which finally opened the door to the First Nations provincial gaming industry.

Conclusion

The history of gaming legislation is characterized by amendments reflecting society's views on gambling. The lottery became the focus of the debate, as two factions, one supportive of lotteries and one in opposition, battled one another. This see-saw struggle carried on until 1969 when federal legislation was introduced legalizing not only lottery schemes, but high-stakes gaming. This was soon followed by the appearance of charitable casinos which, in turn, eventually gave way to for-profit casinos. Gaming is a federally delegated responsibility regulated by the provinces. According to this paradoxical arrangement, First Nations must acknowledge provincial jurisdiction. Campbell points out, however, that "in the federal-provincial negotiations which led to the 1985 amendment and the corresponding transfer of jurisdiction over gambling, it is apparent that First Nations' interests were not considered," adding that ignoring these interests permitted non-native governments to "consolidate jurisdiction over new forms of gambling and the revenues they would generate for private sector groups, for charities, and for provinces." Moreover, "the failure of Canadian legislators to consider First Nations' interests dramatically underscores the lack of foresight and unintended outcomes that are evident in the history of tinkering with gambling law in Canada."[82]

This lack of concern came back to haunt provincial and federal politicians in the early 1990s as First Nations attempted to gain control over reserve gaming.

CHAPTER THREE

The Social, Political, and Economic Context

In 1996, the final report of the Royal Commission on Aboriginal Peoples (RCAP) was released. The most extensive and expensive commission in Canadian history, and the most comprehensive and credible account of First Nations issues, its release corresponded with the birth of the First Nations gaming industry in Saskatchewan and Ontario. Its authors described an urgent need to support self-government and community-based initiatives aimed at rebuilding First Nations economies. Specifically, they warned that "self-government without a significant economic base would be an exercise in illusion and futility." Drastic measures were needed, they wrote, "to rebuild Aboriginal economies . . . severely disrupted over time, marginalized, and largely stripped of their land and natural resource base." Further, they warned, "under current conditions and approaches to economic development, we could see little prospect for a better future." Finally, the authors cautioned that establishing "a more self-reliant economic base for Aboriginal communities and nations will require significant, even radical departures from business as usual."[1] Encapsulated within this overview was one of the prevalent themes to emerge from both the RCAP and the self-government debate of the 1980s: that First Nations and the Canadian government shared a historic relationship that necessitated the two sides working with one another for the mutual benefit of all Canadians.

These same ideas animated First Nations leaders in the early 1980s who were seeking government support and the evolution of federal policies to assist in improving reserve economic conditions. That the government paid scant attention to their requests was, perhaps, not surprising, but it was the lack of concrete changes to Indian policy and the continuing economic suffering of reserve communities that eventually led First Nations leaders to consider gaming as a means of ameliorating the socio-economic deprivation in their communities. The Federation of Saskatchewan Indian Nations (FSIN) was in the vanguard of this movement, particularly Chief Sol Sanderson, who lobbied the Western Canada Lottery Foundation for a working relationship that would see First Nations participating in gaming-related enterprises. Sanderson's successor, Chief Roland Crowe (1986-1994), later claimed, "We tried to get in [at this time] but quite frankly we lacked Indian support."[2] Sanderson and Crowe both understood that an economic base capable of generating the type of revenue required to facilitate nation building was needed if the FSIN was to lobby effectively for increased self-government. From the First Nations perspective, the need to foster economic initiatives to improve reserve conditions was paramount. Over time, First Nations control over economic development through gaming ventures came to be seen as a potential economic means of both stimulating and one day maintaining First Nations economic development and independence within Saskatchewan.

In some respects, gaming may have appeared to First Nations leaders as a last-ditch effort at generating the revenue necessary for reserve economic development. By the mid-1980s, First Nations economic development, but for a handful of communities, was all but invisible; Aboriginal Canadians lagged behind mainstream society in terms of employment and annual earnings. It was during this period that the first reports started to circulate condemning the government not only for its contemporary treatment of First Nations but for its historical neglect of them as well. Something needed to be done. First Nations leaders began to study a wide variety of economic initiatives, and time and again they returned to gaming. It was during this period, too, that the federal government transferred jurisdiction for gaming to the provinces, and the popularity of casino gambling grew, signalling a nation-wide attitude adjustment toward gambling. In such a milieu, is was only natural that First Nations leaders would pose the question, "If Canada and the provinces can utilize gaming to generate revenues for civic purposes, why can't we do the same?"

The Shift from Wards to Self-Governing Nations

It was the late 1980s before First Nations leaders began lobbying in earnest for reserve-based gaming, but their strategy capped an intensive two-decade political struggle that began with the state's attempt at the legislative annihilation of First Nations culture in 1969. Curiously, that decade had begun somewhat promisingly on three levels, beginning with the introduction of the *Canadian Bill of Rights* in 1960, outlawing discrimination on the basis of race, colour, and creed, legislation that also protected First Nations interests. That same year, the extension of the federal franchise and full citizenship rights to all Indians occurred. Unlike previous attempts at wholesale enfranchisement, however, this policy permitted Indians to vote in federal and provincial elections without compromising their status or making participation "conditional upon complete assimilation into Canadian society."[3]

A Special Joint Parliamentary Committee was also established in 1959 to study the *Indian Act*. Although this was the second such committee in 13 years, the federal government suggested that the time was right for First Nations people to "assume the responsibility and accept the benefit of full participation as Canadian citizens." The Joint Committee was mandated to develop recommendations "designed to provide sufficient flexibility to meet the varying stages of development of the Indians during the transition period."[4] All in all, it appeared that federal officials had finally resigned themselves to improving the social, political, and economic standing of First Nations in Canada.

Canadian society was becoming increasingly aware of their federal government's "benign neglect" of First Nations. Media stories of desperate living conditions on reserves became commonplace, and pressure was brought to bear on provincial and federal politicians to improve the situation. The Minister of the Department of Citizenship and Immigration responded in 1963 by commissioning the first of a number of studies to review the situation of First Nations in Canada, with a view to understanding the difficulties they faced in overcoming pressing social and economic problems. Sociologist Harry Hawthorn of the University of British Columbia was approached to establish a research team to study First Nations socio-economic conditions in Canada and to make recommendations for improvement.[5] Co-authored by Marc-Adélard Tremblay, an anthropologist from Université Laval, the report was presented in two volumes: part one in 1966, and part two in 1967. The first part focused on reserve conditions and federal programs that were economic, political, and administrative in nature. In doing so, the Hawthorn-Tremblay report rejected assimilation as a certainty, proposing instead the concept of "citizens plus" to further emphasize that First Nations should benefit from Canadian citizenship while maintaining the rights guaranteed by status and treaty. They were now to be included as "charter members of the Canadian community," as commissioners stressed "a common citizenship as well as the reinforcement of difference."[6]

According to Onondaga scholar David Newhouse, "the report lays the foundation for modern Indian policy. It presents the radical idea that Indians ought to be 'citizens plus'."[7] By 1968, however, a new Liberal government led by Pierre Trudeau took power. According to sociologist J. Rick Ponting, "the new government was imbued with a strong liberal ideology that stressed individualism and the protection of individual rights . . . that emphasized individual equality and de-emphasized collective ethnic survival."[8] Trudeau opposed the direction Hawthorn and Tremblay had charted, and, in 1969, he and his Minister of Indian Affairs, Jean Chrétien, tabled a White Paper entitled *A Statement of the Government of Canada on Indian Policy* in the House of Commons. Claiming its goal was to "enable Indian people to be free to develop Indian cultures in an environment of legal, social, and economic equality with other Canadians," the government was seeking to offload federal responsibilities by devolving bureaucratic control over social programs to the provinces.[9] The government argued that it was First Nations' special status and the policies that had resulted from it that "kept the Indian people apart from and behind other Canadians," and that this "separate road cannot lead to full participation, to better equality in practice as well as theory."[10] All references to the special or separate status of Indians were to be removed from the *Constitution* to promote equality among citizens. Provisions would be made to enable Indians to gain control and acquire title to reserve lands and determine who would share in its ownership.

Resistance to the White Paper was pronounced among First Nations leaders, in particular because the policy took aim at the unique legal relationship that existed between "Indians" and the federal government.[11] Following a brief but vocal period led by the late Harold Cardinal's censure of the Trudeau government's lack of sensitivity, the first written response to the White Paper came from the Indian Chiefs of Alberta, who were at the time attempting to resolve difficulties posed by the ethnic and linguistic discreteness of bands, highly localized band identities, and the geographical separation of reserves.[12] Entitled *Citizens Plus*, this statement came to be known as the Red Paper; it condemned the government for its lack of vision and cited the Hawthorn-Tremblay Report to repudiate the government's proposed changes.[13] *Citizens Plus* presented an Indian political vision of the nature of the relationship between First Nations and the government of Canada. First Nations leaders held a meeting with Trudeau to propose a new and more open relationship between the federal government and the country's First Nations and to formally declare the Red Paper the official First Nations response to the government's policy statement.

The government formally withdrew its White Paper in 1971, but First Nations leaders remained upset that federal officials were arbitrarily dismissing their nationhood claims. Ottawa was now promoting First Nations as one of several ethnicities in need of federal assistance to boost their political participation in multicultural Canadian society. This attitude had stemmed in part from an increase in the number of immigrants to post-war Canada. As a way of maintaining the Canadian national character, immigrant selection criteria correlated to the "absorptive capacity" of various nations and races within a country endeavouring to establish a bilingual partnership between French- and English-speaking Canadians.[14] Anticipating that the new multicultural mosaic would be able to accommodate complex layers of cultural diversity as well as Quebec's demands for greater autonomy, the policy became official in 1971. It was designed to foster a national identity in two ways: first, it was a manner of distinguishing Canada as an independent nation separate from the cultural melting pot of the United States; and second, it sought to cultivate a Canadian cultural plurality by assisting ethnic groups to participate in Canadian society.

Notwithstanding state aspirations for plurality, within one unified Canada existed the problematic notion of a diversity of cultures and their contributions to one nation.[15] Though it promoted ethnic participation in Canadian society, the new policy also functioned to transform ethnic groups into political clientele. As a result, First Nations cultural expressions could be managed without the need to change the dominant federal system in any significant way. The expressed federal desire for increased levels of First Nations participation in Canadian society can be further understood in terms of the concerted resistance to the 1969 proposal to rescind the unique legal relationship. First Nations leaders were reiterating their long-standing treaty message of a nation-to-nation relationship of equals, co-existence with the Crown, a message that contrasted sharply with the view of First Nations as one ethnic group among many in need of federal assistance if they were to contribute to Canadian society.

For the rest of the 1970s the Canadian government struggled to establish a cogent Indian policy. In spite of the rate at which reports and position papers were being produced by First Nations organizations, Ottawa was intent on ignoring claims to Aboriginal rights. Again, the official Canadian position read that First Nations constituted "an ethnic group in the functional sense but they have not reached the level of organizational structure (European style) which would make it possible for government to deal with them through the same approach as would be effective with other ethnic groups."[16] In 1973, however, in *Calder v. the Attorney General of British Columbia*, the Supreme Court of Canada recognized the existence of Aboriginal rights.[17] In the wake of the *Calder* decision and continued First Nations political mobilization, most observers concluded that federal officials should prepare themselves to deal with First Nations issues. The Indian Claims Commission was established in 1974, followed in 1975 by the first modern day treaty signed between Canada and the James Bay Cree Nation. The federal government also initiated the devolution of social control to First Nations by instigating the transfer of responsibility for programs such as education to First Nations organizations and communities by the mid-1970s.[18]

As the 1970s came to a close, First Nations had begun their transition from "wards of the state" reliant on federal handouts, to political players focused on educating the Canadian public and federal politicians about Canada's treaty obligations.[19] First Nations organizations were increasingly influential; this was directly attributable to federal programming that resulted in First Nations concerns becoming more visible, thereby attracting Parliamentary attention. This was seen during the constitutional discussions of the late 1970s that led to the entrenchment of Aboriginal and treaty rights in Sec. 35 of the *Constitution Act, 1982*. First Nations activists had also become increasingly politically conscious and effective. By 1978, for example, the National Indian Brotherhood (NIB), the Native Council of Canada (NCC), and the Inuit Committee on National Issues

(ICNI) were invited to participate in the constitutional discussions. Not satisfied to watch from the periphery, 11 additional First Nations organizations initiated an influential lobby effort.[20] It was during this period that First Nations groups such as the Federation of Saskatchewan Indians (FSI) started to formally articulate the precepts of what would become known as Aboriginal self-government.

Indians and Economic Development: A Brief Overview

First Nations leaders promoted economic development as the remedy for many of the issues demoralizing their communities; a strong economic base was necessary if living conditions were to improve. The Manitoba Indian Brotherhood responded to the White Paper by releasing *Whabung* in 1970, a position paper promoting the idea of increased First Nations self-sufficiency fostered by First Nations, so that they could consider both individual and communal interests. The authors of *Whabung* proclaimed that, "in developing new methods of response and community involvement, it is imperative that we, both Indian and Government, recognize that economic, social, and educational development are synonymous, and thus must be dealt with as a 'total' approach rather than in parts. The practice of program development in segments, in isolation as between its parts, inhibits if not precludes, effective utilization of all resources in the concentrated effort required to support economic, social and educational developments." Also, "the transition from paternalism to community self-sufficiency may be long and will require significant support from the state, however, we would emphasize that state support should not be such that the government continues to do for us, that which we want to do for ourselves."[21] This statement echoes the Hawthorn-Tremblay Report in its call for a comprehensive approach to development. Its authors did, however, take an additional step by further emphasizing reserve economic development as central to First Nations life. At the heart of these statements is the idea that change could lead to self-sufficiency only if First Nations direct this change so that *both* individual and community interests are taken into consideration. This would necessitate governments surrendering some political power and require First Nations people to embrace certain elements of Canadian culture.

Unfortunately, a restrictive *Indian Act* rife with remnants of 19th-century policy continued to guide federal officials. Early Indian policy was designed to remain in place until such time as First Nations had either disappeared or been assimilated into Canada's national fabric, and it was anticipated that both the reserve system and the *Indian Act* would vanish by the mid-20th century. Little thought, therefore, was given to reserve economic development. As Cam Mackie, former co-ordinator of the Native Economic Development Program, explained, following the implementation of the *Indian Act* in 1876, "for approximately seventy-five years the economic development strategy of the federal government was to provide Indian people with a minimum of individual and personal support and through education in residential schools to achieve a level of integration with the larger society."[22] Despite limited attempts to assist First Nations to establish an agricultural base, "for the most part up until the early 1960s little of substance occurred that would lead to any form of economic self-sufficiency."[23]

Living on reserves in certain parts of Canada was not problematic where it was possible to establish and maintain an ongoing, albeit restricted, economy. But the *Indian Act* was limited in scope, especially in terms of economic development. With the exception of permitting First Nations the limited right to hunt, fish, and trap, and the prairie peasant farming experiments of the late 19th century, on-reserve economic development was effectively stifled by myopic federal policies. This did not deter Native leaders from repeatedly petitioning Indian Affairs for support for their economic development initiatives. This constant lobbying, combined with the clear indication that since 1941 the First Nations population in Canada had been showing a pattern of sustained growth, resulted in federal officials agreeing to hear from First Nations leaders.[24]

As early as the 1940s there was a general feeling among Indian Affairs Branch (IAB) officials that the Indian policy — the "civilization policy" — was antiquated and in need of reform, but officials were tied to the official policy. J. A. Glen, the minister responsible for Indian Affairs under Prime Minister William Lyon Mackenzie King, informed King that Indian Affairs was confused, and the Prime Minister later admitted that "there really is need of a shaking up" of the department.[25] In May 1946, former IAB Secretary T. R. L. MacInnes wrote, "two definite schools of thought have developed on the future of the Indian. One favours assimilation; the other envisages a separate Indian racial life with its own distinctive culture and ideology."[26] He added, "Obviously the arguments for and against these respective viewpoints apply, differently and even oppositely in different localities, depending upon the state of advancement of the Indians, and their proximity ratio to the rest of the local population, and other factors."[27] MacInnes's comments demonstrate a marked shift in how the IAB understood First Nations culture. Whereas assimilation had previously been the overriding agenda, it now appeared that federal officials were willing to hear from First Nations people in Canada.

In early 1946, Glen concluded it was time to amend the *Indian Act* and improve IAB services. He also decided not to introduce legislation in the House of Commons prior to a Parliamentary Committee hearing representations concerning the proposed changes. Glen justified his proposal, claiming that it was "imperative, before revision of the *Indian Act* is undertaken, certainly before the revised act is submitted to the house, that existing legislation, together with amendments that may be deemed necessary, be carefully studied, not only from the point of view of the government and the taxpayer, but also from the point of view of the Indian, and in light of his present-day needs."[28]

A draft of the terms of reference for the Special Joint Committee (SJC) was accepted by the House of Commons and the Senate on 13 and 16 May 1946, respectively. The SJC was granted a wide mandate to hear witnesses and gather evidence in relation to eight areas, including any matters concerning the social and economic status of Indians and how to promote their advancement.[29] In particular, members of the Committee were interested in whether First Nations leaders had full command of the political, social, and economic situation they were immersed in, with the hopes their commentary would prove helpful in developing effective solutions. The coherence of concerns of the core five First Nations organizations to present was significant. They all called for improved economic opportunities on reserves. Each described the shocking state of reserve conditions, while emphasizing that there existed an inadequate and diminishing land base to sustain a viable economy.

Reserve economies in the 1940s ranged from agriculture to treaty-secured trapping and fishing rights, in addition to limited IAB assistance in establishing industries. The prairie organizations — the Indian Association of Alberta (IAA), the Union of Saskatchewan Indians (USI), and the Manitoba Indian Association (MIA) — were most concerned with defending what they considered to be treaty-protected rights. In addition, it appeared to First Nations leaders that "little supervision seems to be exercised over the number of fishing permits issued to white fishermen . . . while some supervision is exercised over the gross poundage of the catch."[30] Subsistence economies were still existent in the 1940s, and hunting and fishing were regularly employed to supplement wage-labour ventures. The brief from The Pas Band in Manitoba outlined the issues at play: "Our hunting rights should be extended, and trapping grounds more favourable. Indian people complain that too many white men are being put to trap on the muskrat area."[31] In terms of agriculture, it was the Native Brotherhood of British Columbia's belief that "the need for assistance in the field of agriculture generally is most urgent. Even after centuries of farming life, the white people find it necessary to send their sons and daughters to obtain the most advanced scientific training in farming, fruit growing and gardening," adding that "the Indians, who are just beginning this life, need more practical training along these lines."[32]

The protection of reserve lands was also of concern, although it was dealt with sparingly in each brief. The Native Brotherhood of British Columbia (NBBC) wasted little time in declaring to the SJC that "compensation should be made for lands and timber areas alienated from the Indians," claiming that Indian people were not given "sufficient lands to allow them to be self-supporting and self-sustaining, while, on the other hand, lands contiguous to the reserves have been commercialized and exploited with no benefit to the Indians."[33] The IAA stressed it was "opposed to any further alienation of Indian land for any purpose whatsoever, whether a post-war immigration scheme, land settlement scheme, or any other purpose."[34] First Nations leaders recognized that the loss of land often resulted from government-conducted land surveys, and all written submissions recommended new land surveys be conducted under the scrutiny of community delegates. It was suggested the findings be juxtaposed with the original reserve land allocations described in the written treaties or with official documents housed in Ottawa. As the Shoal Lake brief stated, "We expect that the little Reserve of Bell River Bay (West) as appears on old maps, be returned to us as being part of our reserve."[35]

Despite the impassioned speeches delivered before the Committee and the expressed desire of First Nation leaders to develop local economies, their concerns were literally forgotten. For the next two decades, officials responsible for Indian Affairs were located in the Department of Citizenship and Immigration. It seemed a logical choice, as both displaced European immigrants and dispossessed Indians were in the process of becoming Canadians. Indian agents were pulled from the communities, which were now left to their own devices. Communities thus lost their conduit to Ottawa, and First Nations in many instances were literally lost in the bureaucratic shuffle as they faced increasingly desperate socio-economic realities on reserves. By the 1960s, federal officials had become aware that promoting agriculture and urban employment was inadequate, and in the mid-1960s established a community-development program, which was little more than a revolving loan fund. In the early 1970s, the Department of Indian Affairs created the Indian Economic Development Fund (IEDF) to assist in the establishment of reserve projects. Direct loans, loan guarantees, equity contributions, and advisory services were provided, and both individually and community owned projects were eligible for assistance.[36] However, on the eve of Constitutional inclusion and the beginning of what would become a protracted debate concerning the new idea of Aboriginal self-government, economic conditions appeared to be as poor as ever.

First Nations Statistical Profile: 1980-1990

As the battle for powers of self-government and self-determination gained momentum, the effects of poor economic development on reserves led First Nations leaders once again to turn their attention to economic issues. As of the 1980s, limited government programs combined with issues such as distances from urban centres, a work force with limited labour skills, and a lack of local resource bases were conspiring to limit economic development initiatives in most First Nations communities. Further complicating matters was the slow but steady growth of reserve populations, with many young men and women seeking employment opportunities. Many left the reserve to find work in urban centres; many remained on the reserve in the hope that better economic times were on the horizon. From 1941 to 1979, the First Nations population in Canada grew from approximately 122,000 to 309,000.[37] Within two years, this number had swelled to 335,475.[38] The former period of growth — the Indian baby boom of the 1960s — corresponded with a decline in infant mortality, a trend that continued into the 1970s.[39] Prior to this period, most Aboriginal Canadians lived on reserves, as urban migration was limited. As statistician Andrew Siggner recounts, "as urban industrial growth slackened in the early 1970s and as Indians encountered the barriers of discrimination in employment, housing, and social life, data suggest that a movement back to the reserves occurred, along with a diminution of the out-migration from reserves."[40]

This is not to suggest that First Nations movement into urban centres stopped. The 1971 Regina census reported the First Nations population to be approximately 2,900, whereas sociologist J. Rick Ponting and political scientist Roger Gibbins estimated the 1979 population at more than 20,000.[41] As of 1976, the first Aboriginal baby boomers had reached labour force age, "thereby producing a swelling in the labour force age group, although it was (proportionally speaking) still markedly smaller than its Canadian counterpart."[42] During this period, more than 70 per cent of all bands were considered either remote or rural communities, and these bands represented 65 per cent of the Indian population.[43] As the First Nations population increased, so too did the number of bands with a population of greater than 1,000. From 1977 to 1981, they increased from 13 to 16 per cent. It was estimated that this trend would persist, and that the proportion of bands similar in size was expected to increase to at least 25 per cent before the year 2000.[44] It was further anticipated that 64 per cent of all Indians would be members of these larger bands, up from 44 per cent in 1981.[45]

As of the mid-1980s, urban centres were the major recipients of First Nation in-migrants; they were also the key contributors of a larger number of First Nation out-migrants.[46] Siggner warned that, should economic opportunities fail to "materialize for this growing Indian population, particularly on reserves, the already serious unemployment problem and its related social problems will likely be exacerbated."[47] In 1974, 41 per cent of the on-reserve population was receiving social assistance, and these figures remained consistent despite the fact that two years later it was reported that First Nation bands had received an income of $96.9 million from band enterprises, oil and gas royalties, and interest on government-held trust funds.[48] Nevertheless, from 1970-71 to 1980-81, First Nations social assistance increased from $34 million to over $142 million, a jump of 315 per cent in 11 years. The majority of these payments occurred on reserves.[49] The prognosis for reserve communities by the mid-1980s was not inspiring, the main reasons being the ratio of children and the aged in relation to persons of labour-force age and the scarcity of employment for an expanding labour force.[50] While it was predicted that the First Nations labour force would grow from 190,000 in 1981 to 284,000 by 1996,[51] Ponting and Gibbins warned that reserve unemployment and underemployment was "rampant and Indians living on economically impotent reserves find themselves in the classic state of 'welfare dependency'." Further, "those who do find employment find that it is often seasonal or short-term in nature, and likely to be of the low-paying, unskilled or semi-skilled type in the primary (extractive) sector."[52]

First Nations leaders were well aware of the economic situation facing their communities. By 1981, the unemployment rate was roughly 2.2 times higher than that of the non-First Nations population, a figure that would grow to 2.5 by 1991. For the First Nations population above 15 years of age, the unemployment rate in 1981 was 15.8 per cent, compared with 7.2 per cent for the rest of the population. For those living on rural reserves or settlements, the income disparity with the general population was nearly 1.75. That same year it was estimated that 38 per cent of registered Indians aged 15 and over were employed compared with 60 per cent of the general population. Fifty-four per cent of the First Nations population was not in the labour force, compared to 35 per cent in the general population.[53] From 1980-1990 things did improve on reserves, but First Nations leaders were not satisfied with this limited progress and sought development projects that could infuse working capital into reserve communities.

During the 1980s, individual income levels in Canadian society increased by approximately 4.3 per cent, while in the First Nations population that number dropped by close to five per cent while the average income of the First Nations population dropped from 66 per cent to 60 per cent of the non-First Nations population. Registered Indians watched their average income drop by nine per cent during the same period as their populations grew.[54] It is estimated that only 12 per cent of First Nations men and women living on reserve worked full-time in 1990, compared with 28 and 20 per cent, respectively, for off-reserve men and women. Accordingly, "in addition to carrying a penalty in terms of access to jobs, living on a reserve appears to carry a wage penalty with it as well: those few on-reserve Aboriginals who did work full-time, full-year earned 20 to 25% less than single-origin, off-reserve Aboriginals. Neither the reserve-employment, nor the reserve-wage gap can be entirely accounted for by differences in the observed characteristics of individuals living on and off reserves."[55]

As of the end of the 1980s, First Nations leaders were at an impasse. While the federal government acknowledged that reserve communities were in desperate need of an economic boost, available programs were inadequate to resolve the difficulties. A 1985 study reported that almost half of reserve housing failed to meet basic standards; over one-third was seriously overcrowded in terms of minimal standards; and 38 per cent of reserve housing lacked some or all of the basic amenities, including running water. It was further estimated that upwards of $840 million would be required to correct the problems.[56] At a time when US tribal gaming was beginning, First Nations leaders in Canada started to gravitate toward an economic activity that seemed capable of generating the revenue needed to produce sustainable economies and improve the general standard of living on reserves.

Aboriginal Self-Government and the Need for Economic Development

The 1980s were the most significant political period for First Nations peoples since Confederation, and it appeared that their leaders were up to the challenge. Their lobbying efforts resulted in: the federal government initiating the Parliamentary Task Force on Indian Self-Government in 1982 (the Penner Report), recognizing Aboriginal self-government; the inclusion of section 37 in the *Constitution Act*, mandating the First Ministers Conferences between 1983-87 to define Aboriginal self-government; the Ministerial Task Force on Program Review (the Nielsen Report) in 1986; and the Indian Self-Government Community Negotiations policy statement of 1986.[57] These developments were viewed as a means to "partially reverse hundreds of years of oppressive government policies and neglect, and to improve their intolerable socio-economic condition."[58]

From the beginning, it was clear that Canada's first ministers were reluctant to constitutionally entrench the right to self-government, for it represented a significant departure from the legal and political history of how First Nations people had been traditionally viewed.[59] For close to a decade, however, First Nations had, through a succession of individual reports, been developing the common doctrines that would coalesce into what we today understand as self-government. Much of this had to do with Prime Minister Pierre Trudeau's pronouncement that "we are not here to consider whether there should be institutions of self-government, but how these institutions should be brought into being," and "how they fit into the interlocking system of jurisdictions by which Canada is governed."[60] Providing a sense of legitimacy was the *Report of the Special Committee on Indian Self-Government*, known as the Penner Report. Established by Parliament in December 1982, the committee was "mandated to review all legal and related institutional factors affecting status, development, and responsibilities of band councils on Indian reserves, and to make recommendations in respect to establishing, empowering and funding Indian self-government."[61] The committee travelled throughout Canada to obtain information first-hand from First Nations people. It presented its report in October 1983.

The Penner Report argued for a new relationship with First Nations peoples based on Trudeau's comments at the First Ministers' Conference on First Nations Constitutional Matters: "Clearly, our aboriginal peoples each occupied a special place in history. To my way of thinking, this entitles them to special recognition in the Constitution and to their own place in Canadian society, distinct from each other and distinct from other groups who, together with them, comprise the Canadian citizenry."[62] The report recommended that "the federal government establish a new relationship with Indian First Nations and that an essential element of this relationship be recognition of Indian self-government,"[63] and "that the right of Indian peoples to self-government be explicitly stated and entrenched in the Constitution of Canada. The surest way to achieve permanent and fundamental change in the relationship between Indian peoples and the federal government is by means of a constitutional amendment. Indian First Nations would form a distinct order of government in Canada, with their jurisdiction defined." The report indicated that "virtually the entire range of law-making, policy, program delivery, law enforcement and adjudication powers would be available to an Indian First Nation government within its territory."[64]

In the meantime, as self-government was being defined and accepted by Trudeau and his cabinet, the Native Economic Development Program was created in October 1983, "with the appointment of an advisory board of aboriginal people from all parts of the country." According to Ponting, "the NEDP followed a strategy of attempting to create a pool of capital under the ownership, control, and management of aboriginal people through a series of financial and economic development institutions, including trust companies, loan companies, development corporations, and venture capital operations."[65] Despite such actions, the most widespread criticism among First Nations leaders was "that the DIA's economic development programs are grossly underfunded." Ponting cited, as an example, one district in which the DIA's entire economic development budget for 1985-86 amounted to less than $10,000 per band.[66] He also stated that the complaint of inadequate funds came with additional concerns, including the "inadequacy of funds to hire consultants to do adequate advance planning [which] predisposes many economic development projects to failure; and the department's approach of merely providing 'seed' (start-up) money in a 'band-aid' approach that fails to come to grips with the enormity and gravity of the need."[67]

The Government of Canada responded to the Penner Report in March 1984: "The Committee's recommendations have a special importance because they were unanimously supported by Committee members of all Parties. It agreed with the need to establish a new relationship with Indian peoples." In all, "the effect . . . is to call for the Government and Indian First Nations to enter into a new relationship. . . . Many of the details of the restructured relationship will have to be worked out after careful consideration and full consultation with Indian people." The government agreed, further, "with the argument put forth by the Committee that Indian communities were historically self-governing and that the gradual erosion of self-government over time has resulted in a situation which benefits neither Indian people nor Canadians in general."[68] The government did not yet accept the idea of constitutional entrenchment, although within a decade it would reluctantly read the *Constitution* in such a way as to include the right to self-government.

According to one writer, A. M. Mawhiney, "Since the early 1970s, realities expressed by Indian peoples have been considered in the formulation of Indian policy, at least at a philosophical level. The Penner Report reflected these realities to the exclusion of the more traditional Euro-Canadian views, and recommended a paradigm shift to Indian self-government."[69] The government's response also rejected a number of the Penner Report's recommendations, although the idea of Indian self-government, "as a component in the existing paradigm, was accepted."[70] Despite such optimistic pronouncements, the implementation problems that followed from the recommendations were not addressed.[71] Yet, for the first time, not only were First Nations leaders embracing the concept of the right to self-government, but so was the Canadian government. The result of the Penner Report's recommendations, had they been implemented, "would be that Indian people would determine their own form of government, establish criteria for the self-identification of membership in Indian communities, and exercise jurisdiction in such fields as resources, social services, taxation, and education."[72] Many First Nations leaders interpreted this to mean that jurisdiction for the key ingredient to any successful administration — economic development — had been transferred to First Nations.

Conclusion

First Nations leaders have always understood that they needed public support if their gaming plans were to come to fruition. Public opinion influences public policy, and in the case of reserve gaming, it was anticipated that federal politicians would be reluctant to act unless they had support. The 1985 *Criminal Code* amendment transferring authority for gambling from federal to provincial jurisdictions "was legislated without public input and has been an ongoing source of public controversy ever since."[73] At the time, however, the results of a national poll asking, "On the whole, are you in favour of, or opposed to government-run lotteries?" revealed that 76 per cent of Canadians were in favour, with 16 per cent opposed and 8 per cent uncertain.[74] While it appeared that Canadians supported gaming in general, they had never been confronted with the possibility of reserve casinos. Naturally, the issue of economic development was broached, and this is when gaming began to be presented as a funding mechanism.

As First Nations began to assert their right to self-government, federal officials began to address the corresponding need to build reserve economies to support self-government and improve the general health of the communities. First Nations leaders acknowledged the need to improve reserve economic development, but in many cases were powerless to effect the required change. Again, restrictive *Indian Act* provisions combined with inadequate federal programs left First Nations leaders feeling powerless. As they patiently awaited federal confirmation of their inherent right to self-govern, the US tribal gaming industry was beginning to reap millions in revenues. As these success stories started to penetrate the international border, First Nations leaders in Canada initiated studies to determine the economic potential of gaming, and how to legally put it into practice. They began to investigate gaming as a means of securing the funding necessary to promote sustainable economic initiatives on reserves, and their field of study was the emerging tribal gaming industry in the United States.

CHAPTER FOUR

American Indian Gaming:
A Brief Overview

Despite inauspicious beginnings, the United States tribal gaming industry has in less than three decades become a significant component of many tribal economies, with several states citing tribal casinos as major contributors to their economic prosperity. What began as a small number of high-stakes bingo halls in a handful of states have grown to approximately 360 Indian gaming establishments operated by approximately 220 of the nation's federally recognized 558 tribes.[1] In 2003, Indian gaming generated close to $17 billion — up $2 billion from the previous year. Yet in the early 1980s, when First Nations leaders in Canada began to study tribal gaming, no Indian casinos existed in the US. The Canadians' original goal was to determine the feasibility of the high-stakes bingo operations that were flourishing during this period. The Federation of Saskatchewan Indian Nations (FSIN) in 1985 sent a delegation to Florida to observe first-hand the Seminole bingo venture. Even if the Seminoles did not offer the type of high-stakes gaming that Canadian leaders anticipated one day establishing, the FSIN delegation was nevertheless impressed. On their return, the La Ronge members of the delegation convinced community leaders to establish an off-reserve bingo, setting into motion the First Nations gaming industry in Saskatchewan.[2] However, it wasn't until the late 1980s, when Indian casinos began to dot the American landscape, that First Nations leaders shifted their attention from bingos to larger, high-stakes gaming establishments.

The Pequots of Connecticut in the late 1980s led the development of the US tribal gaming industry, and by the early 1990s had initiated the first phase of construction on the Foxwoods Casino, which would by the early 21st century come to be acknowledged as America's largest casino and one of the world's most profitable gaming establishments. The development of the Indian gaming industry was, however, a protracted process that dated back to the 1970s, following several tribes focusing their attention on high-stakes gaming to foster reservation economic development. Federal officials in most cases resisted these efforts, and Indian leaders at various times found themselves petitioning the courts to determine whether, as self-governing entities, they had the right to operate high-stakes gaming establishments on reservation lands. By 1984, the courts had decided that Indians did have the sovereign right to control reservation economic development, including high-stakes gaming. The Seminoles of Florida and the Pequots followed by constructing bingo palaces. Still, many states resisted Indian claims and employed legislation to shut down upstart gaming establishments. By 1987, the issue of tribal sovereignty and the right to operate casinos had been formally decided in the *Cabazon* decision,[3] which determined that the states had no authority to apply their regulatory statutes to gambling activities conducted on Indian reservations.

Following the *Cabazon* decision, it appeared as though Indian casinos popped up overnight. For First Nations leaders in Canada saddled with lacklustre economic growth, gaming started to look good; the revenues generated could be channelled into community economic development, acting as a catalyst for nation building. One problem facing First Nations leaders was the need for start-up money to fund these projects, and they were wary of the anticipated political fight based on their understanding of the American experience. As they soon found out, the legislative and policy environment from which the American Indian gaming industry emerged differed significantly from that in Canada. Gaming was not without its detractors among First Nations in Saskatchewan, where many communities questioned FSIN officials about their decision. Other First Nations leaders determined it was important to examine the tribal gaming phenomenon to determine its applicability, and to verify why certain models were more successful than others, and thus avoid the pitfalls of the less successful models.

The First Days of Indian Gaming

In the late 1970s, the US experienced a gaming boom as various states voted to legalize casino gambling. As of 1978, Las Vegas was the US gaming capital, dominating the industry, although 14 states were operating lotteries by that time. However, that year New Jersey voters approved by referendum a proposition to legalize casinos, and gambling establishments began to grace the Boardwalk in Atlantic City, attracting large numbers of patrons who were now unwilling to travel to Las Vegas to gamble. Atlantic City's success caught the eye of several state officials and city administrators throughout the country, and from 1989 to 1998 nine additional states — including Mississippi, Iowa, Minnesota, and Connecticut — legalized casino gambling. As of 1995, the US gaming industry was responsible for $37.5 billion in revenue. By 2002, there were 429 non-Indian casinos operating in 11 states, and 40 states as well as the District of Columbia were operating lotteries. By 2004, the industry had grown to include 11 states housing 445 commercial casinos, all of which generated nearly $29 billion in gross revenue that year.[4]

As of 2004, 28 states had become home to approximately 360 Indian gaming establishments operated by some 220 federally recognized tribes.[5] Yet prior to 1979, the number of tribes operating small-scale bingo establishments across the country numbered less than 10; open a couple of nights a week, on average, cash prizes of less than $100 were the norm. The nature of Indian gaming changed dramatically after the Seminole Tribe of Florida opened a high-stakes bingo parlour on their reservation near Miami in 1978. Initial cash prizes were worth thousands of dollars, owing in part to high population concentrations in close proximity to the reservation, providing a huge customer base which, in turn, resulted in higher cash prizes. The Seminole Tribe was soon making several million dollars in annual gaming profits.

In 1981, the State of Florida imposed prize limits, which the Seminoles ignored, resulting in criminal charges being filed as state officials worked to shut down operations.[6] Broward County Sheriff Robert Butterworth took particular exception to the Seminole bingo operation, publicly expressing his concern that it would attract organized crime, create social problems, and do more harm than good to the local non-Indian community. Butterworth also claimed that the Seminole Tribe was bound by a state law that limited organizations operating bingos to a maximum of two nights a week and prize payouts of less than $100 per pot. Challenging state-imposed restrictions, the Seminole Tribe argued before the Federal Court of Appeals that, as a tribe imbued with "sovereign status," they were not bound by the state's gaming regulations.[7] The court agreed, and ruled that the State of Florida could not enforce its bingo laws against the Seminole Tribe's high-stakes operations. The court further ruled that the laws restricting bingos to licensed charitable operations and limiting the hours a casino could remain open and how much money could be won in each pot were "civil/regulatory" laws. Florida is a Public Law 280 state; according to Public Law 280, a distinction is made between a civil law of general application, for which the state has jurisdiction, and a civil regulatory law, which stipulates federal jurisdiction. State laws governing private matters between individuals — including contract law, family law, and tort law — apply on Indian reservations, but general civil regulatory laws exclude states from exercising civil jurisdiction over Indian land. The US Supreme Court upheld this decision following Florida's appeal, acknowledging that the state could not interfere in the economic activities of tribes.[8] The Seminole decision permitted Indian Nations to make use of on-reservation gaming operations to foster economic development by virtue of the US *Constitution* and subsequent federal legislation recognizing tribal sovereignty.

Tribal sovereignty, as a theory, can be traced back to three US Supreme Court decisions involving the Cherokee Nation and the State of Georgia.[9] Often referred to as the "Marshall Trilogy," the legal relationship between the federal government and Indian tribes was described by Chief Justice John Marshall in *The Cherokee Nation* v. *Georgia* as "unlike that of any other two people in existence." Drawing from political theory and international law to resolve the Cherokee's petition to prevent Georgia from dividing their lands into counties and asserting state laws over these territories, Marshall held that an Indian tribe is a "distinct political society" capable of "managing its own affairs and governing itself." In 1832, Marshall held in *Worcester* v. *Georgia* that Indian tribes are distinct and independent political communities, "having territorial boundaries, within which their authority is exclusive." He also noted that, early in the history of North American cross-cultural contact, tribes were treated as sovereign, as evidenced by the treaty relationships that developed. The State of Georgia did not, therefore, have the authority to compel changes to tribal powers, as all tribes kept all the rights and powers they had not expressly given up.

The Marshall decisions determined that Indian tribes had the right to form governments, determine membership, regulate land use, establish mechanisms of law and order, and regulate commerce. Tribal powers of self-government, according to the *Cherokee* decision, were "limited by federal statutes, by the terms of the treaties with the federal government, and by restraints implicit in the protectorate relationship itself. In all other respects the tribes remain independent and self-governing political communities."[10] An Indian tribe, therefore, is considered a distinct political community and retains its inherent powers of self-government absent action by Congress to limit those powers; a state is unable to limit the powers of a tribe. As articulated in the *Cherokee* decision, the federal government also had a unique obligation to Indian tribes, defined as a trust responsibility. As sovereign entities located within the United States, the federal government is obligated to protect all tribes' status as self-governing entities and their property rights. This has come to mean, in part, that the protection of tribal members and the promotion of their economic and social well-being is the federal government's responsibility.

Unlike their Canadian counterparts, US tribes have certain powers of jurisdiction within reservation boundaries, including the powers to "determine their respective forms of government (e.g., craft constitutions), define citizenship, pass and enforce laws through their own police forces and courts, collect taxes, regulate the domestic affairs of their citizens, and regulate property use (e.g., through zoning, permitting, environmental regulation, and the like). And like states, American Indian governments have the power to determine whether they will engage in gaming operations."[11]

The fight over control of reservation gaming at times became heated owing to the stakes that were involved, but by 1986, the Seminole Tribe was operating three separate bingo halls and grossing over $100 million in annual revenues.[12] Following the *Seminole* decision, tribes gravitated to high-stakes bingo gaming in states where bingo was not prohibited by law. By 1987, over 100 tribal bingo facilities were grossing close to $200 million.[13] The *Seminole* decision also offered Indian leaders the hope that tribal gaming could expand to include casino operations. To that point, most Indian gaming establishments were bingo parlours.

Among the exceptions was the Cabazon Tribe of Mission Indians of southern California, which, in addition to bingo, offered poker and other games of chance. The Cabazon leaders' pursuit of gaming was the result of limited economic development rather than a deep-seated desire to open a casino. For example, in 1976 the US Supreme Court determined that state jurisdiction did not extend to Indian lands in California and other Public Law 280 states for the purposes of taxation or regulating business. Several California tribes attempted to capitalize on this geographic advantage, intent on transforming reservations into large-scale retail centres. Four years later these plans were dashed by the Supreme Court when it ruled that tribal sovereignty did not "protect tribes from having to collect state sales taxes imposed on non-Indian buyers. This ruling greatly decreased any advantage native businesses might have had in Indian country."[14] As a result, the Cabazon Tribe accepted its limited economic opportunities and began to offer high-stakes bingo and games of chance, now arguing that they were a sovereign Indian nation and shielded from California laws that restricted bingo and card games under limited conditions.

Like Florida, the State of California acted quickly in an attempt to halt Cabazon operations. Fuelled by concerns of the possible infiltration of organized crime, local and state authorities challenged the Cabazon Tribe's gambling operations, arguing in court that California had state authority over reservation gaming. The Cabazons maintained that state laws did not apply on Indian reservations. As we have seen, the Supreme Court determined that California had no authority to apply its regulatory statutes to gambling activities conducted on Indian reservations. *Cabazon* confirmed that reservation-based gaming activities were permitted in states that had any legalized form of gambling. Indian leadership in the 14 states that permitted gaming watched carefully, and those looking to establish large-scale gaming operations immediately initiated their plans.[15]

The Indian Gaming Regulatory Act (IGRA)

In the wake of *Cabazon* a number of US Indian gaming opponents publicly expressed their concern with the Court's decision. State and local governments, commercial gaming establishments and law enforcement officials "found it unacceptable that Indian gaming was not being regulated by local government."[16] In response, Congress in October 1988 passed the *Indian Gaming Regulatory Act* (IGRA). The IGRA was an attempt to provide a regulatory framework for Indian gaming that officially recognized the right of tribes to establish reservation gaming facilities. In return, tribes were required to negotiate gaming compacts with their home state, codifying what games would be permitted and applicable regulations, while ensuring that tribal governments remained the sole owners and primary beneficiaries of the establishments. The *IGRA* also formally outlined the mechanisms and procedures to be employed in establishing tribal gaming ventures, including the provision that gambling revenues be used to promote the economic development and welfare of tribes.[17]

With the *IGRA*, Indian Tribes were recognized as the primary regulators of Indian gaming, and were responsible for establishing the basic regulatory framework for reservation gaming. But state regulation may also be included in tribal/state compacts, and federal agencies may enforce laws relating to Indian gaming. The agencies involved include the National Indian Gaming Commission (NIGC), the Interior Department, the Justice Department, the FBI, the Internal Revenue Service (IRS), the Secret Service, and the Treasury Department's Financial Crimes Enforcement Network. The *IGRA* also stipulates that gaming revenues are to be employed to fund tribal government operations or programs, to provide for the general welfare of the tribe and its members, to promote tribal economic development, to donate to charitable organizations, and/or to help fund the operations of local government agencies.[18]

The *IGRA* acknowledged Indian sovereignty while at the same time infringing on it by requiring that states create reservation gaming regulations and identify permissible games through the negotiation of a tribal/state compact. Three legally defined classes of Indian gaming were established. Class I gaming permits social games with prizes of minimal value, or traditional forms of Indian gaming that are part of tribal ceremonies or celebrations; it does not involve games of chance. Class II gaming permits games of chance, but is limited to bingo and related games such as pulltabs, lotto, punchboards, tip jars, instant bingo, and some card games; it does not include card games in general, specialty table games, or slot machines. Class III permits all manner of gaming, including slot machines and card games and horse and dog racing. All large tribal gaming establishments have opened according to these guidelines.

Pursuant to the *IGRA*, the NIGC was established as an independent federal agency with special regulatory and investigative powers in relation to Indian gaming. In an effort to shield tribes from organized crime and other corrupting influences, to ensure that Indian tribes are the primary beneficiaries of gaming revenue, and that gaming is conducted fairly and honestly by both operators and players, the NIGC is responsible for regulating all gaming activities on Indian lands. It is also authorized to conduct investigations, undertake enforcement actions, conduct background investigations and audits, and review and approve tribal gaming ordinances.

Originally concerned with Class II gaming, the NIGC's mandate has grown to keep pace with the rapid expansion of Class III gaming. Although Congress intended regulatory issues to be addressed in tribal/state compacts, it left a number of key functions to federal jurisdiction, including approval authority over compacts, management contracts, and tribal gaming ordinances. Congress also vested the NIGC with comprehensive authority to issue regulations in furtherance of the purposes of the *IGRA*. Accordingly, the NIGC plays a key role in the regulation of Class II and III gaming, monitoring all activities in addition to auditing the records. At the same time, it is vested with the authority to determine whether a tribal gaming operation is in compliance with the *IGRA*. Should it conclude that a violation has occurred, it is empowered to issue notices of violation, closure orders, and, in certain cases, impose civil fines of up to $25,000 per day, per violation.

Prior to a Class III facility commencing operations, three conditions must be met: first, the particular form of gaming that the tribe wants to conduct must be permitted in the state in which the tribe is located; second, the tribe and the state must have negotiated a compact that has been approved by the Secretary of the Interior, or the Secretary must have approved regulatory procedures; and third, the tribe must have adopted a tribal gaming ordinance that has been approved by the chair of the commission. Once gaming compacts are in place, the primary responsibility to regulate Class III gambling on Indian lands falls to the tribes. According to the *IGRA*, states may provide some form of regulatory oversight of Class III Indian casinos, but this is not required. This level of interaction is determined by the compact negotiated by the tribe and the state. The result has been the emergence of the Tribal Gaming Commission (TGC), which is responsible for the routine monitoring of gaming activities. According to the NIGC's deputy counsel, "The tribes generally serve as the primary regulators for gambling. They're the ones on the ground. They're the ones that are there 24 hours a day. On occasion states are there 24 hours a day, too, if the tribal/state compact provides for it, but by and large it is the tribes who are doing the primary regulating of Indian gambling."[19]

An additional body, the National Indian Gaming Association (NIGA), is a non-profit body composed of 184 Indian tribes and other non-voting associate members of the 562 federally recognized Indian tribes. NIGA is mandated to advance the lives of Indian peoples economically, socially, and politically, while providing educational, legislative, and public policy resources for tribes, policy makers, and the public on Indian gaming issues and tribal community development. This is considered an essential service in an industry that, in 2005, employed 400,000 persons, of which one-quarter were North American Indians.[20] NIGA assists each community in developing a plan, mapping out how revenues will be utilized for tribal government services, economic and community development, and general tribal welfare prior to filing for a "Revenue Allocation Plan." The Secretary of the Interior must approve any per-capita payments as part of the Revenue Allocation Plan. Currently, some 47 tribes engaged in gaming distribute per-capita payments to tribal members, and those recipients pay federal income tax.[21] Fully three-quarters of gaming tribes devote all their revenue to tribal governmental services, economic and community development, neighbouring communities, and other charitable purposes.

Gaming and Nation Building: The Mashantucket Pequot

First Nations leaders in Canada initially had only the Seminole example to consider as they endeavoured to determine the feasibility of lotteries, high-stakes bingos, and casinos. The overall goal was to generate economic stability for the purposes of promoting nation building and eventually self-government. They also understood that Canada was either unwilling or unable, in the words of sociologist Menno Boldt, to "redesign its industrial society to make room for the traditional ways of Indian life."[22] Boldt acknowledged that "the challenge of living and surviving as Indians is to reformulate the ancient customs and traditions without compromising the enduring truths."[23] This would require of First Nations not taking "over the existing colonial political and bureaucratic institutional structures," but, rather, "to engage their people in planning and developing political and administrative structures and norms consistent with traditional philosophies and principles, i.e. structures that will empower the people."[24] To most First Nations leaders, this meant gaining control of local economies and creating sustainable development.

By this time, the Indian gaming phenomenon had begun to attract academic attention. Harvard University professors Stephen Cornell and Joseph P. Kalt sought to understand the conditions that resulted in sustained, self-determined social and economic development, and how to replicate these conditions in Indian nations. To support this investigation, they formed the Harvard Project on American Indian Economic Development (the Harvard Project). Considered a benchmark in the evolving discussion about First Nations economic development, the project soon became focused on nation building and Indian communities. According to Cornell and Kalt, nation building refers to the policy of legitimate self-rule exercised by Indian tribes in the United States. They defined the key characteristics of nation building as:

- the exercise of *de facto* sovereignty;
- strategic direction;
- effective institutions and policies;
- stable institutions and policies;
- fair and effective dispute resolution procedures;
- separation of politics from business management;
- competent bureaucracy; and
- cultural match.

Tribal gaming — in particular, the impact that casino enterprises had or could have on Indian communities — became their focus.

During this period, Canada's First Nations also began to zero in on tribal gaming, while asking whether gaming was an appropriate salve for the economic difficulties being experienced in the majority of First Nations communities Canada-wide. And in the wake of rapid US tribal casino expansion, the one nation-building success story that American Indian and First Nations leaders closely scrutinized was that of the Mashantucket Pequots of Connecticut. Originally one of the most powerful tribes along the Connecticut coast, Mashantucket was the earliest reservation in what would become the United States when, in 1666, over 2,000 acres were formally set aside for the Pequot's use and benefit. Although tribal leader Robin Cassacinamon requested that the reservation be placed at the headwater of the Mystic River, which the Pequot claimed as their traditional territory, his request was refused. By 1761, the British General Assembly passed a resolution reducing the reservation to 989 acres, and by 1856 it had dwindled to 180 acres following the sale of more than 600 acres at a public auction conducted by the local Indian agent.[25] The Pequot had also witnessed their population drop as a result of disease and the colonial/Indian wars, to the point where, by the late 19th century, they had lost tribal status according to federal guidelines. During the next eight decades, the Pequot reservation was managed by the State of Connecticut, which sold off the land base to pay for the Pequots' upkeep as the population continued to diminish.[26]

In the 1970s, under the leadership of Richard (Skip) Hayward, the Pequots began their tribal resurgence — an exercise that took significant time and resources. Beginning in 1972, there were only two residents on the Mashantucket Pequot Reservation: Elizabeth George Plouffe and her half sister, Martha Langevin Ellal. It was anticipated that, after their passing, the US government would transform the reservation into a state park.[27] Following Plouffe's death in 1973, her grandson Skip quit his job at a nearby New London submarine facility and returned to the reservation to take up residence, promising to improve housing and achieve tribal economic independence.[28] He also began to urge former tribal members to return to the reservation to rebuild the Pequot Tribe in an effort to compel US recognition of their status. Within a year, there were 55 members listed on the tribal rolls, and the tribal government design and its operations were overhauled. Hayward was elected leader of the tribal council at the first annual meeting in 1975, and remained in that position until 1998. His ability to restructure tribal government and entice former community members back to the reservation was impressive. However, the Pequots lost their tribal status. According to legal scholar David Wilkins, "federal acknowledgement is a formal act that establishes a political relationship between a tribe and the United States. It affirms the tribe's sovereign status. Simultaneously, it outlines the federal government's responsibilities to the tribes."[29] Not only did this mean that the Pequots did not have sovereign status, they were also not "entitled to the immunities and privileges available to other tribes."[30]

This became a key issue in the late 1980s when the Pequots decided on gaming as an economic development strategy, for only recognized tribes had exemptions from state laws, enjoyed sovereign immunity, and were not "subject to the same constitutional restraints as are the state and federal governments."[31] The primary goal for Hayward, then, was to regain tribal status for the Pequot, a task that would first require the Pequot to demonstrate demographic stability. Shoring up the membership numbers was clearly the place to start. The most important criterion utilized by the federal and tribal governments for determining tribal membership was blood quantum, a concept first introduced with the 1877 *Allotment Act*, which was designed as a means of transferring communally held reservation lands to private ownership and, in the process, reduce overall tribal landholdings — thereby also reducing recognized tribal populations and the accompanying federal trust relationship. Blood quantum was once again employed in the early part of the 20th century by the US government "as a mechanism to reduce federal expenditures for education."[32] By the mid-20th century, it had become the major factor in determining tribal membership and "whether a given individual is to be excluded from the scope of legislation dealing with Indians."[33] At the same time, there was a certain amount of flexibility when it came to determining tribal membership: individual tribes set their own limits above the federally accepted one-sixteenth minimum blood quantum to make a legitimate claim for tribal membership. Hayward and the Mashantucket Pequot Tribal Council determined that the federal minimum one-sixteenth blood quantum would guide their criteria; as well, they also decided to recognize members who were able to prove Pequot descent from the tribal rolls recorded in the Indian supplement of the 1900-10 census, which listed close to 35 names.[34]

Adding further to the difficulties of determining tribal membership was the location of potential tribal members. The Pequot had gradually moved away from the reservation during the 20th century, and the potential tribal membership was geographically scattered. In addition, many of those same people were also registered as members of the tribal nations with which they were at the time residing. Hayward asked them to move from their adopted communities, where they had firmly rooted and strong kinship ties, back to the Pequot reservation. Many agreed to accept, as part of their membership, two-acre lots on the reservation with the possibility of becoming involved in the proposed tribally owned businesses. Hayward then took the US government to court in 1976, seeking the return of appropriated lands and federal recognition of the Pequot as an Indian tribe.

A secondary goal was to develop the Pequots' economic potential. A number of local economic initiatives were developed by the mid-1970s that began with the Pequots' establishing grassroots businesses, such as maple syrup production, timber resources, and hog farming. The tribe was gradually becoming economically stable, and had a limited economic infrastructure in place when, in 1983, the *Mashantucket Pequot Indian Claims Settlement Act* — the result of a lawsuit first launched in 1976 — was passed, resulting in a $900,000 settlement that could be used to buy back tribal lands. The timing was perfect. After channelling a portion of the compensation monies into a program to improve reservation housing and purchase land, Hayward travelled to Florida to meet with Seminole Chief James Billy. The Seminoles had recently won their landmark court case enabling the tribe to establish a high-stakes bingo enterprise on reservation land. Hayward recognized the case's potential to open up high-stakes gaming on US reservations, and set in motion the development of what would become one of the world's largest gaming establishments.

The small but stable reservation economy that had developed since the mid-1970s provided the Pequot with the capital to build a bingo hall, which netted $2.6 million the first year.[35] Soon afterward, the 1987 *Cabazon* decision opened the door to Hayward and the tribal council to expand their existing operations to include casino-style gambling. Notwithstanding the Pequot nation's sovereign status, the establishment of the IGRA required that the tribe enter into a gaming compact with the State of Connecticut prior to commencing any form of high-stakes gambling. The tribal council early in 1989 approached the State of Connecticut and proposed a state/tribal gaming compact. The state refused. While the IGRA required the Pequot to approach the state, the *Act* also required that the state negotiate in good faith with the tribe. When the state refused a second request, the Pequot took Connecticut to court. The Pequot were briefly vindicated following the court's determination that the state was required to negotiate a gaming compact with the tribe, but still the state refused. Finally, the court appointed a mediator and required the state to submit to negotiations.

Governor Lowell Weicker, Jr., though submitting to the negotiations, argued that the proposed Pequot gaming compact contained provisions for slot machines, an illegal form of gambling in Connecticut at the time. Both parties submitted copies of their proposed compact, of which the Bureau of Indian Affairs (BIA) chose the state's proposal. Eventually, however, the BIA accepted the Pequot compact as binding, and, despite Connecticut's refusal to sign, high-stakes gaming on the Pequot reservation was now permitted. Recognizing that the highest source of revenue in any casino is the slots, the Pequot attempted to establish their casino while simultaneously trying to evade state provisions that made slot machines illegal. A tenuous period of lobbying followed, but eventually Weicker relented and granted permission to the Pequot to include as many slot machines as they desired. In return, however, the State of Connecticut was to receive one-quarter of the Pequot's total slot revenues. Since slots were still illegal in Connecticut, the fact that the Pequots had them resulted in their obtaining a monopoly. By the mid-1990s the State of Connecticut was receiving an average of between $40-50 million each month from 6,500 slot machines.

Once again the timing was apt, for eastern Connecticut in the early 1990s was in the throes of an economic crisis. A downsizing in general manufacturing as well as in the defence industry resulted in a loss of nearly 10,000 jobs.[36] By 1993, projections anticipated the loss of close to 32,000 jobs, resulting in 25 per cent regional unemployment.[37] The change in laws regarding tribal gaming combined with the unique geographic location of the Pequot reservation between two metropolitan areas and the general acceptance of the American public of tribal gaming left Hayward and the Pequot in an unprecedented position to expand their operations.[38] Located a two-hour drive from approximately 20 million people, Foxwoods Resort Casino grew from a small bingo hall into a $60 million gaming facility. When its doors opened, Foxwoods included an expanded 250,000-square-foot bingo hall and a 46,000-square-foot gaming area with 170 tables that employed 2,300 people.[39] During its first year of operations, $4.5 billion was wagered and Foxwoods grossed over $800 million. In 1996, the casino grossed over $1 billion, which represented almost one-fifth of that year's total Indian gaming gross revenue in the United States.[40] The current complex, including gaming and public areas, hotels, and restaurants, is 4.7 million square feet; of this, 315,310 are devoted to gaming.

Foxwoods' impact is significant to the point that it is difficult to fathom what Connecticut's socio-economic state would be without it. The casino sees 41,000 visitors a day and employs 12,934 people; casino operations result in $252 million spent yearly. The $193-million Mashantucket Pequot Museum, a leading cultural attraction in the area, attracts more than a quarter of a million visitors a year, of which more than 40 per cent come exclusively to the museum, and generates more than $800,000 in total revenues. The Pequot also own off-reservation businesses; the Pequot Hotel Group employs an additional 797 people, resulting in $7.4 million in local purchases. Since the opening of Foxwoods, the State of Connecticut has collected more than $1 billion in slot revenues, $2.3 million annually in property taxes paid to neighbouring towns, and an additional $4.4 million in regulatory fees. It has been estimated that every new Foxwoods job supports roughly 1.23 additional non-casino jobs, meaning that 20,017 new jobs have been created in New London County, where the casino is located.[41]

A recent University of Connecticut study revealed that "the Mashantucket Pequot Tribal Nation plays a major role in the regional economy, contributing 41,000 jobs to the State, with 31,000 of those in New London County, generating $1.2 billion in Gross State Product, and adding $1.9 billion to the State's aggregate personal income. Of these amounts, New London County captures $800 million in GRP and $1.1 billion in personal income."[42] Foxwoods plans to open two championship golf courses and recently began construction of a $100 million addition that would add 825 slot machines in addition to more parking, restaurants, and retail stores.[43]

Conclusion

The story of tribal gaming does not end with the Pequots. For every success story, there are dozens of tribes that failed to establish successful gaming enterprises. In a statement to the National Gambling Impact Study Commission in 1998, Joseph Kalt expressed his amazement at how the success of a handful of tribes had coloured the public's perception of Indian gaming. He went on to note that, in 1996 alone, "more than half of all Indian gaming revenues were generated by only eight tribes' operations."[44] The revenues generated by tribal gaming establishments are impressive and can facilitate nation-building and economic stability, both of which have long evaded US Indian leaders. However, the Canadian situation differs significantly from that of the US, where American Indian tribes are considered sovereign entities, enabling Indian control over reservation gaming. There is also a centralized bureaucracy dealing with gaming, and specific legislation to guide the industry's evolution. First Nations brought home many of these lessons and continued to monitor the situation. As they would soon find out, however, the lessons they learned in the United States would be of limited help to them in Canada.

CHAPTER FIVE

Ontario: The Legal Ramifications

Criminologist Colin Campbell suggests that Canada's current legal regime is antiquated and out of step with popular forms of gambling. He has argued that the pith and substance of contemporary legal responses to gambling were shaped during the first 25 years of the 20th century, when exemptions were made regarding gambling at racetracks which, in turn, established the political, moral, economic, and legal contexts for later amendments to the *Criminal Code*.[1] Legislators of the time could not have anticipated the emergence of First Nations' interest in gaming. It was the 1990s before Canadian law pertaining to First Nations gaming was established, and then it was the provinces that were given jurisdiction over gaming, empowering provincial officials to choose what order of gaming establishments they would sanction and what the prize limits would be set at, while gaining control over the number and nature of events that could be held. This corresponded with reports from the United States indicating that gaming revenues from tribal casinos totaled $212 million in 1988 (a figure that jumped to $6.7 billion by 1997),[2] and First Nations leaders began to promote gaming more aggressively as a cure for the economic and social ills in their communities.

Despite the financial figures filtering into Canada, federal officials were reluctant to authorize First Nations gaming. In response to First Nations lobby efforts, the Ontario government eventually acquiesced, not anticipating the cost and time that would be spent in court delineating each party's responsibilities. Nevertheless, on 31 July 1996, Casino Rama opened to an eager public curious to inspect Canada's largest First Nations-operated casino. Since being chosen in 1994 as the host community, the Mnjikaning First Nation had become the focus of the national media and Ontario First Nations looking to cash in on a portion of gaming revenues. During the next 18 months, events unfolded according to schedule. Then in June 1995, following the election of the Progressive Conservatives, Ontario First Nations lost, in NDP leader Bob Rae, their strongest supporter. It was Rae who had initiated discussions leading to the creation of Casino Rama. Following Rae's defeat at the polls, Premier Mike Harris started dismantling the original Ontario-First Nations gaming agreement. The most egregious revision was his imposed 20 per cent Win Tax on gross revenues generated by Casino Rama. An initial period of political interaction between the provincial Progressive Conservatives and Ontario First Nations slowly devolved into a relationship distinguished by animosity and distrust.

The Genesis of First Nations Gaming in Ontario

Prior to engaging in any discussion about Casino Rama, the 10-year period preceding the NDP's announcement that it would support a First Nations casino must be reviewed, for it was during this decade that First Nations gaming policy in Canada was forged.

The Shawanaga First Nation in Ontario was the first to challenge the federal government for the right to conduct reserve gaming. Their position was that gaming was a constitutionally protected Aboriginal right. Not unlike other First Nations communities, Shawanaga, located approximately 30 km northwest of Parry Sound, boasts a population of 550, with 209 living on-reserve, and total land holdings of 3,377 hectares.[3] In 1986, the construction of a recreation complex began on reserve land with the aid of provincial and federal funding. Many band councillors deemed the federal support inadequate, and suggested that the funding could be supplemented by establishing a gaming house. The federal government, however, refused to allow the proposed high-stakes bingo operation to proceed, despite declarations by Shawanaga officials that revenues would be directed toward alleviating reserve socio-economic conditions and a subsequent increase in reserve employment. Despite inadequate funding, the recreation centre was completed in 1987, and soon started being used as a gaming house.

Shawanaga leaders acknowledged that they would have to develop a legal strategy in anticipation of a negative response from the government. If court proceedings were initiated, they would cite the *Indian Act* in support of their claim to jurisdiction over reserve gaming. To subvert provincial jurisdiction, Shawanaga leaders argued that section 81 of the *Indian Act* provided for band "control and prohibition of public games" and "other amusements," a strategy many First Nations leaders considered key to their future prosperity.[4] According to the *Act*, the Canadian government accepted First Nations' right "to control public games," including high-stakes bingos.[5] Then, in 1985, the federal government delegated authority for gaming to the provinces. According to the *Criminal Code*, then, bands interested in gaming were required to obtain a provincial license prior to commencing gaming activities.[6]

Federal and provincial officials were not caught unawares, for the Shawanaga had long advocated local control of gaming. In 1981, two band resolutions were passed establishing the Shawanaga First Nation Lottery law followed by a community policy to establish the Shawanaga First Nation lottery authority vested with the authority to name its members.[7] These actions suggest that community officials believed their unique status permitted them to operate outside provincial jurisdiction. Gaming operations commenced, and band councillors pronounced Shawanaga an independent nation within Canada with the inherent right to self-government. They claimed that Canadian laws, as they related to First Nations gaming, did not extend to reserve communities. Acting on their professed self-governing jurisdiction, the Shawanaga First Nation Council passed two resolutions in August 1987 which, according to section 81 of the *Indian Act*, authorized the band council to pass local gaming by-laws:

> Be it resolved that the Shawanaga First Nation Government officially advises the Federal Government of Canada and the Provincial Government of Ontario that the Shawanaga First Nation Government does not recognize these governments' laws having any application or jurisdiction on our sovereign land base set out in the 1850 Robinson Huron Treaty which was set aside and held by our people.

> Be it resolved that the Shawanaga First Nation rejects any enforcement officer entering Shawanaga First Nation lands to enforce federal or provincial laws without first signing a treaty agreement with the Shawanaga First Nation Government giving these governments jurisdiction on our lands.[8]

Community centre bingos eventually sparked an Ontario Provincial Police (OPP) investigation. At first the OPP warned Chief Howard Jones and the band council that they were in violation of the *Criminal Code* — specifically, that they had failed to procure a provincial gaming license. Jones ignored the warnings, choosing to initiate a media blitz to inform the public of his community's dilemma. In a September 1987 interview, he claimed that the band netted $20,000 per month from its operations, and that cash prizes of nearly $20,000 were awarded at weekly events that drew upwards of 400 people per night. Jones also stated that the gaming revenues would aid in the construction of a school and a health care facility. Arguing that government grants "for these things" always come with "strings attached," he added that gaming revenues helped to support local programs aimed at improving housing on the reserve and in nearby Parry Sound, and that his community would continue to bus in gamblers from all over the region at its own expense.[9] By then, the reserve bingo halls were situated in three large circus tents where customers were charged admission ranging from $100 on one day to $50 on another.[10] The OPP charged Chief Howard Pamajewon and former Chief

Howard Jones with running an unlawful gaming house later in 1987.

Meanwhile, leaders of the tiny Eagle Lake First Nation in western Ontario were facing similar issues in their attempts to establish a high-stakes bingo operation. The chief and council of the community of 225 located near Dryden had passed a resolution in 1985 authorizing the band council to establish a lottery law and regulate gaming activities on the reserve. Although the band had run a small-scale bingo operation since the 1950s, bingo had recently become big business at Eagle Lake, beginning with once-a-month "monster bingos" that paid upwards of $90,000 and generated net profits of up to $50,000 per night. Soon crowds of up to 1,000 people were attending these events, many entering the community on chartered buses.[11] By the early 1990s, the Eagle Lake operation was employing more than 21 full- and part-time people and generating more than $1.2 million annually in revenue. Bingo profits were channeled into band programs to help pay for an elementary school and gymnasium, a tourist camp, a hockey arena and community centre, and improved housing.[12] On 3 November 1990, the OPP charged Chief Arnold Gardner and band members Allan Gardner and Jack Pitchenese with running a bingo operation without a provincial gaming license.

As these events transpired, the Supreme Court of Canada was occupied with *R. v. Furtney*, a case originating in Ontario in which the accused — Philip Furtney, Scott Furtney, Diane Roy, Hugh Chamney, and Diamond Bingo Inc. — were charged with counselling licensees of bingo lottery schemes to violate the terms and conditions of their licences, specifically the so-called 15-20 per cent rule, whereby a maximum of 15 per cent of the revenues can go to management costs and a minimum of 20 per cent must go to the charity. The trial judge found that the provisions of the *Criminal Code* purporting to delegate power to the Lieutenant Governor in Council were *ultra vires* — acting beyond the scope of its powers — and dismissed the charges. On appeal, however, the Supreme Court concluded that the provinces were simply asserting their constitutional powers according to section 92 of the *British North America Act* of 1867.[13]

The court in *Furtney* held that both the federal and provincial governments held jurisdiction over gaming. The federal government prohibited gaming generally, but permitted exceptions through the delegation of administrative responsibility for gaming to the province. Nonetheless, *Furtney* stands for the proposition that a provincial legislature has jurisdiction to enact laws in the gaming area subject only to Parliament's paramountcy in the case of a clash between federal and provincial legislation.[14] It is important to note that there is a limitation on a provincial legislature's jurisdiction in this area, and, according to the court, the province cannot prohibit and punish in the interest of public morality, because such legislation is criminal law.[15] In a related case, the Alberta provincial court ruled in *R. v. Gladue and Kirby*[16] that the *Indian Act* did not supersede "the application of the criminal code to gambling on a reserve."[17]

Now that it appeared that avenues challenging the provinces' right to license gaming on reserves had been effectively closed off, gaming proponents were forced to devise a new strategy. The struggle would now turn to establishing that First Nations had an inherent right to conduct reserve gaming enterprises. Shawanaga Chief Roger Jones was vociferous in his support of the Aboriginal right to self-government. "We regard ourselves as a sovereign nation," he said, "we sign treaties and we have the right to pass laws in our lands and if we wish to pass a law that's going to generate revenue for our community in whatever manner we see fit, we have the right to do that."[18]

Jones also addressed the concept of sovereignty and self-government before the Royal Commission on Aboriginal Peoples (RCAP) in 1993:

> Sovereignty is difficult to define because it is intangible, it cannot be seen or touched. It is very much inherent, an awesome power, a strong feeling or the belief of a people. What can be seen, however, is the exercise of Aboriginal powers. For our purposes, a working definition of sovereignty is the ultimate power from which all specific political powers are derived.[19]

Steadfast in its claims to sovereignty and self-government, the Shawanaga band council was also pragmatic in its belief that the province did not have the right to control First Nations gaming. Although it was not entirely clear how provincial legislation would affect a reserve gaming establishment, the Shawanaga First Nation took the time to meet with the OPP and the Ontario Lotteries Corproration (OLC) to determine the extent of provincial jurisdiction. Somewhat surprisingly, the OLC offered the band a license to conduct gaming operations, which Shawanaga representatives politely declined, claiming that the establishment of any reserve economic initiative was an inherent right of a self-governing nation.[20] By accepting a license from a provincial agency, the Shawanaga First Nation would be compromising their political authority.

Jones and Pamajewon were convicted in March 1993 of keeping a common gaming house, contrary to section 201(l) of the *Criminal Code*.[21] Later that year, in November, Chief Arnold Gardner, Jack Pitchenese, and Allan Gardner of the Eagle Lake First Nation were convicted of conducting a scheme for the purpose of determining who were the winners of any property, specifically a bingo, contrary to section 206(1)(d) of the *Criminal Code*. Shawanaga legal counsel David Nahwegahbow foreshadowed these events following his defeat in *R. v. Jones* in 1991 by stating that he would pursue the case to the Supreme Court, because in his mind the issue was a constitutional question dealing with whether or not the provinces had the right to regulate First Nations' interests.[22] He further stated that, though the band may be considered guilty "in the eyes of the public," he believed that "the political arena is still open" and an "avenue we have to look at."[23]

Supreme Court of Canada Justice William Stevenson countered Nahwegahbow in his response in *Jones*, indicating that "such a mistaken belief was no answer to the charges since ignorance of the law is no defence to breaking it." Stevenson noted that the band did not challenge the validity of the *Criminal Code* gaming section, although it did request that the court not make any statements that may adversely affect legal issues concerning Aboriginal self-government.[24] The next stage would be to wait for the appeal process to runs its course.

The Evolution of First Nations Gaming in Ontario

In 1992, Ontario Premier Bob Rae announced his intention to open a reserve casino, as he had promised during his election campaign. He envisioned the establishment of a high-stakes casino to be operated by provincial First Nations as a source of revenue to improve the poor socio-economic conditions of most reserves. Rae initiated discussions, and took the controversial step of forgoing the province's share of the revenue, agreeing instead to direct all casino revenues to the First Nations. Mocked by the press and vilified by the Opposition, Rae maintained his belief in gaming as a means of assisting First Nations in reserve economic development. Despite the premier's position, the Ministry of Consumer and Commercial Relations was slow to involve First Nations in discussions or negotiations. Responding to the apparent lack of government interest, Union of Ontario Indians (UOI) delegate Joe Miskokomon spoke before the Ontario Legislative Assembly about the proposed *Ontario Casino Corporation Act* in September 1993. Miskokomon informed members that "both procedurally and substantially, we have been disappointed by the approach of the Ontario government to casino development and implementation." In particular, "the ministry has not entered into any formal negotiations on casinos with the first nations." Fearing that the Ontario casino industry, if established without First Nations participation, could overwhelm centrally located communities while not helping more geographically isolated reserves, Miskokomon expressed his desire to see First Nations and the Ontario government work together: "I believe that the keys to success of the gaming industry in Ontario are co-operation, co-ordination and control." Co-operation, he said, would "ensure the greatest benefit for both the government of Ontario and the first nations, which will in turn ensure that the industry is effectively controlled." At the time of Miskokomon's testimony, there were 45 reserve school projects on hold owing to a lack of financing. Further, additional funding was needed to improve community infrastructure, including basic services "such as roads and sewers that are in desperate need of repair or construction." Miskokomon ended his statement by stressing the need for Ontario to maintain its responsibility "to ensure that this industry is developed in a careful and conscientious way."[25]

The ministry eventually met with representatives of 24 First Nations and developed five criteria pertaining to the establishment of a First Nations casino:

1. it would support a single First Nations pilot casino;
2. the pilot casino would be situated on a reserve;
3. the casino would meet the same standards of integrity and security as the planned Windsor casino;
4. the First Nations pilot casino would operate in conformity with the *Criminal Code of Canada*; and,
5. all casino revenue profits would be shared among the province's First Nations.

If questions about gaming's potential remained, a 1993 Ontario Casino Project study conducted by Coopers and Lybrand Consulting Group should have assuaged any fears; it projected that an aggregate of seven casinos throughout Ontario would generate more than $850-million in annual revenues. Spin-offs would include casino patrons spending upwards of $1.4 billion on non-casino purchases, of which 60 per cent of revenues would result from visitors from outside Ontario. The construction industry would benefit from 13,000 person-years of employment and, once operational, the casinos would create 97,000 full-time jobs.[26] While the report dealt with issues such as pathological gambling and its associated problems, they were the only social costs mentioned.

In late 1993, the NDP and provincial First Nations were still negotiating for the construction of a First Nations casino. The Mnjikaning First Nation decided that their community was perfectly suited to house a casino, and band manager Ted Williams and cultural advisor Mark Douglas aimed their lobby efforts at the premier's office. The largely untapped Toronto gambling market was a source of optimism to a community whose main industry was a band-owned business making portable toilets, and local unemployment hovered around 65 per cent.

The Mnjikaning (Rama) First Nation is located 15 km east of Orillia in Ontario's cottage country, and 135 km north of Toronto. The community is situated on 2,350 acres of land divided into eight separate parcels, with a membership of 1,266 people, of which 505 live on reserve.[27] The written history of the Mnjikaning First Nation can be traced to 1690, when Chippewa leaders agreed to assist the Huron-Wendat people in a war against the Iroquois. After the brief war was over, the people decided to remain, owing to the prevalence of food provided by the local fishing weirs. The Chippewa supplemented their lifestyle by hunting and trading with other First Nations and British and French traders. Eventually an onslaught of settlers into modern-day Ontario resulted in their encroachment onto and eventual occupation of Mnjikaning territory, which was desired by settlers for the same reasons that attracted the Chippewa: an abundance of fish and good hunting. The Chippewa happened also to be situated beside a central transportation hub long utilized by a myriad of First Nations travelling in this region of Ontario. Not lost on local colonial administrators was the fact that Mnjikaning land was considered rich farmland with unlimited agricultural potential.

In 1818, colonial administrators hatched a plan to open up Ontario for settlement, and immediately approached Mnjikaning leaders to propose an exchange. In return for a perpetual annuity of £1,200 in both currency and goods, Mnjikaning Chief Mesquakie (William Yellowhead) agreed to cede 1,592,000 acres to the colonial government to be opened up for settlement. Colonial officials upheld their end of the deal, but the Chippewa soon found themselves contending with unchecked colonial settlement. Such was the case in much of eastern Ontario, and the threat of hostilities began to take root. Wary of the near-constant threat of war and settler complaints, Lieutenant-Governor Sir John Colborne created a plan in 1829 aimed at settling all of the "nomadic tribes" into two settlements located at Coldwater and the Narrows (near Orillia). Upon his arrival at the Narrows, Mesquakie and his people were ensured that this was the last time they would have to relocate, and were encouraged to take up farming. But again, unchecked settler movement into the region and pressure to open up the Narrows to large-scale farming resulted in Mesquakie and his followers once again relocating, this time to Ramara Township, where they purchased 1,600 acres of land. By 1846 the Chippewa had 300 acres under cultivation and a settlement of 20 houses, four barns, and a school house. By the 1870s, the community was known to the government as the Chippewas of Rama, a name that stuck until 1993 when the community formally changed its name to the Mnjikaning First Nation.

With the exception of subsistence farming and the local fisheries, little in the way of economic development occurred at Mnjikaning prior to the late 1960s, when a trailer park and convenience store opened and some fishing guides moved into the region. In the 1980s, the chief and council, working with the community's newly struck economic development team called "Living Effectively in Rama Now" (LERN), began to promote to the community the need to invest in new and innovative economic initiatives. In what were described as informal "kitchen-dialogues," community members met to determine priorities while also developing coping strategies. The result of these discussions was a 10-year plan whose intent was to see the installation of a local water system, a new community centre, a new church, and a local newsletter. RAMCOR was then created to promote business and economic development, although there were still a number of obstacles that had to be overcome. For instance, Mnjikaning was situated in the heart of cottage country, effectively shutting the door to industrial development, and the limited land base would not permit large-scale industrial farming or mineral extraction. However, one off-reserve community member closely monitoring the US tribal gaming industry eventually convinced the band council to consider establishing a bingo. The Mnjikaning First Nation initiated discussions with the American entertainment conglomerate, Bally's, about building a community casino.[28]

The band's economic development team and select members of the band council preserved a secret relationship with Bally's. Community members acknowledged the proposed casino's economic potential. Many, however, were concerned that the casino would result in higher crime rates and increased traffic, or that the casino would become the centre of the community, outstripping the best interests of the people in lieu of maintaining profit levels. Even though most people believed that strategies could be developed to ameliorate future problems, community members were soon divided into pro- and anti-casino camps. A protracted period of information sessions and community discussions followed, and it was decided that a referendum should be held to determine community support. From 14-16 September 1994, 120 community members travelled to Foxwoods, America's largest tribally owned and operated casino, to witness first-hand gaming's potential. This was followed by three information sessions sponsored by the chief and council, the casino economic development team, and Bally's representatives to answer the community's questions. At one of these sessions, word leaked out that the band council had signed a management deal with Bally's, stipulating that the Mnjikaning band council was obliged to partner with Bally's in the event the casino project was accepted and given permission by Ontario to begin construction. Despite this public relations setback, one week later, on 28 September, the community voted 71 per cent in favour of the casino.

By February 1994, 14 provincial First Nations had submitted proposals to host the casino. At this time the Ontario government announced that a First Nations fund would be established to administer the gaming profits to the province's First Nations. Negotiations continued, despite pressure from First Nation's leaders to force the Ontario government to recognize First Nations' jurisdiction over gaming. Premier Rae announced on 5 December that the Mnjikaning First Nation had been selected as the site. The casino would be situated on First Nations land (the Mnjikaning reserve) and would be run by an established corporation during its first 10 years of operations. Unfortunately for Bally's, the province instructed Mnjikaning leaders to terminate their relationship with the entertainment consortium. A casino operator was nevertheless required, and a request for proposals was sent out which stipulated that the operator's costs prior to construction would include the construction of a recreational facility, a senior's home, and the establishment of a trust fund to develop a gambling addictions program. Bally's was permitted to compete in the selection process, but in the end the selection committee chose the Miami-based Carnival Hotels and Casinos. Bally's did not follow through on a threat to sue the Mnjikaning band council for breach of contract.

The Mnjikaning proposal was considered the most attractive for a number of reasons, the most important being the revenue-sharing formula, which would see

65 per cent of net revenues split among the province's 133 First Nations. Of this, half would be distributed by population: 40 per cent would be distributed equally among all First Nations, and 10 per cent to those communities designated as remote. The remaining 35 per cent would remain with the Mnjikaning First Nation to deal with issues ranging from the impact that increased traffic would have on reserve infrastructure to ensuring the funding of local programs to deal with problem gaming in the community.

Following site selection, a development and operations agreement was reached between Ontario, Carnival Hotels and Casinos Canada Ltd. as casino operator, and the Mnjikaning First Nation. Construction on the $42-million Casino Rama began in 1995, and the facility was slated to open in May 1996. However, following the announced opening date, the First Nations of Ontario found themselves embroiled in a number of disputes, all of which resulted from the NDP's defeat at the hands of the Progressive Conservatives on 8 June 1995. During the campaign, Mike Harris had promised that his party had no intention of altering the gaming agreement and that the First Nations could keep the casino profits. Following the election, Harris rescinded his promise and imposed a 20 per cent Win Tax on Casino Rama gross revenues. He argued that it was standard operating procedure, and that his government simply wanted the same 20 per cent it currently received from the Windsor casino and would obtain from the proposed Niagara Falls casino. When First Nations leaders refused to renegotiate, Harris responded by shutting down construction in February, and the province halted casino financing until an operating agreement had been formalized.

Mnjikaning Chief Lorraine McRae claimed that the process did not conform to the original agreement between the Ontario government and the provincial First Nations. The promise, she said, "was that the Native people would benefit — all 131 First Nations — and that the province was not to benefit from this in any way at all."[29] NDP MPP Tony Silipo told the media that "the Tories have taken a deal negotiated in good faith, and reneged — without consultation, without notice and at the 11th hour."[30] Even Orillia's Mayor, Clayt French, expressed his dismay with the government's new demands, stating, "I think at this stage of the game, it's pretty horrible. That's like changing the rules halfway through the game."[31] Nevertheless, the Chief's Committee and the Planning and Priorities Committee agreed to set aside 20 per cent of future revenues in a trust account in order to continue their consultations with provincial officials, the goal being to keep construction on track.

While negotiations continued, 300 workers were laid off within a week of construction coming to a halt.[32] Economic Development Minister Bill Saunderson announced to the media in March that a deal had been reached to resume construction; unfortunately, the delays pushed the casino's opening to July 1996. Saunderson also stated that the province would impose the Win Tax, which at the time was approximately $650 million over the next 10 years.[33] Gord Peters, regional chief of the Chiefs of Ontario, claimed that, while an agreement to resume construction had been reached, First Nations still rejected the Win Tax: "From our point of view, we've never agreed with the 20 per cent the province is taking. It was a unilateral decision on their behalf."[34] Nevertheless, in April the final Development and Operating Agreement was signed between the provincial First Nations and the Ontario Lottery Gaming Corporation. The Harris government compelled First Nations to sign an acknowledgement that Casino Rama would remit the required 20 per cent Win Tax to the Consolidated Revenue Fund.[35] Casino Rama opened its doors to the public on 31 July 1996.

The Shawanaga/Eagle Lake Appeals

As Casino Rama was preparing for its grand opening, the Shawanaga appeal was winding its way up to the Supreme Court. The First Nations' legal team presented three points of defence. First, they argued that the Crown had not proved the essential elements of the charge, which was running a bingo operation without a provincial gaming license. Second, they argued that section 15 of the *Criminal Code* provided a defence, for they were establishing and enforcing laws by right of sovereign power. Third, they argued that the laws of Canada were of no force or effect pursuant to the Shawanaga First Nation's inherent right to self-govern.[36] Defence lawyers argued that gambling existed prior to extended European contact for both ceremonial and celebratory purposes, thereby permitting the appellants to operate and regulate high-stakes gambling on reserves. The Ontario Court of Appeal on 21 December 1994 declined this argument and upheld the conviction.[37] The Supreme Court upheld the Ontario court's decision on 22 August 1996, concluding that the essential elements of the charge had been proven. The Court also held that "the appellants had not demonstrated either that they were acting in 'obedience' to the Shawanaga First Nation's lottery law (it did not require them to act as they did) or that the band council had *de facto* sovereignty."[38]

The court concluded that, in order for gaming to be recognized as an Aboriginal right, the activity in question must be an element of a tradition, custom, or practice integral to the distinctive culture of the Aboriginal group claiming the right. Directed to determine whether the activity in question could be said to be a defining feature of the culture in question prior to contact with Europeans, the court articulated that gaming was not, in fact, an integral part of the distinctive cultures of the Shawanaga or Eagle Lake First Nations. As such, gaming was *not* an Aboriginal right, and therefore reserve gaming facilities were not exempt from provincial legislation according to Sec. 35(1).[39] This, in effect, created a situation whereby only the manner or method of exercising the activity would be permitted to evolve while the activities themselves would not.[40] Justice Claire L'Heureux-

Dubé indicated that gaming in its current context must be weighed against the historical record to establish whether the Aboriginal right to gaming existed. The Justice determined that gaming

> should not be characterized as "the rights of the Shawanaga and Eagle Lake First Nations to participate in, and to regulate, gambling activities on their respective reserve lands." The proper inquiry focuses upon the activity itself and not on the specific manner in which it has been manifested. The claim must be broadly characterized: do the appellants possess an existing aboriginal right to gamble? If such a right can be shown to exist it would oblige the government to justify the infringement upon that right by the Criminal Code, which essentially prohibits gambling.[41]

Responding to her own question, Justice L'Heureux-Dubé stated: "The evidence presented did not show that gambling ever played an important role in the cultures of the Shawanaga and Eagle Lake First Nations. Gambling as a practice was not connected enough to the self-identity and self-preservation of the aboriginal societies involved here to deserve the protection of section 35(1)." As such, "[i]t was unnecessary to consider whether section 35(1) encompasses a broad right of self-government which includes the authority to regulate gambling activities on the reservation. Even if some rights of self-government existed before 1982, there was no evidence that gambling on reserve lands generally was ever the subject matter of aboriginal regulation."[42] Justice Antonio Lamer concurred:

> The most accurate characterization of the appellants' claim is that they are asserting that section 35(1) recognizes and affirms the rights of the Shawanaga and Eagle Lake First Nations to participate in, and to regulate, gambling activities on their respective reserve lands. Characterizing the appellant's claim as an inherent right of self-government was considered too general, and must be related to a particular custom, practice, tradition or activity.[43]

Citing *R. v. Van der Peet*, Justice Lamer concluded that "Aboriginal rights, including any asserted right to self-government, must be looked at in light of the specific circumstances of each case and, in particular, in light of the specific history and culture of the aboriginal group claiming the right."[44] As such, the "evidence presented at trial did not demonstrate that gambling, or that the regulation of gambling, was an integral part of the distinctive cultures of the Shawanaga or Eagle Lake First Nations at the time of contact. The activity was therefore not protected by s. 35(1)."[45]

The original claim, that gaming was an inherent Aboriginal right, was answered. Of note, the case was also related to self-government as an Aboriginal right, and not to self-government as an exercise of Aboriginal title. The possibility of the recognition of Aboriginal rights occurring in another case as well as to the exercise of self-government as part of Aboriginal title have not been exhausted. In sum, the Supreme Court articulated that gaming was *not* an Aboriginal right and that on-reserve gaming facilities were not exempt from provincial legislation according to Sec. 35(1). Currently, even should reserve gaming activities and the corresponding by-laws receive federal consent, the provinces argue that the *Criminal Code* applies to all Canadians, First Nations notwithstanding, and since the *Code* gives regulatory power over gaming to the provinces, First Nations would be forced to observe provincial regulations and licensing provisions.

The Métis Sue the Ontario Government

In May 1996 the Ontario provincial government was once again embroiled in a gaming lawsuit. This time the legal action was initiated by Métis and non-status Indians who claimed they were being discriminated against by virtue of their not being included in the Casino Rama revenue-sharing agreement. Robert Lovelace, a member of the Ardoch Algonquin community located near Kingston, and 1,200 individuals filed suit, seeking a portion Casino Rama's anticipated $100-million annual revenues, although the casino had not yet opened its doors. The province informed Lovelace that the casino's proceeds would be distributed only to Ontario First Nations communities registered as bands under the *Indian Act*. Métis and non-status Aboriginal leaders argued that, at the individual level, their communities included members who "have, or are entitled to, registration as individual 'Indians' pursuant to the *Indian Act*."[46]

Among the appellants were the Be-Wab-bon Métis and Non-Status Indian Association, the Bonnechere Métis Association, self-identified as Métis communities, and the Ontario Métis Aboriginal Association (OMAA), a non-profit organization representing the interests of off-reserve Aboriginal peoples.[47] They argued that Métis and non-status Indians living off reserve were effectively frozen out of an estimated $100 million a year in profits, the result of a decision by provincial officials to include only "Indian bands recognized by the federal government."[48] All gaming assets were frozen until the case was finalized, which would take four years. At trial, the judge accepted the argument concerning Ontario's unconstitutional actions in denying the Métis and non-status Indians' participation in the negotiations. The judge held that, by excluding the Métis, Ontario had violated section 15(2) of the *Charter of Rights and Freedoms*, and that the province's actions were *ultra vires* the *Constitution Act, 1867*. The judge ordered that the Métis be allowed to participate in future revenue distribution negotiations.

The Ontario Court of Appeal subsequently set aside the decision, finding that "the motions judge had misapprehended the facts and made errors in law."[49] Since the key objective of the casino project "was to ameliorate the social and economic conditions of bands," the court held that "the casino project was authorized by s. 15(2) of the Charter and could not therefore constitute discrimination under s. 15(1)."[50] Furthermore, "the Court of Appeal held also that the province did not act *ultra vires* the *Constitution Act, 1867* as the province simply exercised its spending power."[51] The Métis and non-status Indians launched an appeal. The heart of the case was the revenue-sharing agreement, despite Métis spokesperson Henry Wetelainen's claim that the First Nations Fund was peripheral to the larger issue of the status of the Métis and non-status Indians. "We want to have the same rights as all aboriginals," he was quoted as saying, "and for many years we've been looking for a constitutional case like this, in which we could challenge to have those rights."[52]

On 21 June 2000, the Supreme Court published its decision upholding the Ontario Court of Appeal judgement, indicating that the province of Ontario was not violating Métis and non-status Indian rights by choosing to negotiate only with First Nations leaders. Four years after the lawsuit was initiated, one media article finally offered some insight into this complex topic:

> At issue in the case was the group's contention that their exclusion as non-status Indians from the Ontario First Nations profit-sharing project violates their rights under Section 15 of the Charter of Rights and Freedoms. . . . The section states everyone is equal and protected under the law, including those who are disadvantaged by race, sex, colour, age, ethnicity or physical or mental disability.[53]

The author concluded by offering the Supreme Court's rationale that "section 15(2) says any efforts to help any specific disadvantaged group cannot be regarded as discriminatory against another."[54]

In a similar case, this one concerning the Métis right to hunt, the Métis were recognized by the Supreme Court as possessing Aboriginal rights in 2004. The case in question, *R. v. Powley*, was initiated by father and son, Steve and Roddy Powley in 1993 after they were charged with hunting moose without a license and unlawful possession of moose meat contrary to Ontario's *Game and Fish Act*. The Métis Nation of Ontario determined to test *Powley* to establish the existence of Métis hunting rights. A two-week trial in 1998 resulted in the judge determining that the Métis community at Sault Ste. Marie had an existing Aboriginal right to hunt protected by section 35 of the *Constitution Act, 1982*. He also found that Ontario's regulatory regimes unjustifiably infringed on the Métis right to hunt. The Powleys were acquitted. Two appeals followed, and on 19 September 2004 the Supreme Court of Canada upheld the lower courts' judgements and formally recognized that the Aboriginal rights of the Métis exist.[55]

Mnjikaning First Nation Sues the Ontario Government

In April 1996, Ontario's First Nations reluctantly agreed to Premier Harris's 20 per cent Win Tax in an effort to get the casino up and running. Arguing that they were pressured into accepting Harris's proposal, First Nations leaders did not waver in their position that the Win Tax violated a legal agreement with the province of Ontario. The money being lost was significant. During its first two months of operation, Casino Rama played host to 889,200 gamblers — an average of 14,200 people each day — generating $66.3 million in gross revenues.[56] The annual payroll for the 2,663 employees, 700 of whom were Aboriginal, was tabbed at $60 million. The casino's benefits were felt immediately. Unemployment at Mnjikaning dropped from 70 per cent to eight, and band staff jumped from 50 to 230. By 2000, there were close to 25 private and band-owned businesses operating.[57] The Mnjikaning Kendaaswin Elementary School opened in 1998 to both First Nations children and those from neighbouring non-Native communities, followed by the community building its own fire department, establishing a first-response emergency unit, and creating a tribal police unit that works in conjunction with the OPP. Water and sewage treatment facilities were also constructed to service the local community and the needs of nearby businesses.[58]

In July 1998, the Chiefs of Ontario filed a Statement of Claim in an effort to recover the 20 per cent of gross revenues lost since the implementation of the Win Tax two years earlier. The claim was tied up in court until the first revenue-sharing agreement lapsed in 2001. A new agreement was immediately signed by all parties, but First Nations reiterated their displeasure with the Win Tax. On 24 October 2001, lawyers representing the Mnjikaning First Nation filed notice, claiming that declarations made "that withholding of the 20 per cent win tax was unlawful" were inaccurate while also seeking "an order directing payment to or for the benefit of the Ontario First Nations of all such amounts wrongly withheld since July 31, 1996."[59] The Mnjikaning First Nation accused the Progressive Conservative government of blocking construction of the casino in early 1996 to force the band to turn over 20 per cent of the annual revenue to the province: "The province ordered a halt to construction of the interim casino facility, in order to put pressure on Mnjikaning to agree to its decision."[60] In its statement of defence filed 31 December, the Crown denied "that at any time in connection with the development, construction, or operation of the pilot commercial casino at Rama, or in connection with the distribution of revenues from that casino, it acted in bad faith, or for any improper purpose, or unlawfully . . . insisted that it did not coerce the Mnjikaning First Nation into signing away the contested twenty per cent of the gross revenue from Casino Rama," while also denying "that the Plaintiff (Mnjikaning) was 'pressured' into executing the Agreements."[61]

The Chiefs of Ontario also decided to revisit the original revenue allocation which had granted 35 per cent of gaming revenues to the Mnjikaning First Nation. These monies were to be set aside for casino upgrades and to help ameliorate the anticipated negative impact that the increase in vehicle traffic would exact upon the community's infrastructure and the need to finance programs to deal with social problems resulting from casino operations. In the last week of June 2001, at an all-chiefs conference held on Walpole Island, provincial First Nations voted to reduce Mnjikaning's share to the same level as every other band in the province.[62] Mnjikaning Chief Sharon Stinson Henry protested that the original split was fair. "This isn't the old Rama, that serene community," she said. "We have 12,000 cars coming in every day."[63] The Mnjikaning First Nation rejected the chiefs' decision, allowing the revenue-sharing agreement to lapse while filing a lawsuit against the Ontario government, the second party to the revenue-sharing litigation, to retain their 35 per cent share. An escrow account was opened to bank 35 per cent of future gaming revenue, pending a legal ruling.[64]

The casino project also resulted in community factionalism, specifically over the Looking Far Ahead trust fund established in 1996. As of 2001, $32-million was in the fund; a faction in the community felt that the fund should be opened and $10,000 distributed to each community member. Chief Stinson Henry had been elected in 2000 on the platform of breaking the trust fund and establishing a per-capita annuity from the accrued interest, without touching the principal. At that time, Rama seniors told her that, while the casino brought jobs for the younger people, they received little. According to Stinson Henry, "I didn't look at it as giving money, I looked at it as listening to my people."[65] Opposing her was Byron Stiles, the band's addiction co-ordinator, who feared that band members had yet to learn the financial skills to handle such a large sum of money. Nevertheless, in December 2000 the Mnjikaning First Nations held a referendum, and the majority of voters chose to open up the trust. A one-time payment of $10,000 was distributed to each band member over 18 years of age, and this was followed by an undisclosed annual payment in following years.[66]

Following the 9/11 attacks on the World Trade Centre, the SARS crisis, and the Iraqi war, all of which led to increased border security, the soaring Canadian dollar and the summer 2003 blackouts resulted in the Ontario casino industry taking a considerable financial hit. During the period 1999-2000 to 2003-04, Casino Niagara revenues dropped from $641 million to $499 million. From 2003 to 2004, Casino Niagara and Casino Windsor each suffered drops in revenue of nearly $100 million. As of 2005 the provincial casinos were down $172.5 million in revenue from 2002-03. Casino Rama was the lone Ontario casino to hold strong, increasing its revenue by $25 million during the same time period.[67] With this information, the Mnjikaning First Nation and Chief Stinson Henry began speaking of one day operating Casino Rama under federal jurisdiction, which would result in Ontario losing its 20 per cent Win Tax, which amounted to $18 million annually. According to Stinson Henry, "since the province has been difficult to deal with, we're covering all our bases. We're researching when the federal government turned the responsibility for gaming over to the provinces."[68]

During the next five years, Casino Rama operations continued. As of January 2005, however, and following five years of arbitration, the outstanding issues had yet to be resolved. The Ontario Lottery and Gaming Corporation at one point proposed a new revenue-sharing scheme whereby First Nations would receive a share of all provincial gaming proceeds, rather than having to rely solely on Casino Rama, an alternative scheme that OLGC Director of Public Relations Joe Vecsi believed could settle the outstanding litigation between the government and First Nations. In early 2005, Liberal Finance Minister Greg Sorbara recognized the importance of working "closely with Ontario's First Nations to build a stable source of funding for community, economic and cultural development, health and education."[69] That February, former Liberal Ontario Premier David Peterson was appointed to mediate discussions with the intent of formalizing a new revenue-sharing agreement — an appointment that paid $1,000 a day.[70] Tired of ongoing litigation and arbitration, provincial First Nation leaders are also interested in seeing the long-running dispute over Casino Rama revenues reconciled.

In a joint announcement with Anishinabek Nation Grand Council Chief John Beaucage, Chief Stinson Henry indicated that the Mnjikaning First Nation agreed to participate in the proposed mediation process, with the intention of producing a new revenue-sharing formula. The goal was to settle the matter out of court. Mnjikaning representatives and a special chiefs' committee agreed to work with Peterson to create a "mutually agreeable" revenue-sharing formula within 60 days. But according to Stinson Henry, the provincial government once again employed pressure tactics to compel mediation. She claimed that during a meeting she attended with OLGC CEO Duncan Brown and a number of Ontario chiefs, Brown intimated that the casino's operating license might not be renewed when it comes due in 2011 if all litigation is not resolved. The province would then assume control, and all First Nations would receive an unspecified share of all gaming revenue for an unspecified period of time.[71] As of this writing, both the lawsuits and mediation are still active.

Conclusion

Despite the animosity of the parties involved, Casino Rama persists, and is today Ontario's most profitable casino. And while First Nations leaders insist on resolving outstanding claims, no party to date has attempted to shut down operations, recognizing that revenues for community economic development would also end. Everyone appears willing to keep the money flowing as each party works at resolving their concerns. Tensions continue to emerge from time to time as the issues drag on. The history of First Nations gaming in Ontario is one of confrontation and the use of the courts to resolve issues. The Shawanaga First Nation's argument that control over gaming on reserve was an Aboriginal right was denied by the Supreme Court of Canada, forcing all First Nations developing casino projects to acquiesce to provincial jurisdiction. Then came the lawsuits: one filed by the Métis seeking inclusion in the revenue-sharing pact, another resulting from Premier Mike Harris altering the province's gaming agreement with First Nations.

The tenuous nature of First Nations gaming is illustrated, but so, too, is its potential for economic revitalization. And while the events chronicled in this chapter are unique to Ontario, similar dynamics have influenced the creation and evolution of the prairie First Nations gaming industry, suggesting that First Nation leaders must seriously consider the potential issues before adopting gaming as an economic endeavour. Internal factionalism and jurisdictional disputes with provincial and federal authorities are but a few of the issues that could ultimately derail a project. As well, the casino's host community is forced to contend with additional issues, including, but by no means limited to, problem and pathological gambling, higher crime levels, and the impact of increased traffic on the community infrastructure. How is the money being channeled to the province's First Nations being used? Is it benefiting the communities? These and other questions warrant additional research.

CHAPTER SIX

Saskatchewan and Manitoba: Early Days

In the early 1990s, community leaders and a number of academics started to focus on improving reserve economies. Studies such as the Aboriginal People's Survey (1991, 2001) and the Royal Commission on Aboriginal Peoples (1996) demonstrated limited reserve economic development and the need for a significant infusion of capital to assist in building up reserve infrastructure across the country and develop educational programs for a work force that was slowly coming of age. Reserve economies were largely a consolidation of limited wage labour combined with the vestiges of historic economic practices such as hunting, trapping, and fishing. The proliferation of high-tech industry followed by its movement into regions previously largely occupied by First Nations oftentimes left local communities in worse shape. This led federal and provincial politicians to consider the most effective means of incorporating First Nations into the modern economy. By no means was this a new question, but it took on greater significance as statistics confirmed that the modern Canadian economy was leaving First Nations in its wake.

Critical analyses of various gaming-related issues were soon initiated by both opponents and proponents of First Nations casinos. Gambling advocates argued that casino revenues could potentially reduce First Nations' economic dependence on provincial and federal government transfers through revenue distribution and increased employment. Arguably, casinos represented an untapped source of revenue that could bolster the quality of life in First Nations communities. A variety of examples were cited supporting the initiative, not the least of which was the increasing reliance of provincial governments on gambling, specifically lotteries, to generate revenue. Canadian First Nation leaders turned to American case studies investigating how successful various cities and towns with casinos and other types of gambling were in their efforts to boost their economies and raise government revenues without paying more taxes.

Gambling was becoming big business in both Canada and the United States during this period. In 1993, for example, 70 million Americans visited ballparks while 92 million visited casinos. In 1994, casino patrons spent more than $400 billion in total wagers for poker and slot machines in addition to horse tracks and lotteries.[1] Statistics Canada reported that Canadians wagered $2.7 billion in 1992.[2] In 1992-93, construction costs for the fledgling gaming industry were tagged at $69 million, while more than $78 million was spent annually on wages.[3] Despite the economic potential, opponents argued that casino revenues were a limited and unstable revenue base. *The Economist* declared that, in spite of government claims of gaming's economic benefits, many citizens were afraid that the hidden costs — such as additional policing and the social impact of gambling addictions — would outweigh the benefits.[4] One author asserted that gambling had a negative economic effect, estimating its cost to each adult in America at $110-$300 annually.[5] Policy makers were beset with warnings that casino gambling taxes placed a proportionately heavier burden on low-income groups. Concerns about the increased numbers of problem and pathological gamblers were cited, as were the costs of financing the infrastructure to deal with them. Most researchers agreed that there was a high level of problem gambling among Canadian adults, adolescents, and First Nations, suggesting that policy analysts needed to question more effectively whether the social costs of creating an Aboriginal gaming industry exceeded the potential monetary benefits.[6]

From a community perspective, concern was expressed that casino success could quickly outstrip a community's ability to manage the revenue flow, while questions were raised about a strategy that would see US-based casino management companies operate First Nations casinos in Canada. Gambling was also seen as a negative influence that could undermine the integrity of First Nations culture, leading to community fragmentation. Early reports emphasized the need to consider whether traditional values were being replaced by materialism, or perhaps simply greed. Relying on US examples, the Canada West Foundation's *Gambling in Canada Project* declared First Nations casinos a potentially disruptive force that could reduce the gambling revenues at existing Alberta casinos. This would have the effect of reducing funding to the non-profit sector through gambling grants and charitable gaming. The report noted that close to one-third of the non-profit organizations that participated in the study cited gambling-related grants as their top funding source, while half claimed gaming grants to be one of their top three sources of funding.[7] Opponents cited the increased availability of gaming as a catalyst for increased problem gaming.

It is evident that both First Nations leaders and provincial and federal government officials were aware of the issues attendant on the creation of reserve casinos. This, in a variety of ways, influenced the development of the First Nations gaming industry in the late 1980s and early 1990s. The context was now set for the rise of the First Nations casino industry in western Canada.

The FSIN Tackles Gaming

The Federation of Saskatchewan Indian Nations (FSIN) member communities were among the first to seriously consider reserve casinos. Since the late 1970s, the FSIN and Treaty 6 signatories had championed self-determining powers, believing that treaty making with the Crown was "indicative of mutual recognition." By signing Treaty 6, it was argued, Canada implicitly recognized the signatories as nations: "both the representatives of the Crown and those of Treaty First Nations recognized each others' authority and their capacity to enter into treaties on behalf of their respective peoples."[8] The FSIN also considered each individual nation to be vested with the self-governing powers required to foster internal economic initiatives to promote nation building. The FSIN affirmed this position in the late 1970s: "No one can change the Indian belief. We are Nations; we have Governments. Within the spirit and meaning of the Treaties, all Indians across Canada have the same fundamental and basic principles upon which to continue to build their Governments ever stronger."[9]

One of nationhood's key principles is control over economic development; gaming was something FSIN leaders promoted in the early 1980s as the economic engine that could stimulate development and eventually maintain First Nations' independence within Saskatchewan. The leaders of several First Nations communities in the early 1980s expressed an interest in establishing casinos and approached provincial officials to begin discussions. The timing was opportune, for the Saskatchewan First Nations gaming movement corresponded with the early stages of the US tribal gaming industry. The mid-1980s was a period in which American Indians were beginning to promote more forcefully their claims to internal sovereignty by establishing high-stakes bingo operations, and, later, reservation casinos. Interestingly, the general First Nations population in Saskatchewan was cautious. This led First Nations leaders and officials from the Province of Saskatchewan to initiate a research program to investigate US tribal gaming. Each body independently determined that First Nations gaming establishments were a viable economic development, but no formal commitment developed.

The FSIN continued to monitor the US tribal gaming situation and found some remarkable developments. In one year alone 23 states established state/tribal gaming compacts that resulted in 115 reservation casinos.[10] Spurred on by these events, FSIN leaders nevertheless understood the vagaries of tribal gaming. Although they did not anticipate that they could generate similar revenue levels in Saskatchewan, what caught FSIN leaders unaware was the apparent level of influence now enjoyed by US tribal leaders, something they desired in Canadian politics. In addition to improving community infrastructure and financing social programming, the money generated by gaming was being used by various tribes to promote economic ventures on reservation lands, since it was now possible to secure venture capital from entrepreneurs who had previously avoided financial ventures on reservation lands.[11]

First Nations resistance to gaming at the community level persisted, but the FSIN insisted that it was an option they could no longer ignore. Citing evidence from the US demonstrating how once-destitute tribes were now reaping dividends from gaming, First Nations leaders claimed that gaming improved self-governing capacity which, in certain instances, led to economic expansion beyond the reservation. As First Nations leaders lobbied the provincial government to consider reserve casinos, gambling was becoming increasingly popular in Canada. Beginning in the mid-1970s, lotteries had generated close to $2-billion in total revenue by the late 1980s. As the growth of provincial lotteries leveled off, consumer interest shifted to Video Lottery Terminals (VLT) and high-stakes casinos. From 1992 to 1997, total national revenue from gambling increased from $2.7 billion to $6.8 billion. So, too, did government profits, which increased over the same time period from $1.7 billion to $3.8 billion.[12]

By the early 1990s, it appeared that Saskatchewan First Nations were well positioned to lobby the provincial government. They had the research in hand, and were well versed in the political dynamics that underpinned FSIN/provincial relations. In 1991 the people of Saskatchewan elected the New Democratic Party under the leadership of Roy Romanow. This would prove significant to First Nations leaders with gaming interests. Following the Progressive Conservatives' ruinous period in office, the NDP took over at a time of low public confidence and trust in elected officials. Romanow capitalized on past Conservative failures to promote economic development, and soon the NDP was being portrayed in the media as pro-business. First Nations leaders watched Romanow's actions closely, and in the end were pleased with what they saw. In their estimation, First Nations gaming initiatives corresponded with the Premier's resolve to stimulate economic development. The NDP's publicly demonstrated compassion for First Nations concerns convinced the FSIN and community leaders that Romanow was accessible and perhaps willing to consider their gaming initiatives.[13] Chief Roland Crowe commented at the time, "This historical relationship meant that the Native leadership felt comfortable initiating a discussion regarding a Native casino gambling policy with the NDP government, which demonstrated an impressive level of trust in the Romanow government."[14]

Despite parallel initiatives aimed at economic development, the NDP and the FSIN dealt cautiously with one another. For years the FSIN had demanded that existing provincial gaming policies be revamped to permit casinos and high-stakes gambling. Romanow did not dismiss FSIN demands, but he was reluctant to acquiesce to First Nations lobbyists. The Aboriginal population's general lack of support for the gaming industry did little to help matters. Arguably, the resulting inability of the FSIN to speak on behalf of many of the province's First Nations, tribal councils, and individual band councils rendered the organization less effective than it might have been. As a result, the FSIN's suggested changes to provincial gaming policy were largely ignored, and little headway was made. Recognizing that they could ill afford to delay negotiations, the FSIN changed tactics, and, despite the lack of community consent, approached provincial officials directly. They sought to establish a working relationship that would lead to new gaming policies that would benefit the FSIN and its affiliate communities. By taking a proactive stance, the FSIN hoped to be able to convince their constituents of gaming's probative value.

Romanow experienced similar opposition in his cabinet. Nevertheless, as time passed, he was able to begin working behind the scenes with First Nation leaders, and it soon appeared that the two parties were working toward creating a provincial gaming initiative. In February 1993, the NDP government published an internal document that promoted the expansion of provincial gaming policies. The document made specific mention of First Nations people and their involvement in what was described as a "joint-venture framework" with the provincial government.[15] Three overriding goals guided the NDP's policy:

1. the control and regulation of gaming was to remain with the provincial government;
2. the issue of government revenue generation would be met through gaming enterprises in support of overall deficit reduction goals; and
3. provincial gaming policy would be structured to help revamp the hospitality industry, the catalyst of which was future casino development.[16]

Market research led the NDP to accept gaming's potential and the role First Nations could play in the successful expansion of both the hospitality and tourism industry.[17]

It was with this policy proposal in mind that Janice MacKinnon, Minister in Charge of Gaming, initiated preliminary discussions with the chiefs of several tribal councils concerning their involvement in casino projects. No official negotiations took place; rather, each side sought to determine the other's level of interest in and compatibility with the gaming industry. It was a positive meeting, in that the voluntary interaction demonstrated both sides' intention to establish a working relationship. Unfortunately, MacKinnon became increasingly confrontational with Native leaders and the FSIN during this period, and Romanow replaced her in March 1993 with Eldon Laudermilch, the fourth Minister in Charge of Gaming in as many years. This laid the groundwork for the establishment of the government negotiating team consisting of Dave Innes, vice-president of the Saskatchewan Liquor and Gaming Authority; Victor Taylor, Assistant Deputy Minister of the Saskatchewan Indian and Métis Affairs Secretariat; and Andrew

Thomson, Chief of Staff to the Minister of the Saskatchewan Liquor and Gaming Authority. Negotiations were initially held with the chiefs of Prince Albert, the Battlefords, Saskatoon, the Touchwood File Hills, Qu-Appelle, Meadow Lake, Yorkton, and Agency Chiefs.[18]

As the FSIN and the NDP began to establish a working relationship, opposition to casino expansion was quickly mounting in the province. Ironically, it developed outside Saskatchewan. A Vancouver-based splinter group known as the Citizens Against Gambling Expansion (CAGE) established a Regina chapter and began to weigh in on the debate. Their strategy was to emphasize the immoral nature of gambling, and they delivered a petition to Regina City Council demanding a municipal ban on future casino development. They also filed a court injunction to halt casino construction, but it was dismissed by the Saskatchewan Court of Appeal.[19] CAGE's initial failure represented an important moment in the casino expansion debate, for "The ineffectiveness of Citizens Against Casino Gambling Expansion and their methods to halt casino expansion demonstrated to the provincial government that opposition to the casino project, at least in Regina, was not strong."[20] This gave the government time to develop an effective public relations strategy to augment existing public support.

Clearly, both the provincial government and the FSIN were prepared to handle the onslaught of complaints. Both parties promoted gaming's economic viability, pointing to the US tribal gaming industry as an example. Provincial officials produced statistics demonstrating how much money — some $7 million annually — was being spent outside Canada by Saskatchewan gamblers. This money could be better spent in the province, officials claimed. Laudermilch insisted that "there was a massive bleeding of gaming dollars" from Saskatchewan into the United States, and that immediate measures were required to ebb the flow.[21] The FSIN, the NDP, and provincial First Nations leaders agreed on gaming's potential to promote economic development and increased self-government. An FSIN report confirmed that the average personal income for First Nation individuals was roughly one-half that of non-First Nation individuals. Only 31 per cent of First Nations individuals of labour-force age were employed; 60 per cent of First Nations people over the 15 had failed to obtain a high school degree; and infant mortality rates were 2.5 times the national average.[22]

The data clearly indicated that gaming could not only ameliorate socio-economic problems on reserves, but could stimulate the entire provincial economy. The FSIN warned that if First Nations' birth and education rates continued at their current pace, the resulting increase in First Nations unemployment, decreased personal incomes, and increased reliance on government assistance would be detrimental not only to Saskatchewan First Nations but the provincial community as whole.[23] This simply reinforced what provincial officials had long been aware of: the socio-economic disparity that existed between First Nations and non-First Nations. A long-term objective was developed that would see the social capital put in place for a healthy future for First Nations communities, to which gaming was considered the best strategy.

The White Bear Casino Raid

As provincial and First Nations politicians carefully considered their next steps, the chief of the White Bear First Nation, Bernie Shepherd, along with Brian Standingready and several band councilors, announced their intention to build a casino. Located 13 km north of Carlyle in the southeast corner of Saskatchewan, White Bear had a registered population of just over 2,000 and limited development potential. Provincial officials, reacting negatively to the announcement, contacted Shepherd, who was told that the provinces were responsible for all gaming activities, including reserve casinos. Shepherd was persistent. He cobbled together a loose collection of American partners and proceeded to open a casino inside White Bear's golf clubhouse on 26 February 1993. Anticipating resistance, Shepherd preceded the casino's opening by informing both the media and provincial officials that the people of White Bear were vested with an inherent right to engage in a gaming enterprise. Further, since the casino was located on reserve land, which is federal Crown land, Shepherd claimed that their actions were effectively shielded from provincial jurisdiction. The band council claimed that they had obtained the necessary business experience by conducting research visiting US tribal casinos.

The government did not accept Shepherd's argument, reiterating, through the media and official correspondence, the province's jurisdiction over gaming. Aware that the casino was an illegal gaming house according to the *Criminal Code*, Shepherd informed provincial officials that he would voluntarily shut down the casino and petition the provincial court for a determination of the casino's status.[24] Romanow ignored the offer, and on 22 March sent in the RCMP to conduct a 4:00 a.m. raid on the White Bear casino. A 36-member RCMP tactical team clad in camouflage and armed with assault rifles and supported by a surveillance helicopter shut off power to the reserve and blocked access to and from the community. They seized 115 slot machines, six card tables, on-site financial records, and between $70,000 and $125,000 cash.[25] The casino maintenance crew, security, and a handful of employees tabulating the evening's receipts were the only people on site. Many of those arrested were women who were forced, with guns pressed to the back of their heads, to lie face-down with their hands behind their backs.

Band councillors Edward Little Chief, Standingready, and his wife Brenda were at the casino when the raid began; all were arrested and detained at the Carlyle Police Station. Although they were released before noon the next day, all three, according to policy analyst Warren Skea, had been denied the right to contact a lawyer while incarcerated. Charges were ultimately laid against Shepherd, Stand-ingready, Alan King, the band's consulting partner from the United States, and his business partner, Susan Alsteen. The manner and the abruptness of the casino's closure generated public sympathy for the people of White Bear. By the time the trial commenced later that fall, the judge ruled that Shepherd and his associates truly believed that the White Bear First Nation had the jurisdiction to regulate gaming on its lands and did not have the guilty intent required for the trial to proceed. All charges were dismissed.

The events at White Bear accentuated the fact that First Nations considered economic stability the key component of Aboriginal self-governance, but it was only after the RCMP raid that the provincial government and the FSIN began to study gaming extensively. If anything, the White Bear incident motivated Romanow and FSIN leaders to finalize a preliminary gaming agreement. Romanow took the ini-tiative and approached FSIN leaders, proposing a partnership that would see the establishment of casinos, the revenues from which would be allocated to provin-cial First Nations, exhibition associations, and the province. By January 1994 the provincial government had established the Minister's Advisory Committee on the Social Impacts of Gaming, and commissioned Fox Consulting of Reno, Nevada, to address the public's concerns. The final report, *Economic Feasibility of Casino Gaming in the Province of Saskatchewan*, estimated visitor projections, casino tax revenue, the average amount spent per visitor on gambling, direct and indirect employment, and the amount of money that was anticipated to filter into the larg-er Saskatchewan economy. Perhaps the most important conclusion was that the province could only support one first-class casino, and that "if the casino is built on an Indian reserve and is staffed by reserve residents, then limited taxes are esti-mated."[26] Fox Consulting concluded that a Crown-owned casino would maximize government revenue and control over operations and development.[27]

First Nations leaders took heed of the Fox report and proceeded slowly. A year of FSIN/Saskatchewan negotiations followed. During this period, a provincial policy was struck making it illegal for First Nations bands to operate their own casinos, although they would receive more than one-third of future casino-generated net revenues. A proviso was also included that would guarantee at least one-third of all casino jobs at the newly announced Casino Regina and Casino Saskatoon would be set aside for individuals of Native ancestry. In January 1994, the province announced that a gaming agreement had been struck with the FSIN that involved the province allocating $1.75 million to the partnership, anticipating that gaming would generate the revenue required to help "build and renew the infrastructure that has sadly been ignored by governments since the treaties were signed over a hundred years ago."[28]

The arrangement called for the construction of two full-scale casinos in Saskatoon and Regina. Gaming revenues would be split among the province, the

FSIN, the Métis Nation of Saskatchewan, and provincial exhibition associations. Owing to the premier's trepidation in navigating the jurisdictional waters around the construction of reserve casinos, the original deal in principle dealt with off-reserve gaming. Immediately, four First Nations communities announced their disapproval, and banded together to form the First Nations Gaming Alliance, with the intention of raising casinos on each of the four reserves in question. According to Warren Skea, Romanow petitioned the provincial court to pronounce on the legality of operating on-reserve gaming establishments; the court ruled that the bands were legally entitled to operate reserve casinos. The province appealed the decision, on the grounds that the original provincial court decision was ambiguous and inconclusive.[29]

In the meantime, First Nations leaders lobbying to build on-reserve casinos discovered how expensive such a venture could be. When a lack of capital funding stalled development, community leaders returned to the negotiating table, proposing a partnership with the province. The Saskatchewan government would provide the start-up capital, the FSIN would provide the labour force, and a revenue-distribution formula would be established. Such a partnership would grant the FSIN a controlling interest in the role each party would play, while also leading to greater FSIN control of casino operations, management, and overall decision-making.

The two sides set to work developing the foundational principles that would see First Nations gaming become a reality in Saskatchewan. Two agreements were signed in 1995: the Gaming Framework Agreement (GFA), and the Casino Operating Agreement (COA). At the heart of the GFA was the revenue-sharing formula, including a set of guidelines delineating how the revenues were to be spent by recipient First Nations. Specifically, 37.5 per cent of net revenues were to go to the provincial government, 37.5 per cent to the First Nations Trust, and the remaining 25 per cent to four provincial Community Development Councils (CDC). Each CDC was established to aid in the distribution of one-quarter of the net profit share pursuant to the GFA in an effort to stimulate First Nations economic development, fund reserve justice and health initiatives, finance reserve education and cultural development, improve community infrastructure, and develop senior and youth programs and other charitable purposes. Each CDC was to be recognized as a corporate body with a board of directors.[30]

The first casino, The Gold Eagle at North Battleford, opened its doors on 1 March 1996, followed by the Northern Lights Casino at Prince Albert on 6 March. The Bear Claw Casino on the White Bear reserve opened in November, followed by the Painted Hand Casino at Yorkton in December. During the first full year of operations (1997-98), the four First Nations casinos generated $57.6 million and realized a total profit of $20.3 million.[31] Everything appeared to be proceeding smoothly. Things were going so well that plans for a downtown Saskatoon casino were in the works. In the spring of 2000, however, the public's perception of the Saskatchewan Indian Gaming Authority and the Saskatchewan First Nations gaming industry changed.

The Dutch Lerat Affair

In May 2000, the Saskatoon *StarPhoenix* ran a banner headline that read, "Casino books opened." The focus of the story was the FSIN's compliance with provincial requests for a full disclosure of all financial statements related to the distribution of casino revenues. FSIN Chief Perry Bellegarde had challenged the government, declaring that "we're going one step above the requirements right now," referring to the financial disclosure provisions of the 1995 GFA.[32] But in early 2000, SIGA's and the FSIN's spending habits came under government and media scrutiny — largely a result of persistent criticism from the Canadian Taxpayers Association. Fuelling the fire was an unofficial report of financial discrepancies contained in an independent audit of SIGA's books. This information was forwarded to officials at the Saskatchewan Liquor and Gaming Authority (SLGA), who forwarded it to the FSIN in early April. Over the course of the next month, the affair was played out in the provincial and national media as relations between Bellegarde and Saskatchewan gaming Minister Doreen Hamilton became increasingly strained.

Given that First Nations educational and economic standards lagged behind those of mainstream Canadian society, it is hardly surprising that, during the early days of First Nations gaming, there was among Saskatchewan First Nations a general lack of the expertise required to operate casinos. Few individuals living on reserve had the education or the skills to establish or operate large gaming enterprises. This resulted in the emergence of two trends. The most popular approach was to hire a casino management company to run the day-to-day gaming operations. At Casino Rama, for instance, the US-based Carnival Hotels and Casinos Canada Ltd. was contracted by the provincial government and Ontario First Nations to direct casino operations. They were paid a percentage of the revenues and, to date, few difficulties have arisen. The second approach was to establish a gaming authority, such as the Saskatchewan Indian Gaming Authority (SIGA), in which the 72 First Nations who were party to the provincial gaming agreement were responsible for selecting a board of directors to manage what has grown to be four First Nations casinos. SIGA members, of course, had little experience operating casinos.

The focus of the investigation quickly zeroed in on SIGA CEO and chairman Dutch Lerat, a former FSIN vice-chief. Lerat was initially accused of receiving upwards of $360,000 in unauthorized debit and credit card purchases, and on 16 June his gaming registration was suspended by Minister Hamilton. She also requested that an interim CEO be appointed, and publicly questioned SIGA's effectiveness while threatening to fire the association's primary officers. She further declared that Bellegarde's resistance would result in the shut-down of all slot machines in the casinos, though such actions were considered beyond the scope of Part 7 of the GFA, which addresses dispute resolution. Bellegarde refused to acquiesce to Hamilton's demands to suspend Lerat, claiming that the province had overstepped its authority. But Bellegarde was under extreme pressure, and eventually gave in, firing Lerat on 22 June. Lerat, in the meantime, had quietly resigned two days previously. He was temporarily replaced by Prince Albert Grand Council Chief Gary Merasty. The verbal fireworks early in the investigation led to an atmosphere of distrust and acrimony, and Bellegarde and Hamilton did little to hide their disdain of one another. As they bickered through the media, two independent auditors were hired to look into SIGA's — and specifically Lerat's — spending practices.

In a journalistic feeding frenzy, SIGA and Lerat became the focus of local, provincial, and national media animus, and all SIGA-related expenditures eventually came under scrutiny, from legitimate political campaign contributions to a computer purchase for a young First Nations student. Provincial auditor Fred Wendel investigated SIGA's books, and by summer's end released the Saskatchewan Indian Gaming Licensing Report. According to newspaper reports, Wendel stated, "Our audit found improper and questionable use of public money. The problems are serious and the government needs to correct the problems quickly."[33] According to Wendel, Lerat had taken $360,000 in unauthorized debit and credit card advances in addition to his $150,000 salary. He also owed $811,906 to SIGA for unsupported expense claims and a number of suspect business trips. Wendel was critical of SIGA as well, highlighting how little research was conducted prior to SIGA initiating a $12-million advertising campaign. Unaccounted for was an additional $1.7 million that was originally destined for Saskatchewan's First Nations Fund, Métis organizations, and the province. Finally, SIGA had paid $875,000 to Saskatchewan Indian Gaming Licensing (SIGL), a body that had no authority to grant licenses.[34]

Wendel's criticism was not reserved for SIGA and Lerat alone, however; he was equally critical of the Saskatchewan government's role, pointing out that Saskatchewan officials ignored a 1999 report by provincial auditor Wayne Stelioff recommending that the SLGA work with SIGA "to establish proper conflict of interest guidelines; ensure inspections and audits are completed as planned or document why the plan was changed; receive an external auditor's report within 90 days of the adequacy of SIGA's internal controls and receive and approve SIGA's budget on a timely basis, with procedures in place for approaching changes to the budget." Wendel concluded that, had the SLGA "fully acted on the recommendations we made in our 1999 spring report to the Legislative Assembly, it would have prevented some of the improper use of public money."[35] The report

and ensure gaming integrity, and have the power to suspend or cancel licenses.[44] Representing each community or a grouping of several communities interested in pursuing gaming, each commission would allow licensing of reserve gaming while permitting First Nations control of their own gaming endeavours. In January 1989, the OCN became the first First Nation to sign a First Nation Gaming Agreement in Canada, formally establishing the OCN Gaming Commission, an entity appointed by the chief and council and authorized by Provincial Order-in-Council. All the while, the OCN maintained its lottery operations, grossing an estimated $5.8 million in 1991.[45]

The gaming agreements provided "for the appointment and establishment of an Indian Gaming Commission with authority to exercise powers similar to the [Manitoba Lottery Foundation] in licensing charitable or religious organizations under section 207(1)(b) of the Criminal Code. Among the Commission's powers is the exclusive power to set and collect license fees."[46] Under the leadership of Pawley's successor, Progressive Conservative Gary Filmon, the province in 1990 made official its gaming policy aimed at resolving jurisdictional disputes with First Nations.[47] Soon after the OCN signed their agreement, the Manitoba government legalized the placement of VLTs in rural Manitoba, followed quickly by a provincial policy permitting their use on reserves. As a result, the OCN signed the first First Nation VLT Agreement in September 1992. By August 1993, 14 Indian Gaming Commission Agreements were in effect, representing 20 First Nations, eight Video Lottery Terminal (VLT) site holder agreements, and 74 lottery licenses for reserves with 24 First Nations.[48] With the exception of a 10 per cent cost-recovery fee paid to the province, VLT revenues remain with First Nations.

Manitoba officials acknowledged First Nations socio-economic difficulties and, in turn, initiated work on an Aboriginal policy framework. In June 1993 it was noted in the Manitoba Legislature that "these programs and agreements are integral to the sustainable development and long-term growth of new enterprise in the North and in our native communities." These comments paralleled the Manitoba government's desire to work with First Nations "to ensure that northern residents and Aboriginal people have a greater voice in the institutions that serve them and greater administrative control over specific programs," and to live up to "our responsibility to consult with a broad range of men and women from Manitoba's northern and native communities." Officials also admitted that there was a need to provide "a solid foundation for the future through sustainable development that must include targeting areas for economic development and diversification, as well as improvements to local infrastructure."[49] According to political scientist Kathy Brock, the overall goal was "to enhance quality of life through improved living conditions, economic development, and the creation of jobs."[50]

The distribution of VLTs provincially incensed a number of grassroots non-First Nations groups concerned with what they perceived to be the growing incidence of problem gaming in Manitoba. Concerted lobbying efforts led in 1993 to a moratorium on further expansion of VLTs and casino sites. This was followed by a January 1994 RCMP raid of five Manitoba reserves that resulted in the seizure of 48 VLTs and other gaming equipment and tickets.[51] The RCMP claimed that the raids were aimed not at halting unlicensed gaming, but were "directed to information that we had been provided with in respect to the acquisition of weapons."[52] No weapons were seized. The Assembly of Manitoba Chiefs (AMC) accused both the police and Manitoba officials of using the weapons rumour as "an excuse to eliminate the competition for provincial gambling revenues," and called for "a boycott of the Winnipeg's Crystal Casino and other provincially-sanctioned gambling."[53]

During this period, First Nations leaders for the first time were presented with data suggesting that, even should they be successful in constructing casinos, Canadians were reluctant to patronize them. A 1993 Angus Reid Group survey of 2,129 Canadian adults demonstrated that 59 per cent of respondents strongly opposed and 14 percent moderately opposed the expansion of casinos on Native land.[54] A mere 15 percent of Canadians showed interest in gambling at a First Nations casino. While four per cent claimed they were "very interested" and 11 per cent "somewhat interested," half of the 40 per cent of respondents who had visited a casino in the past year expressed an interest in visiting a First Nations casino.[55] While these numbers varied regionally, and general interest in and support for First Nations gaming was substantially higher in Manitoba, Saskatchewan, and British Columbia, the statistics represented political barriers that required careful navigation.[56]

Early on, the AMC had expressed a desire to negotiate all gaming agreements on behalf of the host communities. The Native Affairs Secretariat and the Native Gaming Section preferred to negotiate with individual First Nations, taking into account the different needs of each community. In an attempt to resolve the issue, First Nations requested that the AMC establish "a First Nations Gaming Commission and to secure a federal *Criminal Code* amendment to recognize First Nations jurisdiction on-reserve."[57] The AMC responded by promoting the establishment of the First Nations Gaming Commission, an umbrella organization responsible for regulating gaming, with the authority to negotiate market share agreements to ensure that small First Nations communities also benefited from casino projects.[58] The AMC also promoted the FNGC in an attempt to reconcile the province's desire to maintain a monopoly over gaming and First Nations' desire to develop their own industry. In March 1995, Manitoba established a 14-member Lottery Policy Review Working Group to review existing gambling policies. The Working Group's report, released in January 1996, led to the establishment of the Manitoba Gaming Control Commission (MGCC). As evidenced by events in Ontario and Saskatchewan, First Nations casinos had become a hot topic, leading the Working Group to recommend a separate review focusing specifically on First Nations gaming. This recommendation established the notion that matters related to reserve gaming were to be viewed independently of other gaming policy issues. It was decided in 1996 to proceed with First Nations gaming.

The First Nations Gaming Policy Review (the Bostrom Report) followed, recommending that the Province of Manitoba support First Nations economic development by helping to establish upwards of five reserve casino operations. The goal was to ensure sustainable First Nations economic benefits and opportunities, to act as a catalyst for economic development for the host community and surrounding area, to provide revenues to all First Nations in Manitoba, to promote tourism and the hospitality industries, to create jobs, and to provide substantiation of mitigating measures to address social impacts that might occur.[59] The Bostrom Report also recommended that the revenue be allocated as follows: First Nations, 90 per cent; the Province of Manitoba, 10 per cent.[60] The following year, the First Nations Casino Project (FNCP) was initiated, followed two years later by the establishment of a formal Selection Committee. The committee consisted of representatives of the Assembly of Manitoba Chiefs and the province, and was mandated to review and recommend potential casino proposals. Following its review of twelve eligible proposals, the committee recommended in June 2000 that five should advance to the development stage: the OCN, the Brokenhead First Nation, the Nisichawayasihk First Nation, the Sioux Valley First Nation, and the Swan Lake First Nation.

Of the five proposals, the OCN's progressed the quickest. A six-member partnership was established by the OCN, Chemawawin, Grand Rapids, Wuskwi Sipihk, Mosakahiken, and Marcel Colomb First Nations, which then selected the OCN as the host site. A $6-million proposal was developed that would see the casino housed in a refurbished bingo hall and create upwards of 150 jobs. Mayor Gary Hopper of The Pas publicly announced that the community fully supported the project. He inquired about The Pas becoming a partner in the project, but was turned down because the consortium believed it was large enough.[61] The proposal included a revenue-sharing agreement that would allocate 70 per cent of the profits — which, as stipulated by the province, must go toward economic development projects — to the six partners. The remaining profits would be divided between a trust fund to benefit all First Nations (27.5 per cent) and a First Nations addiction foundation.[62] Following a year of negotiations, the OCN proposal was accepted and an agreement between the province and the Aseneskak Casino Limited Partnership was reached on 7 September 2001. Approval soon followed, permitting construction to begin on the $4.6-million, 20,000 square foot facility.

The Aseneskak Casino

The OCN was not unlike many First Nations communities in Manitoba. From the beginning, OCN leaders and local casino proponents made it clear that, while they wanted their community to be chosen as the casino site, they were not dependent on it, as other First Nations may have been. Starting in the late 1960s, the OCN chief and council decided to pursue local political autonomy, and they understood that it would require economic stability. They devised a community development strategy which was designed to strengthen the reserve economy and improve its members overall quality of life. The strategy involved:

1. developing administration and program delivery;
2. strengthening local government authority; and
3. developing local enterprises.[63]

OCN administration was established in 1968 following DIAND's partial devolution of the band's financial and administration services. By the spring of 1969, the OCN had its own Social Assistance Department. Throughout the early 1970s, the OCN began to assume responsibility for a number of federal programs, including reserve economic development and some components of public works.[64] The third of the strategy's key components — the development of local, band-owned enterprises — began in the late 1960s with the creation of a gravel-hauling company that eventually expanded into a general trucking enterprise.[65] This planted the seeds for further initiatives. OCN members Gordon Lathlin, Joe Ross, Malcolm McGillivary, and Henry Wilson proposed the construction of an on-reserve shopping mall in the early 1970s. The four men recognized that, even though The Pas was home to the majority of the lumber conglomerate's workforce, the town housed a limited number of businesses to serve the local community. In other words, The Pas had no major outlet mall. The OCN established the Otineka Development Corporation in 1973 with the intention of developing a community grocery store.

What people did not count on was the support the proposal would receive from neighbouring First Nations, the majority of whom witnessed considerable leakage of reserve dollars into neighbouring non-Native communities.[66] The proposed $8-million project soon found support, and plans were then expanded to develop a large-scale shopping centre. The Otineka Mall opened in 1975, a complex of 225,000 square feet located on nearly 13 acres of commercially designated reserve land, comprising an indoor shopping centre, recreation facilities, and business offices. The Otineka Mall continues to act as the region's retail and business centre. OCN-owned and operated IGA and SAAN stores are both housed in the mall, as are several retail stores, a 30-machine Video Lottery Centre, and the OCN administration offices. The mall is also home to the Paskwayak Business Development Corporation, the OCN Chief and Council Offices, the Swampy Cree Tribal Council, the Cree Nation Child and Family Caring Agency, the Opaskwayak Educational Authority, and a number of provincial offices. Soon after the mall's opening, regional road construction made the OCN accessible to previously isolated communities such as Grand Rapids, Easterville, and Moose Lake. Members of surrounding communities soon began flocking to the OCN, creating a market centre that was promoted as a tax-free zone for status Indians.

The mall's success led to the formation of the Paskwayak Business Development Corporation (PBDC) in 1987. The OCN chief and council announced that year the establishment of the PBDC to encourage regional economic development. The OCN wholly owns the PBDC, which fosters commercial and investment initiatives, and guides the development of the OCN business portfolio. The PBDC is also mandated to assist band members who aspire to open their own businesses while helping current owners expand their enterprises through capacity building.

The $8.2-million, 60-room Kikiwak Inn opened on 1 July 1996. The hotel has meeting facilities, a swimming pool and hot tub, an exercise room, as well as a full-service restaurant, lounge, and VLT area, and currently employs 60 people.[67] The Pas Food Town, located off-reserve within The Pas township limits, opened 3 December 1997. The principle business is groceries, produce, fresh meat, and tobacco. The 5,000-square-foot store employs ten people.[68] The OCN Shell Gas Bar opened 1 November 1998, with eight pumps and a 1,800 square foot building that houses a convenience store. The Gas Bar currently employs 20 people.[69] The community also owns and operates a Dollar Store that employs 10 people, recently adding a trailer court and building centre to its portfolio.[70]

With the acceptance of the OCN casino proposal, provincial officials established a number of strict regulatory measures. The agreement permitted the government to conduct unscheduled audits, and it forced the casino to be up and running and fulfilling the partnership's proposals within two years (by 2002).[71] The Manitoba Lotteries Commission (MLC) was given responsibility for security and surveillance, as well as controlling gaming proceeds and setting policies, while also setting the mix and number of games.[72] During the time construction began, the Manitoba government sponsored a training program to prepare OCN members to assume skilled jobs once the casino opened, including security, surveillance, slot attendants, cashiers, dealers, accountants, and clerical and management positions.[73] The Aseneskak Casino opened 15 February 2002. One year later, the AMC posted on their website an article written by Bill Redekop encapsulating the previous year's highlights. The article stressed that the casino provided 180 jobs, of which 82 per cent were held by Aboriginal people. The tenor of the article was nevertheless dour, with Redekop quoting casino manager John Gauthier as saying, "We're hoping for no loss, but there may be a little."[74] Seven months later, the

CBC ran a story indicating that the Aseneskak Casino lost close to $900,000 in its first year of operations. Chemawawin First Nations Chief Clarence Easter was quoted as saying, "The province should sit down and give us a fair deal. Instead of a one-way deal, it should be a two-way deal, where they benefit and we benefit as well." [75]

The casino fared better in its second year, rebounding with a $400,000 profit. Yet the problem was not so much government interference as it was geography. The casino was not situated anywhere near the province's tourist traffic. It was originally anticipated that tourists would account for 80 per cent of casino revenues, but it was evident that it was local residents who were contributing the 80 per cent. Gauthier clearly indicated that the casino "cannot support itself on just local traffic." [76] As demonstrated in the United States, the success or failure of tribal gaming correlates directly with geography. The reason Foxwoods and the Mohegan Sun casinos have become so successful is a direct result of their proximity to large populations. The drive to Connecticut from New York (pop. 9 million) is two and a half hours, from Boston two hours (pop. 3.4 million), and one hour from Hartford (pop. 121,578) and Providence (pop. 173,618). [77] There are more than 13 million potential customers within a four-hour drive of both casinos. Of the existing high-stakes First Nations casinos in Ontario, Saskatchewan, and Manitoba, the most successful is Casino Rama. Situated on the Mnjikaning First Nation, the casino is located 135 km north of the Greater Toronto Area which boasts a population of more than five million. [78] It is also located in Ontario's cottage country, where the population blooms each summer; in nearby Peterborough, the resident population of 60,000 grows to nearly 250,000 in the summer, a direct result of an influx of cottagers from the US and Greater Toronto. Similar trends occur in Orillia and nearby vacation spots surrounding the Mnjikaning First Nation. The Aseneskak Casino, on the other hand, is located near a regional population that numbers less than 7,000. The nearest urban centres are Flin Flon (pop. 6,000), a one and a half hour drive; Thompson (pop. 13,256), a four-hour drive; and Dauphin (pop. 9,186), a two-hour drive. [79]

The South Beach Casino

Following the acceptance of the OCN proposal, all other proposals were denied, with the exception of the Brokenhead First Nations submission, and this was not without delays. The deal had been scuttled in December 2003 after Gaming Minister Tim Sale, acting on the Manitoba Gaming Control Commission's advice, declared that the Brokenhead proposal did not meet the financial requirements listed in their agreement with the Assembly of Manitoba Chiefs. Six months later, on 20 July 2004, the MGCC reversed its decision and tentatively approved the $24-million proposal that would see construction of an 18,000-square-foot casino and a 50-room hotel roughly 65 km north of Winnipeg. Following an extensive investigation that included criminal record checks, a review of financial records, and personal interviews with the people and organizations involved in the proposed resort, the project was accepted. The first phase was finished in May 2005, with 300 gaming machines and 30 gaming tables, a bingo hall, a restaurant, a lounge, and a sports bar. The second phase will see an expanded entertainment area, while phase three is designated for hotel construction.[80]

On 29 May 2005, the South Beach Casino opened for business, with 172 employees, two-thirds of whom are of First Nations ancestry. Within 90 minutes of opening its doors, more than 472 gamblers were inside. The next day, the casino was packed with 3,000 patrons, to the delight of Southeast Resource Development, an umbrella corporation representing the seven partner First Nations of the Southeast Tribal Council: Bloodvien, Brokenhead Ojibway Nation, Hollow Water, Black River, Little Grand Rapids, Pauingassi, and Poplar River.[81]

In the months prior to South Beach opening, member communities of the consortium suddenly found themselves the focus of the smoke-free debate. South Beach operators as well as management at the Aseneskak Casino in The Pas came under fire from politicians, business owners, and citizens alike for sanctioning smoking in their casinos. Manitoba had established legislation the previous October effectively banning smoking in all public places, including bars and restaurants. In May, NDP Premier Gary Doer was widely criticized for what his political opponents perceived to be a lack of resolve for failing to sanction casino operators in violation of provincial statutes. In particular, Stuart Murray, leader of the opposition, argued that the premier had the power "to say to them [Brokenhead casino consortium] that you will not receive the government's approval to establish a casino unless the licensing agreement includes the condition the facility is smoke-free." Doer countered that, "while provincial jails such as Headingley are governed by provincial policy, federal institutions such as Stony Mountain are governed by federal jurisdiction," and other areas of federal responsibility, "including military bases, First Nations reserves, airports, et cetera, would be excluded."[82]

Question Period in the Manitoba Legislature focused on the smoking issue, and the premier did his best to explain the exigencies involved. Gaming Minister Tim Sale elaborated:

There are a number of First Nations communities in Manitoba, well over 50. Chiefs and councils have jurisdiction in those First Nations communities in regard to by-laws, in regard to a whole range of issues with which they have a fiduciary relationship with the federal government. When they pass a by-law, when they do anything in regard to Indian lands, they have to get the permission of the federal Minister of Indian Affairs. Now that is an anachronism in my view, but that is the law. The law is that on the reserve, chiefs and councils are the government. We respect governments: federal governments, First Nations governments. It is a jurisdiction issue.[83]

He added, matter of factly, "We do in fact have the right to regulate gambling under the *Criminal Code of Canada*. That is very clear." But the provincial government did not "have the right to regulate behaviours of a variety of kinds in First Nations communities. That is the chiefs' and councils' responsibility."[84]

During Question Period the following day, Dave Chomiak, Minister charged with the administration of *The Gaming Control Act*, added:

> The federal minister responsible, Andy Scott, has indicated that they will not enforce a non-smoking by-law on Saskatchewan First Nations communities and, in fact, that has come from the federal government. I also remind the member there was an all-party task force that signed an agreement with respect to a smoking ban that did not apply to First Nations communities nor did it apply to military establishments under the jurisdiction of the federal government.[85]

Even so, just days before the casino was to open, Conservative deputy leader Glen Cummings asserted that the province should step in and force the South Beach Casino to go smoke-free. He proposed rewriting the existing agreement while suggesting that all future First Nations interested in pursuing a reserve casino agree to make their complex a smoke-free environment as a condition of obtaining a gambling license.

The First Nations casino smoke-free debate has also been a source of acrimony in Ontario, Saskatchewan, and Alberta. In Yorkton, for instance, town officials passed a by-law banning smoking in public places in 2004. A provincial ban followed on 1 January 2005, which, according to provincial Health Minister John Nilson, applied throughout the province. The FSIN responded that its casinos were under First Nations jurisdiction and the bands would set their own laws. The Sakimay First Nation subsequently passed a band by-law permitting smoking in the Painted Hand Casino, which is located within Yorkton's city limits and is classified as an urban reserve. Federal Indian Affairs Minister Andy Scott has said he would refuse to block a First Nations bylaw permitting smoking in casinos.

Conclusion

First Nations leaders in Manitoba and Saskatchewan studied the US tribal gaming industry, followed events as they took place in Ontario, and decided to construct reserve casinos to foster economic development. The focus of this chapter is to highlight the differences in how two provincial governments chose to respond to First Nation desires to implement reserve gaming, and ultimately how this influenced the resulting regulatory environments and, in turn, the success of First Nations gaming in each province. It also demonstrates the lengths that officials of each government went to in order to maintain authority over provincial gaming. Yet it also illustrates how, in the Dutch Lerat case, gaming needs to be treated as more than a quick cure for economic ills, while highlighting the need for professional casino managers to guide the industry. Outside experts may be required in the early days of casino operations.

Casinos are not always successful. The Aseneskak casino lost close to $1 million in its first year of operations, owing not so much to poor management as poor location, a lack of local patronage, and limited tourist traffic. While the jury is still out on the South Beach project, it is likely that summer tourist traffic into Manitoba's beach cottages will be its saving grace.

Both First Nations and officials in Saskatchewan and Manitoba took to gaming as a tool of economic development. First Nations, however, considered gaming to be a right, and, as such, outside provincial jurisdiction. Following the White Bear raid and a corresponding court judgement, it was clear to all that negotiations represented the best strategy. In Manitoba, provincial officials asserted jurisdiction over gaming and informed First Nations that their ambitions rested on both positive and successful negotiations. This is a continued sticking point, as First Nations in both provinces maintain that reserves are Crown land and therefore immune to provincial legislation. This is seen in the current debate over anti-smoking legislation.

Owing to the newness of the industry, it is difficult to conclude whether or not gaming is a positive or negative influence, either within First Nations communities or the provinces at large. The initial revenues from Saskatchewan are quite impressive, and the OCN casino made close to half a million dollars in profit in its second year of operations. A recent announcement from Saskatchewan indicates that two new First Nation casinos have been approved for Swift Current and Whitecap First Nation. Lacking further research, it remains unclear as to whether the costs outweigh the benefits.

CHAPTER SEVEN

First Nations Gaming in Alberta

On 19 November 2004, Chief Sandford Big Plume of the Tsuu T'ina First Nation addressed the Calgary Chamber of Commerce. Speaking of the advantages of building a reserve casino, Big Plume was candid in telling those in attendance that the casino would fall short if Calgary citizens failed to patronize the complex. He highlighted the central role the municipality would play in the project's success or failure, calling the residents of Tsuu T'ina and Calgary "partners in the development of the region. In responding to Calgary's need to grow, and our need to prosper." He also indicated his optimism that a "spirit of co-operation and goodwill" would result in a solid relationship between the two communities for generations to come. With their proposal in the final stage of the approval process and investors already lined up, the Tsuu T'ina community considered the casino to be the revenue generator necessary for what the chief described as "an ambitious, and sometimes intimidating master development plan,"[1] but they needed the people of Calgary to participate, both as customers and as municipal neighbours. The same holds true of the Enoch Cree, located just west of Edmonton, where the construction of a $132 million casino resort is nearing completion.

Gaming has become big business in Alberta, as the statistics will confirm. In 2003-04, sales on casino table games totaled $621.9 million, of which $499.1 million was paid out in prizes, leaving $122.8 million to be divided among facility operators, advisors, trustees ($85.9 million), and charities ($36.9 million). Additional sales on slot machines in casinos and racinos totaled $9.3 billion. Of this amount, $8.6 billion was paid out in prizes, leaving a net of $683 million to be divided among the Alberta Lottery Fund ($479 million), casino and Racing Entertainment Centre (REC) operators ($102.3 million), and provincial charities ($95.1 million).[2]

Alberta's First Nations leaders have long been interested in establishing a provincial gaming industry. Following the announcement in 2001 that the province was prepared to review First Nations casino proposals, several were submitted.

With the exception of the Enoch proposal, all the remaining casino proposals have reached stage six in an eight-stage process; the Tsuu T'ina, Alexis Nakota Sioux Nation and the Stoney Nakoda Nation anticipate approval by the end of 2006. (The Blood Reserve proposal was formally withdrawn in 2005.)

Approved on 19 January 2001, the First Nations gaming policy allowed for the operation of reserve casinos according to Alberta's charitable gaming model. Under the policy established for the Alberta Gaming and Liquor Commission (AGLC), reserve casinos are required to adhere to the terms and conditions established for other charitable casinos in the province. The eight-step proposal format is as follows:

1. An interested group or individual expresses formal interest in developing a casino in a community.
2. The AGLC issues a notice of expressed interest for a traditional casino or a First Nations casino, as the case may be, determined by the location of the community. The AGLC places an advertisement in a local newspaper, advising interested parties that the AGLC will accept expressions of interest from other groups or individuals for this licence. This process allows all interested parties in a specified area an opportunity to make an application for a casino facility licence in that area and be considered at the same time as the original applicant. The AGLC will advise all municipal and band councils in the surrounding community of the interest in the proposed facility.
3. The AGLC conducts an initial assessment to determine if the responses have merit and meet basic criteria related to market demand and benefit to charitable groups. At this stage, the AGLC does not require municipal land use, zoning, or development approval for an expression of interest to be deemed valid. Applicants are expected to defer seeking appropriate municipal approvals until advised in writing by the AGLC.
4. The Board of the AGLC considers community support — or the lack thereof — as expressed through the municipal or band council, and may conclude the process if, in the Board's view, the council does not support the concept of a new casino facility in the community. If the council is silent and there is no demonstrated opposition, the Board, at its discretion, may decide to continue the application process.
5. The AGLC accepts detailed proposals from applicants who have expressed an interest in the development of a casino in the community under consideration. The proposals must include a business plan, and the applicant must demonstrate to the Commission that the proposal has taken into consideration factors that may affect the community and adjacent communities. The applicants are also required to issue a public notice of their application for a casino facility licence. The

AGLC will advise all councils in the surrounding community of any proposals received.

6. Proposals are evaluated by a selection committee using stringent criteria, and the best proposal is selected.

7. A thorough due diligence investigation is conducted into the proponents and other key persons or organizations associated with the selected proposal.

8. If all requirements for a gaming facility have been met (federal and provincial legislation, regulation, and policies, and municipal requirements, permits, licences, or authorizations) the AGLC will make a recommendation to the Board respecting the issuance of a casino facility licence to the successful applicant. [3]

Once a First Nation community or band council has decided that casino construction is an appropriate course of action, the consent of the First Nation by way of band council resolution is required. There is also a need to determine the level of acceptance of the proposal by members of the First Nation. Since all casino gaming must be conducted and managed within the province's charitable gaming model, and the rules for casino gaming consistently applied among all casinos in the province, the remaining steps in the proposal process are the same as those for other types of licensed gaming facilities. A First Nations casino proposal for a reserve gaming facility requires the same type of information as all other submissions, and is evaluated accordingly.[4] Under the First Nations gaming policy, however, all reserve casinos include slot machines to generate charitable gaming proceeds for First Nations.

The development of the current Alberta First Nations gaming industry dates back to the early 1990s. This chapter traces this evolution from the first super-bingos held at Tsuu T'ina and Enoch in 1993 through the remainder of the decade as the debate concerning on-reserve casinos heated up.

The 1990s was a period of extended consultation with Premier Ralph Klein, who worked with First Nations to help them realize their vision. The vagaries of the provincial First Nations Gaming Policy will be discussed, and the chapter concludes with three case studies examining some of the issues the leaders at Enoch, Tsuu T'ina, and Stoney continue to face in their efforts to establish casinos. The First Nations gaming industry in Alberta has yet to move from concept to reality, and much of the available literature deals with anticipated socio-political outcomes and economic projections. Even so, it is possible to evaluate the process to date and provide a foundation for future studies to shed light on current processes that are, as yet, immeasurable.

The Genesis of First Nations Gaming in Alberta

The genesis of the Alberta First Nations gaming policy can be traced back to 1993 and the lobbying efforts of officials from the Tsuu T'ina First Nation, located southwest of Calgary, and the Enoch Cree First Nation, located west of Edmonton. Intent on holding a super-bingo, a large-scale event guaranteeing jackpots exceeding $10,000, Tsuu T'ina officials approached the Alberta Gaming Commission (AGC) in 1993 seeking a license to hold the event. At first, their application was denied on the grounds that provincial gaming regulations did not allow for super-bingos. Soon afterward, Deputy Premier Don Kowalski, who was also the Minister Responsible for Gaming as well as the Minister of Economic Development, reviewed his decision.[5] He granted the Tsuu T'ina a license in time for the band to hold its August super-bingo, an event that was widely publicized for its $100,000 grand prize. Admission to the 2000-seat event was $100 which included six cards, while additional cards could be purchased at six for $30 or nine for $45.[6] In total, 1,850 players participated, resulting in an estimated $100,000 profit — and calls for the creation of an independent First Nations Gaming Commission.[7]

Watching events unfold, Enoch Cree officials followed the Tsuu T'ina lead and applied for a license to hold their own super-bingo. Kowalski knew he would be unable to deny the request after issuing the Tsuu T'ina license, and the Enoch held their super-bingo that fall. Despite the success of both events, neither band at the time seriously considered establishing a high-stakes casino. Then word filtered west that US tribal casinos such as the Pequot-owned Foxwoods Casino Resort in Connecticut were reaping staggering profits. Alberta First Nations began to study more closely the US tribal gaming industry. Both Tsuu T'ina and Enoch leaders also struck up a political relationship with Kowalski.

Little did leaders from either community realize the role they would play in generating support for a provincial First Nations gaming industry. At the time, leaders from both communities acknowledged the economic potential of living next to cities with high populations. Tsuu T'ina economic development officer Peter Manywounds had long considered the band's proximity to Calgary advantageous for starting a ski hill, a hotel, and an industrial park. With the help of Brian Barrington-Foote, a Saskatchewan lawyer who had worked with First Nations on sovereignty issues, Manywounds pitched his vision of a First Nations-owned casino complex to the Tsuu T'ina band council.[8] The selling point was the fact that, since the casino would technically be located on federal land, the band did not have to comply with provincial gambling policies.[9] Unfortunately, in 1995 Manywounds was removed from office, and the casino project lost its most influential and vocal proponent. The project did not die, but it was several months before casino advocates re-established their agenda. As these events unfolded, the

Enoch Cree watched with interest, and, paralleling the actions of their southern neighbours, declared an interest in developing a reserve casino.

While Enoch and Tsuu T'ina officials lobbied for a First Nations gaming policy that would allow them to control revenues, the leaders of several geographically marginalized bands came forward to support them. Several chiefs promoted a policy model in which all provincial bands would benefit equally from casino developments on any reserve. After Ralph Klein had led the Progressive Conservatives to power in June 1993, he informed one chief that they should go ahead and build a casino and he would support them. Klein then instructed his Minister of Gaming to research the economic potential of First Nations gaming and what licensing changes would be needed to promote the expansion of such an industry in Alberta.

Immediately, a representative of the provincial gaming industry demanded that First Nations gaming policies conform to existing provincial criteria — specifically, the disbursement of proceeds. First Nations casinos needed to be on a level playing field with existing facilities, they argued, and the financial process must be transparent. The group supported an open, competitive process for establishing new casinos. Representatives of a municipal association then came forward to express their concern about the potential impact First Nations casinos would have on local community infrastructure, particularly roads, and suggested that provisions to compensate municipalities for these hidden costs should be included in any agreements. Municipal delegates further promoted the need to treat First Nation casino operators in the same manner as existing ones. When, in December 1994, Klein established the Alberta Lotteries Review Committee to develop policy recommendations, committee members immediately became aware of the growing public resistance to First Nations gaming. Committee chair, MLA Judy Gordon (Lacombe-Stettler), proposed that a separate First Nations gaming report be produced, to which Klein agreed.[10]

During the summer of 1994, the seven tribal council chiefs of Alberta decided to hold a Chiefs' Summit in November. This first summit was attended by a number of provincial ministers and officials, the Minister of Indian and Northern Affairs Canada (INAC), and all Alberta's First Nations chiefs. The summit accomplished little more than to introduce the major players to one another. The second Chiefs' Summit, held 14-17 March 1995, resulted in the Minister of Family and Social Services, Mike Cardinal, declaring that provincial First Nations leaders "should take a leading role" in determining if a casino industry will exist, "because it's their project." He added, "I think Native leaders should propose what they'd like to see in Alberta and then we'll negotiate."[11] The third Chiefs' Summit took place 8 November 1995. First Nations leaders were intent on establishing an agreement outlining a First Nations/government gaming relationship that would also affirm existing Aboriginal and treaty rights. The resulting *Understanding on First Nations-*

Canada Relations was signed by Minister of Indian Affairs Ron Irwin and the Chiefs of Alberta. Later that day, Klein and Cardinal appended their signatures to the document. It appeared that all sides were creating a relationship of trust that could eventually lead to a First Nations gaming policy.

The agreement was somewhat surprising, considering that two months earlier the First Nations Gaming Congress had announced that Alberta bands were demanding $100 million from the provincial government in exchange for halting casinos construction. Spokesperson Willie Littlechild, a lawyer and former Progressive Conservative Member of Parliament, was clear in his demands: if Alberta did not wish bands to construct their own casinos, perhaps "a share of what we put into the provincial coffers" — the amount the Congress estimated First Nations were spending annually on gambling — be returned.[12] Littlechild and the FNGC notwithstanding, a Tsuu T'ina plebiscite held in December resulted in 73 per cent of band members voting in favour of the casino proposal.[13] In January, Klein and Gordon met with Chief Whitney and the Tsuu T'ina band council, and all parties agreed that final arrangements about "casino size, location, construction dates, and revenue-sharing possibilities still needed to be discussed."[14]

As preparations were being made for a second summit, Klein had met with Tsuu T'ina leaders in February 1995, promising band members that he would place First Nations gaming on the agendas of several upcoming meetings with southern and northern First Nations leaders. Gordon and First Nations leaders considered such a meeting necessary, although Gordon also had to contend with the request that only those committee members who also happened to be MLAs be on hand for the discussion. Gordon complied, and on 3 April 1995 northern First Nations leaders and committee members met at Edmonton House, while officials met with southern leaders at the Tsuu T'ina band office on 12 April 1995. Leaders on both sides decided that, prior to making a final determination about First Nations gaming, it would be wise to visit a US tribal casino. On 12 June 1995, the committee traveled to Mystic Lake Casino in Minnesota and the Coeur d'Alene Tribal Bingo Association in Idaho. The trip was considered a success and, despite some public comments opposing the quick establishment of reserve casinos, most committee members were impressed with what they had witnessed.

The committee submitted its report to the government in April 1996, recommending that the province limit casino expansion to four First Nations reserves in order to assure the viability of casinos as a source of revenue for non-profit organizations. It was also determined that future First Nations casinos must be licensed on reserves, or areas contiguous to the reserve — the latter point was one no provinces had yet considered. The key recommendation was that, "First Nations casinos must be government regulated and retain their non-profit status."[15] First Nations casinos, then, would be subject to the same rules, regulations, and legislation as other charitable casino gaming initiatives. This meant that, as charity casinos, 40 per cent of all revenue must be directed to First Nations charities, 10 per cent to a First Nations trust fund to be shared by all provincial bands, while the remaining 50 per cent would be used for casino management and be directed to the casino operator.[16] Premier Klein endorsed the recommendations in June 1996, and during the next five years a number of First Nations expressed interest in reserve casinos. Even with the policy initiative on the table, further discussions with First Nations and Commission representatives were required to clarify the requirements for casinos under Alberta's charitable model.

The First Nations Gaming Policy announced in 2001 was adopted in response to a recommendation of the Gaming Licensing Policy Review to examine the bingo industry and the charities that take part in bingo activities. The aim of the review was to construct policies that set out procedures and processes to address proposals related to the growth or expansion of gaming activities. The Alberta Gaming and Liquor Commission developed their eight-step application process in 2002-2003[17] as a means of promoting controlled and managed growth of the provincial casino industry. Twenty-seven applications were submitted in the first year. None of the applications made it through the process prior to licensing that first year, and during that time provincial officials worked toward establishing the framework for the First Nations Development Fund with the provincial First Nations, Alberta's satellite INAC office, and Alberta Community Development. Funded by provincial revenues from electronic gaming in casinos on First Nations land, it was anticipated the revenue would provide opportunities for investment in social and economic development on reserves, as well as social, health, education, and infrastructure spending.[18] Alberta's share of the proceeds from First Nations casinos would be deposited in the Alberta Lottery Fund for traditional lottery programs and to provide funds to the new First Nations Development Fund.[19]

The Enoch Cree Nation Casino

Located three km west of Edmonton, 10 km southwest of St. Albert, and 20 km north of Devon, the Enoch Cree boasts a population of 1,628 on two non-contiguous reserves. Their existing land base was limited, amounting 8,800 acres for agriculture, 200 acres for grazing, 25 for industrial development, 10 for recreation, and 2,586 acres of forest.[20] The one exploitable resource available to the community was their proximity to large amounts of disposable income: the Edmonton population. Community leaders recognized this advantage in 1993 when they held their first super-bingo. Rather than aggressively pursuing a reserve casino project, Enoch officials instead chose to watch patiently from Edmonton as Tsuu T'ina representatives wrangled with provincial officials over the issue. During this foundational period, Enoch leaders carried on discussions with the province. As the media and government focused on the Tsuu T'ina, the Enoch began developing their proposal. Following the release of the First Nations component of the Alberta Lotteries Commission Report in 2001, community leaders knew that it was only a matter of time before First Nations casinos would become a reality. Then, in 2002, the Alberta government announced that it was prepared to accept casino proposals from provincial First Nations, and the Enoch submitted one of the first.

In January 2004, the Enoch Cree reached a $52 million settlement with the federal government for land that covers a large district of west Edmonton.[21] Contending that the original agreement resulting in the sale of a parcel of land in 1910 should have included provisions ensuring the band's interest in subsurface and mineral rights, it was determined that Ottawa was derelict in its duty to protect the Enoch Cree's interests; as a result, Canada settled the claim and the band ratified the agreement.[22] On 15 April 2004, the AGLC approved the band's application to construct a $132 million on-reserve casino. According to Chief Ron Morin, "This agreement is the culmination of years of discussion and dialogue between the government and Alberta First Nations. It is also the first major economic agreement secured collectively by First Nations, with either the provincial or federal government."[23] Within moments of the announcement, CBC Canada broadcast a story of what they interpreted to be the Enoch Cree's triumph and the catalyst that would soon see the emergence of a provincial First Nations gaming industry.

Lost amid the media reports was the story of more than a decade of fighting for the right to conduct reserve gaming. Few newspapers were privy to the battle with Edmonton city council over the cost of servicing the casino; fewer still were the television and radio reports of the last-ditch efforts by residents of Lewis Estates, a golf-course community west of Edmonton, to halt casino approval. The focus of the stories could be distilled into two main themes: (1) the potential for revenue generation; and, (2) the potential for problems associated with all gaming facilities. The latter theme was quickly forgotten as the media began to highlight the various statistics attached to the project, which were impressive. The proposal projected a 255-room, four-star hotel, a sports complex with two NHL-sized ices rinks, several restaurants and bars, and meeting and conference space, in addition to a 60,000-square foot casino with 600 slot machines, 40 table games, and a high-limit gaming lounge.[24]

The project was also expected to employ 700 people, with an annual economic spin-off of $29 million for Edmonton. An additional $34.4 million would filter into the Edmonton market through labour, lottery fund revenues, and vendors and services, while an estimated $11.6 million would flow outside the greater Edmonton area.[25] Robert Morin, president of the Enoch Community Development Corporation, stated that 90 per cent of the construction costs would stay in the greater Edmonton area, generating 865 jobs with a combined payroll of $35 million.[26] The Enoch Cree Nation's partner was Nevada-based Paragon Gaming, which operates the Augustine Casino in Palm Springs, California for the Augustine Band of Cahuilla Mission Indians. Paragon also has gaming projects in New Mexico, Oklahoma, and Nevada, and is in the final stages of a licensing agreement with Alexis First Nation.[27]

As the proposal proceeded through the AGLC's eight-stage approval process, it became apparent that the community stood a good chance of receiving provincial approval. Almost immediately, people living in Lewis Estates came forward in opposition of the casino, claiming it would result in increased neighbourhood traffic — upwards of 17,000 cars per day — as well as higher crime levels.[28] These complaints led Edmonton city council's executive committee to recommend in November 2002 that the city halt negotiations on hooking up municipal utilities to the reserve until the casino met the city's development standards. In what *Gambling Magazine* claimed was a bid to win some control over a massive casino complex, city council's executive recommended halting discussions with the Enoch Cree Nation. City officials admitted that Edmonton may have been legally obligated by legal precedent set in British Columbia to at least talk about providing services to neighbouring municipalities, but Mayor Bill Smith stated that council could ignore the precedent and withhold services to Enoch.[29]

City council then announced that all construction and connection costs were to be borne by the Enoch Cree Nation, while long-term operation and maintenance costs were to be covered by monthly drainage services utility payments. The fee would be based on metered sewage generated from the development or metered water consumption.[30] The debate continued into the summer. At a city council meeting on 9 July, 24 presentations were made in support of and opposition to the casino. Catherine Twinn, widow of Sawridge First Nation's Chief Walter Twinn, said, "The process that I see imposed on First Nations is one that I see as being driven by racism in that impossibly high standards of perfection are imposed on First Nations, that no other could meet."[31] Mayor Smith replied that, although personal opinions were permitted, "you're not going to challenge or accuse anybody here of racism," adding that he was "very disappointed" with this turn of events.[32] The meeting ended with councillors declaring a six-week moratorium on all discussions concerning the Enoch casino until the executive committee could meet and put forward additional recommendations. At the next meeting, the decision was once again delayed.

Rather than wait for provincial approval, the Enoch Cree with Paragon Canada chose to take a proactive stance, a decision based on the estimated length of time it would take to resolve the issues with Edmonton. Both partners wanted to begin construction and have the casino operational as soon as possible subsequent to provincial approval. As their legal counsel, Janice Agrios, stated,

"This development will proceed with or without city services."[33] Chief Morin was equally firm in his resolve, claiming that the project's development would not be halted but simply delayed by Edmonton's tactics, adding, "Enoch is not, and will never be, subject to Edmonton's bylaws," adding that Edmonton sells its services to other communities without attaching conditions, but seems to follow a different standard for First Nations than, say, Sherwood Park or St. Albert.[34] City administrators had by this time begun to endorse the plan, claiming that their concerns about the development had been addressed. This was followed by the recommendation that an agreement for road, water, sewer, police, and fire services be negotiated with the Enoch Cree Nation.[35] The Enoch Cree offered to pay the city $1.4 million for water, sewer, and firefighting services for its proposed casino. According to Curtis Treen of the Lewis Estates Community League, which opposed the casino, the final decision was predictable "but very disappointing." He elaborated: "There has been political will on the provincial and federal side, we believe, to move this ahead, despite the concerns of the community here."[36] Edmonton city councillor Karen Leibovici informed the media that the city would try to mitigate those concerns during its negotiations. She nevertheless admitted that, "The federal government said it was OK to have a casino on that site and the province seems to be approving the license, so I think what we do at this point is to try and mitigate the impact on our citizens in the west end."[37]

At one point, Enoch representatives indicated that they would consider moving the complex an additional 200 metres away, and though Treen said he was encouraged by the band's willingness to negotiate, he had been hoping for a little more distance.[38]

The non-contiguous nature of the Enoch Reserve restricts the band council's plans for economic development, suggesting that casino revenues cannot realistically be funneled into reserve economic development. There remain only 21 acres for additional development, and while this land can, in turn, house an assortment of buildings, thereby diversifying the Enoch Cree economy, the band council will have to determine how it will use the anticipated gaming revenue. A number of options are available, but the Enoch Cree have yet to make their goals public.

The Tsuu T'ina Casino

Unlike the Enoch Cree, the Tsuu T'ina are currently playing a waiting game in anticipation that the community will receive approval from the AGLC to proceed with casino construction. If their plan comes to fruition, the Tsuu T'ina expect the $30 million, 75,000-square-foot casino will bring in close to $100,000 a day in revenue.[39] Unlike the Enoch, the Tsuu T'ina band council does not see the casino as the chief source of revenue; the money will be used to fund a 30-year,

$700 million economic plan to further diversify a growing reserve economy. This plan entails developing a 940-acre parcel of land to build a seven-storey, 190-room hotel with a water park and convention facilities, big-box retail stores, a mall and heritage centre, a number of restaurants, beverage rooms, and a neighbourhood pub, plus an entertainment centre featuring a 225-seat theatre for live acts. Finally, two million square feet of new office and light-industrial space will be developed with the intention of attracting 15,000-20,000 new jobs to the area.[40] In short, it is nation-building fuelled by casino dollars.[41]

Descended from the Athapaskan-speaking people, who include the Navajo and Apache of the south and the Dene and Chippewa of the north, the Tsuu T'ina hereditary chief Bull Head signed Treaty 7 in 1877 on behalf of his 255 followers, agreeing to share a reserve with Blackfoot and Blood bands near Blackfoot Crossing. Relations became strained, however, and in 1883 Bull Head and his people moved onto a 174-square kilometre parcel of land southwest of modern-day Calgary.[42] Settler movement into the west radically altered First Nations economies, and by the early 20th century the Tsuu T'ina were largely dependent on government rations and treaty annuities. Population numbers dwindled until the 1940s, when they began to improve, and limited agriculture and land leases were used to help stabilize the reserve economy. By the 1970s, the Tsuu T'ina leadership was becoming increasingly politically and economically active, first establishing the band-owned Sarcee Development Ltd. followed by what has grown into an upscale residential community on Bragg Creek, Redwood Meadows. Construction of a golf course followed, as did smaller projects during the 1980s.[43] In the early 1990s, community leaders began to consider gaming as an option, and by 1993 the Tsuu T'ina had held a successful super-bingo and begun to lobby Alberta officials for permission to construct a reserve casino.

The casino itself will consist of a single building that will include gaming, food, and beverage facilities, retail shopping, and support areas. Surrounding landscaped areas will accommodate 1,000 vehicles. Located on decommissioned Department of National Defence lease lands, an existing access road and pre-existing infrastructure, including electrical, gas, sewage, and water lines, may be tied into the City of Calgary's infrastructure.[44] With a population close to 1,500, of which 60 per cent per cent are under the age of 25, the Tsuu T'ina chief and council anticipate an increased demand for housing, education, and social services.[45] They decided to develop a long-range economic plan to take advantage of anticipated revenues. The construction of more than 250 houses at Tsuu T'ina will be required over the next five years to keep up with demand.[46] Exacerbating issues is the local unemployment rate: 80 per cent, and it rises another 10 ten per cent in winter. Although the Tsuu T'ina currently operate 21 reserve businesses, the 500 new casino jobs will result in a large number of reserve residents with access to regular, full-time employment that does not necessitate driving to

Calgary and other nearby communities.[47] Training programs will be established to ensure that reserve residents have the skills necessary to work in the casino.[48]

With no business taxes on band-owned business on reserve, the Tsuu T'ina hope to reduce rental costs by upwards of one-quarter in comparison to Calgary. A Tsuu T'ina Heritage Centre is planned, and 300 acres of public green space along the Elbow River has been designated for protection, and will connect the city's existing pathway system across the reserve. It is with all this in mind that band members voted 73 per cent in favour of the 15-acre site for the proposed casino and the 30-year economic development plan.[49] In addition to approving the casino project, it also mandated the band council to negotiate the final stages of an agreement with the province to allow a ring road across its land south of the city. An agreement in principle has been signed, permitting the transfer of reserve land to the provincial government for the purpose, potentially ending a decades-old debate about Calgary's transportation future.[50] The Alberta government anticipates that $26 million will be directed from the casino to improve provincial charities' access to funding.[51]

The Stoney Nakoda Nation Casino

Like the Tsuu T'ina, the Stoney Nakoda Nation is also a Treaty 7 signatory. The Stoneys are descendants of the Dakota Sioux who lived in three groups, the Bearspaw, Chiniki, and Wesley. After separating from the Sioux, the Stoneys gradually moved west to the foothills of the Rocky Mountains. Their contact with the Blackfoot Confederacy was limited, owing in part to their military alliance with the Cree, the traditional Blackfoot enemy. Nevertheless, living in close proximity to the Blackfoot Confederacy led to their invitation to meet at Blackfoot Crossing in September 1877 to participate in treaty negotiations. After the allocation of three separate reserves, federal officials promoted the adoption of farming and a sedentary lifestyle on reserve, and pressured the Stoneys to surrender their lands. According to a report published by the federal Department of Indian Affairs, the Stoney people as of 1885 were self-reliant through "hunting furbearing animals and game," while also purchasing a "large herd of cattle, which is annually increasing in number."[52]

Unlike the Tsuu T'ina, however, reserve land was continually added to the overall Nakoda land base. The original reserve at Morleyville was 175.5 square km in total, located along the Bow River between the Kananaskis and Ghost Rivers. A number of separate land allocations followed during the next four decades; the Rabbit Lake Indian Reserve was added in 1914, covering approximately 1,200 acres; then in 1948, in partial fulfillment of treaty land promises, the 5,000-acre Big Horn Reserve was established. That year, the 4,180-acre Eden Valley Ranch was purchased, which in 1958 was transformed into the Eden Valley Reserve.

Nakoda Nation officials in the 1960s began to use natural resource revenues, particularly from the burgeoning oil and gas industries, to purchase nearby ranch lands. By the 1970s, the Stoney Nation became one of the first in Canada to start a cultural program aimed at preserving the Stoney language in schools and promoting university-level education. It was during this period that the Stoneys started to expand their business enterprises, first by opening a wilderness park and then by taking advantage of their location. Ready access to the national First Nations' community led to annual conferences and powwows, which in turn permitted Native people throughout North America to visit the small community nestled in the foothills of the Rocky Mountains.[53]

Just as it appeared that the community was making economic headway, the Stoney First Nation was confronted with a potential public relations disaster. Following the suicide of 17-year-old Sherman Labelle in May 1998, reports began to surface indicting the band for funneling money from social programs to pay a band debt that was estimated to be between $5.6 and $9.1 million.[54] An inquest into Labelle's death found that the Stoney band council and INAC "apparently did nothing about the lack of educational opportunity, the lack of programs for mental health and alcohol treatment and the abuses of power by [the] tribal government."[55] INAC initiated a forensic audit of the Stoney Nation, and the accounting firm KPMG unearthed evidence of financial misconduct related to the management of the band's oil revenues. Following the review, auditors requested that the RCMP investigate 43 allegations of possible criminal activity, citing evidence that not all Stoney money was spent on authorized programs and that community members received unauthorized money from the Nation.[56] The RCMP investigation ended with no charges related to mismanagement being laid, but it took INAC two-and-a-half years to hand back responsibility for band finances to the Stoney First Nation. An independent firm was retained to ensure the band's leaders followed the rules and there was no mismanagement.

Following Alberta's announcement that it was prepared to accept First Nation casino proposals, the Stoney band council immediately prepared and submitted an application. On 22 June 2005, the *Calgary Herald* reported that the Stoney proposal was about to receive final approval, permitting construction on a $27 million, 110,000 square foot casino and hotel resort to be built on reserve lands at the corner of the Trans-Canada Highway and Highway 40.[57] Although the Stoney proposal is in stage seven of the eight-stage process, preparations are under way to begin construction. For the small community of 4,000 living on the Morley, Rabbit Lake, Eden Valley, and Big Horn reserves, the casino is expected to draw upwards of 400,000 visitors while generating approximately $23.8 million in net revenues the first year.[58] The Stoneys recently purchased 234 acres from TransAlta that will house the casino complex, complete with 15 gaming tables and 300 slot machines — with room to expand to 600. The proposal also calls for a 92-room hotel, a 320-seat restaurant, lounge, and entertainment complex, a 150-person conference centre, and a water park. The project has been designed so it can be expanded to fill the entire 240-acre site with more hotel rooms, casino, and retail space.[59]

Mayfield Consulting Canada, Inc. has been selected as the casino operator, a provision required by the AGLC. Each band owns one-third of the casino. Current directors are Bearspaw Chief Darcy Dixon, Chiniki Chief Aaron Young, and Wesley Chief Ernest Wesley. A chief who happens to be defeated in an election will remain on as a director, but only to serve out a three-year term. All three bands voted in favour of the casino project, and it is anticipated that 20 per cent of the resort's workforce will be filled by members of the Stoney nation, a number that is expected to increase over time. The anticipated $23.8 million in year-one gambling revenue will be divided as follows: $6.4 million go to the casino operator; $4 million set aside for the Mini Thni Community Foundation to be disbursed on the Stoney First Nation; $11.4 million split evenly between the Alberta Lottery Fund and the Stoney Nakoda Nation Development Fund, and the remaining $1.9 million disbursed to non-gaming First Nations in the province.[60]

Community leaders hope the revenue can be channeled into community economic development. They have a ten-year option with TransAlta to purchase the town of Seebe, a 150-acre community currently enclosed by the Stoney First Nation. The town comes with 22 houses, a 17-suite apartment building, a water treatment plant and sewage lagoon, a curling rink, a one-room school house, and a baseball diamond. The Calgary Power Company originally purchased the land from the Stoneys in 1911 to build the Kananaskis Dam on the Bow River. The hydro plant at the time was considered too far a commute from major population centres, and the company decided to provide housing as a way of attracting employees to a rural area. When TransAlta took over from the Calgary Power Company, business operations grew, and so did the town. But as the dam site was modernized, fewer workers were required. When subsidizing the community became financially prohibitive, TransAlta subdivided the site and put both parcels on the market. The Moondance Land Company and the Stoneys subsequently purchased 539 acres south of the town site for $11 million. According to Stoney-Moondance spokesperson Trez McCaskill, the land is earmarked for "a planned residential community, a satellite suburb with a golf course," adding that "whether there's a hotel or not will depend on the market."[61]

Conclusion

Owing to the nature of the First Nations gaming industry in Alberta — one that exists only on paper until such time as a casino formally opens — this chapter has been restricted to tracing the general chronology of events leading up to the decisions that resulted in the creation of the AGLC's eight-stage casino application review process. It has been further limited to discussing the anticipated benefits of the three high-profile casino projects: Enoch Cree, Tsuu T'ina, and Stoney. Interestingly, the process leading to the establishment of reserve casinos began in 1993 following Premier Ralph Klein's ascension to power, and 13 years later we have yet to see any First Nations casino operational in the province. The process took 12 years in Manitoba, whereas Saskatchewan politicians expedited the process and had four First Nations casinos operating within five years. Similarly, in Ontario, Casino Rama was operational within five years of the NDP government's announcement. What the delay in Alberta means is as yet unknown. What we do know is that the Enoch Casino will be operational by the end of 2006, and the Stoneys appear on course. Currently, the Tsuu T'ina project has been sidetracked by a three-decade debate about the placement of a ring road on reserve land, which appears no closer to being resolved.

A broader public discourse has begun to emerge in Alberta concerning what both gaming advocates and opponents see as the proliferation of casinos, both on and off reserves, and the need to consider the ramifications of unchecked expansion. The current regulatory framework is of concern, for it appears that all casino proposals are going to be successful, yet there are no criteria for treatment programs as part of the application process, and provincial officials have yet to create a policy for similar programming. The question of what the economic, political, and social impact a failed casino will have on a small community seeking gambling revenues to jump-start a stagnant economy is, as yet, unanswerable, but it remains salient. The First Nations gaming industry in Alberta is in a transitional stage between concept and reality, and until casinos are operational, many of the questions about the efficacy of the overall process will simply have to wait.

CHAPTER EIGHT

Social and Political Responses
to First Nations Gaming

Despite the spate of lawsuits resulting from the Casino Rama project, the success of the casino indicated that there was both political and social support for reserve casinos. The growth of the Saskatchewan First Nations gaming industry further indicated that citizens in western Canada had caught the gambling bug. Nevertheless, the general response to First Nations gaming was less than enthusiastic. Provincial governments were reluctant to relinquish jurisdiction, and prairie premiers employed the RCMP to enforce their position. In Manitoba, the RCMP raided the Opaskwayak lottery operation in 1986, and they laid charges against two members of the Cross Lake and Roseau River First Nations following a 1992 raid of an unlicensed gaming establishment. In Saskatchewan, a 36-member RCMP squad raided the White Bear reserve in March 1993.

The negative reaction of western provincial officials was not unique. A February 2000 Canada West Foundation poll indicated that only one per cent of respondents believed that First Nations should operate gaming establishments. Paradoxically, 52 per cent supported reserve gaming, as opposed to 34 per cent who did not. In the prairie provinces, 49 per cent of respondents supported reserve gaming if it was regulated by government, while 55 per cent of respondents who had gambled in the previous year agreed (32 per cent strongly agreed) that only the provincial government should be permitted to license reserve gambling. The data seemed to indicate that the public would support First Nations gaming as long as it was confined to the reserves.

A major obstacle arose among First Nations themselves. In the United States, host communities have at times become factionalized. An extreme example occurred at the St. Regis Mohawk Reserve in New York, where rival factions briefly went to war over the casino debate, resulting in the deaths of two men in a gun battle.[1] Though similar events have not occurred Canada, one disquieting trend has emerged: First Nations leaders proposing reserve casino projects consistently find themselves at odds with neighbouring non-Native communities. A municipal referendum in 1994 indicated that 52 per cent of Saskatoon residents opposed a downtown First Nations casino. In 2001, the town of Headingley, west of Winnipeg, twice voted to prohibit the proposed Swan Lake First Nations project. Further north that year, the people of Thompson rejected a similar proposal by the Nisichawayasihk (Nelson House) First Nation. Recently, community opposition to the Enoch First Nation casino proposal was sparked by Edmonton citizen's groups and city council members. For the most part, First Nations leaders have remained undeterred and continue to forge ahead with their plans. The moral of the story to date seems to be that First Nations gaming is fine so long as it remains government regulated, on reserves, and away from mainstream Canadian society.

Race-Based Politics

As the Manitoba government began to sift through First Nations casino applications in the early 1990s, the selection committee was impressed with the Swan Lake proposal. Swan Lake is a community of 1,145 located 115 km southwest of Winnipeg. In 1995, the community was awarded a $10.4-million Treaty Land Entitlement (TLE) payment to purchase a minimum of 484 acres to be added to the reserve land base.[2] The Province of Manitoba and the federal government owed Swan Lake the money in lieu of land it was supposed to have received in the 1880s under the terms of a treaty. Following the resolution of TLE negotiations, the community established Swan Lake First Nation Enterprises and initiated an economic development project. The provincial government announced that it would pursue the establishment of reserve casinos following the 15 October 1997 release of the Bostrom Report supporting the creation of a First Nations gaming industry. The finalization of several years of study by Swan Lake officials coincided with the report's release, and the community decided to purchase the Alpine Motel in the Rural Municipality of Headingley, a community of 1,600 located immediately west of Winnipeg. The 25-acre parcel was earmarked for casino development. The land would have to be designated an urban reserve by the federal government, but casino advocates believed this would pose few difficulties. It was anticipated that the provincial government would soon issue a request for proposals (RFP) for casino projects, and Swan Lake was poised to expedite matters and develop a $100-million complex that included a hotel, a 7,000-seat arena, and a conference centre. The proposal appeared destined for quick acceptance and immediate construction.

The Swan Lake proposal was one of three that would be located off-reserve, the other two being the Nisichawayasihk in Thompson, and the Sioux Valley proposal to be located in either Sifton or Brandon. According to lawyer and former Progressive Conservative cabinet minister Darren Praznik — the Tories had been defeated in the September 1999 provincial election — the RFP issued by the new NDP government was poorly worded and did not distinguish between rural and urban reserves. The selection committee therefore had no contingency plan for proposed casino construction on land located off reserve, even land that had been purchased by First Nations intent on conversion to urban status. "Quite frankly I think the government has made a major mistake," Praznik said, adding that the government's ability to press forward with the proposal "would be much easier in the community if they weren't requiring that the land be made reserve land."[3] These words would become prophetic, for by March 2000 a significant number of Headingley residents were openly protesting casino construction in their community. Many cited the Bostrom Report:

> prior to a proposal being considered for evaluation, a proposal must demonstrate community support (resolution of council) from the local government in which the proposed gaming facility is to be located. If a proposal does not contain the necessary community approval documentation, it will not be considered for evaluation.[4]

The fact that Headingley's elected officials supported the Swan Lake proposal did not deter casino opponents from forcing a plebiscite. After weeks of sometimes racially charged lobbying by casino opponents, the people of Headingly voted down the proposal by a substantial margin, with 85 per cent voting against it.[5] Headingley's town council withdrew its support.

A number of reasons were later cited for the failure of the proposal. *Winnipeg Sun* writer Tom Brodbeck highlighted shifting criteria. The provincial gaming policy was being developed simultaneously with the review of First Nations gaming proposals, and the two processes sometimes clashed. For instance, after the initial RFP time period had elapsed and First Nations had submitted their plans, the government announced that successful casino bids would require the support of adjoining communities, a condition that had not been spelled out in the original RFP. According to Brodbeck, "Nobody really knew what that meant or whether the support had to be in the form of a plebiscite," adding that, "it was nearly impossible to get that support because there was a government-imposed gag order on all casino proponents." Brodbeck asserted that "the process was made worse by the NDP's insistence that the casinos had to be on reserve land — for what reason nobody could explain."[6]

Following the plebiscite, Swan Lake leaders lobbied the Headingley town council for the opportunity to educate community members about the casino's benefits. They also requested that Premier Gary Doer's office ignore the plebiscite results.[7] While town councillors were prepared to consider Swan Lake's request, the premier was less than willing. As far as he was concerned, "Headingley now in my view does not meet the conditions, period."[8] On 7 June, he stated further that he would not allow casino proponents to continue trying to earn public support when it was clear that support was not forthcoming, and that he did not favour holding continuous plebiscites to obtain the desired result. The Minister in charge of administering the *Gaming Control Act*, Steve Ashton, later confirmed to the Manitoba Legislature that his office had written a letter to the municipality of Headingley indicating that the premier's office accepted the results of the plebiscite.[9]

Undeterred, Swan Lake officials worked during the last week of November in an attempt to allay community fears. The distribution of 700, 20-page booklets detailing the project and offering testimonials about First Nation casino operations in communities such as Prince Albert, Saskatchewan and Deadwood, South Dakota did little to sway public opinion. On 6 December, a second plebiscite was held and the people of Headingley once again voted against the casino proposal. This time 69 per cent of eligible voters participated in the plebiscite, with 53.9 per cent voting against the casino. This was a far cry from the original 85 per cent opposition.[10] Nevertheless, as the Premier's office indicated in June, the results of the April plebiscite were binding and the Swan Lake proposal was dead. On 7 December 2001, the Swan Lake First Nation formally withdrew its Headingley casino proposal followed by the Manitoba government declaring that the project would not proceed.

The Swan Lake casino proposal and the reaction of the people of Headingley made national news in Canada. Even the celebrated environmentalist, David Suzuki weighed in on the issue:

> I am saddened by the idea of native-run casinos. It doesn't reflect their core beliefs as people. It depends on some weird addiction that is both damaging and dangerous to society. . . . Instead of bringing in Wonderbread to native communities, they should have Mabel, who's good at baking bread, start her own bread-baking business. Instead of buying $10,000 coffins from outside the community, they should have local carvers build them.[11]

Swan Lake Chief Roy McKinny advised Suzuki to "get with the times."[12] The notoriety of the project was a black mark on the Doer government and the provincial FNGP. The failure of the Swan Lake proposal was the first in what would be a string of failed casino bids in Manitoba. Of the initial five proposals, only the Aseneskak and the Brokenhead casinos in the end became operational.

The proposal's failure raised the spectre of racism following an aggressive lobby campaign led by casino opponents supported by the Manitoba Jockey Club. A pamphlet attacking the casino asked readers, "Why did residents choose to live in Headingley?" The response was, "to enjoy a quieter rural lifestyle. Will there be a residential area developed to accommodate employees from Swan Lake

Reserve — where will they reside?" Manitoba Jockey Club President Harvey Warner claimed that the under-used Assiniboia Downs had "the square footage and the infrastructure; we could produce an environment at a much lesser cost and be up and running quicker, with none of the opposition that is being received now." Swan Lake business advisor and casino project manager, Rick Wenaus, was distressed by what he portrayed as unethical commentary that "plays upon the old idea that reserves are broken down shacks and old cars. Swan Lake is a very progressive, up-to-date and business-like reserve." Wenaus also expressed frustration at the selection process: "We operate under a very different set of rules than any of the other casinos — I don't think there was a plebiscite or vote held when the Downs put in their machines. . . ."[13]

On 17 December 2003, AMC Grand Chief White Bird and several other chiefs met with Premier Doer to discuss the FNGP's failure. A position paper was prepared outlining some of the issues related to revamping the process. Doer established a two-member committee to investigate the FNGP, and on 30 June it released its report. The committee was critical of the premier's office and of the overall process, which it claimed was flawed from the start. The original RFP had not limited site locations beyond stating that the casinos must be located on reserve prior to becoming operational. This did not take into account the proposals that depended on the conversion of off-reserve holdings into urban reserve land.[14] The committee accepted that, in those cases where potential First Nations casinos could be located off-reserve, community support would be vital to their success, but it indicated that a plebiscite was not required to obtain the support of municipalities and local governments. Instead, the committee urged municipalities and local governments

> to consider their support of First Nation casino development as they would for any other business ventures proposed within their jurisdiction. Early formal support for development should be secured and articulated as part of an expression of interest process to clarify and confirm the economic development interests of local governments and communities, minimize pre-development expenses, and affirm mutual economic benefits.[15]

The committee's final report advocated permitting elected officials of First Nations communities to determine on behalf of their constituents the proper path. In the end, Swan Lake opened a reserve casino, which currently operates 40 VLTs and employs four full-time staff and on-site security — a far cry from the proposed $51-million complex that was cut short by outside interests.[16]

Gaming Troubles at Dakota Tipi

Northeast of Swan Lake, near Portage la Prairie, lies the Dakota Tipi Nation. A community of less than 100 members living on a reserve of 30 acres, the Dakota once lived within the Portage la Prairie city confines. The land they occupied had been purchased by the ancestors of the current residents from money earned as regional farm workers. In the 1950s, at the request of the city, the Dakota moved south of town onto their current reserve site.

Like many First Nations in Canada, the Dakota were beset by economic difficulties that eventually led to social problems in the community. Recognizing the need to improve living conditions, in the early 1970s the community established a reserve bingo under the leadership of Chief Dennis Pashe. The bingo soon became the Dakota's most profitable business, employing 10 people. The profits went toward alcohol and drug abuse programs, a playground on the reserve, and community housing. The success of the bingo led the band to open a casino in 1986, which was promptly shut down by provincial authorities.

Little was heard from Chief Pashe or the Dakota Tipi for much of the next decade. During this period, the Pequots opened Foxwoods, Casino Rama opened in Ontario, and four First Nations casinos opened in Saskatchewan. In Manitoba, the OCN had signed a gaming agreement with the province in 1990 followed by a VLT agreement, permitting the placement of one-armed bandits on reserves. In 1994, the Dakota entered into a gaming agreement with the Province of Manitoba, which granted responsibility for the licensing and control of on-reserve charitable gaming to the band. The agreement limited reserve gambling to lottery schemes, which did not please Pashe, who had by now publicly stated his desire to expand his 1,000-seat bingo hall to include blackjack, dice games, and slot machines.[17] But provincial gaming policy and federal legislation offered little flexibility. The province would not rescind the gaming agreement, nor would it alter its provisions.

In July 1999, as Winnipeg was preparing to host the Pan Am Games, provincial authorities discovered that the Dakota intended to open an unlicensed reserve casino, and that it would house a number of slot machines. When Pashe learned that the news had leaked, he announced to the media that any attempts to shut down the casino would result in his band blocking the Trans-Canada Highway, impeding motorists travelling to Winnipeg for the Games. He was quick to condemn Premier Gary Filmon, declaring him a racist and anti-Native for failing to respect his promise to license two First Nations casinos. He is reported to have said that "The only thing missing from Filmon's head is a pointed white cloth."[18] Frustrating Pashe further was Filmon's recent $66-million commitment to refurbish two Winnipeg casinos.[19] Despite warnings that band officials faced prosecution if they proceeded, on 23 July the Dakota Tipi opened a new casino.

Following a six-week investigation, RCMP entered the Dakota Tipi reserve on 16 August and seized 25 slot machines from the makeshift casino housed in the community bingo hall. Officers claimed that Pashe and his supporters smuggled the machines into Canada from North Dakota and now faced penalties under the *Customs Act*, including a possible $500,000 fine and five years in prison. The RCMP inspected the machines in an effort to determine whether they had been modified to accept Canadian currency and if the payout had been lowered. According to Sergeant John Fleming, "This action was one step in our continuing investigation under the *Customs Act* in respect to the illegal smuggling of gaming machines into the province of Manitoba from the United States." Pashe rebutted: "There's a lot of hypocrisy by the provincial government. On one hand they say they have no jurisdiction to provide services to you, such as recreation programs, housing programs, social services, then on the other hand they say they have jurisdiction to stop us from raising money. They can't have it both ways." Pashe threatened that members of the Dakota Tipi might retaliate by blocking rail lines in the province. [20]

If the premier's office thought Pashe was all bluster, the railway companies took him seriously and petitioned the courts for a restraining order. On 19 August, both Canadian National and Canadian Pacific Railways were granted court injunctions prohibiting Dakota Tipi members or their sympathizers from blocking rail lines. [21] Pashe responded by taking out a full-page advertisement in the *Winnipeg Sun* accusing the Tories of giving gaming contracts to individual and group campaign contributors. [22] In October 1999 Gary Doer's NDP defeated Filmon's Conservatives, taking 32 seats to the Tories' 24. The Liberals took one seat. On 5 October 1999, Doer was sworn in as Premier of Manitoba.

During the next 18 months, Pashe attempted to foster positive relations with the Doer government. He also took advantage of new provincial First Nations gaming policy to apply for a license to install 25 VLTs in the bingo hall. In January 2001, Dakota Tipi entered into a site-holder agreement with the Manitoba Lotteries Commission (MLC) to operate the VLTs on reserve, the proviso being that the Dakota comply with the 1994 provincial/First Nations gaming agreement. Pashe and the band council were prepared to make a strong bid for a reserve casino. However, rumblings of discontent concerning Pashe's leadership began to be heard beyond the community. In 1997, community members Corrine Smoke and Leona Freed had claimed that the chief and council used the band identification number of departed residents to obtain increased federal transfers. They also alleged that band members were misappropriating money from the bingo hall for their personal use. The heart of the debate was Pashe's claims that, when he accepted the role of chief in 1978, he did so through hereditary succession. According to Sec. 74 of the *Indian Act*, elections by band custom are permissible; hence, Pashe was not required to call an election. For the next 20 years, he handed out what some community members argued were privileges to his supporters, including access to education money, bus services, jobs, and social assistance. A workfare program Pashe initiated in 2001 resulted in social assistance cheques being withheld by the band administration and people were forced to work for food vouchers.[23]

In December 2001, 30 community members led by Chief Pashe's 67-year-old mother, Elsie, his eldest bother, Steven, two of his sisters, the mother of three of his children, and the small band's holy man, passed a no-confidence motion and elected Pashe's sister, Marjorie Prince, as interim chief. The group also demanded that the council open the books to determine how the estimated $10 million a year generated by a gas bar, a bingo palace, VLTs, and government funding was being spent. Pashe refused demands to call an election, claiming that such practices "are against our history." According to community member Corrine Smoke, however, "the whole band custom concept is phony. It's alien to our culture. Plains Indians like the Dakota were always democratic; we chose leaders based on merit and decisions were made by consensus."[24] With the community increasingly factionalized, the Christmas break was marked by periodic gunfire and internecine violence. The Dakota Ojibway Police Service, established in 1977 to serve First Nations communities in southwestern Manitoba, investigated at least six shootings on Christmas and New Year's Eve involving Pashe, his ex-wife, and the nephew of interim Chief Marjorie Prince. Finally, in May 2002, the Minister of Indian Affairs invoked Sec. 74 of the *Indian Act* to impose third-party management on the Dakota Tipi to resolve the conflict and investigate allegations of financial impropriety.[25]

The month before, April 2002, the Provincial Council of Women of Manitoba and several reserve residents had petitioned the premier's office to investigate Dakota Tipi for the misuse of gaming revenues. These requests, combined with the growing political instability on the reserve, led the Manitoba Gaming Control Commission (MGCC) to initiate contact with the band's chief and council, community representatives, and the band's legal counsel, INAC and other organizations in an attempt to resolve the conflict. By mid-July, further allegations surfaced linking gaming revenue and criminal activity on the reserve. The province suspended the band's gaming privileges later that month. In September, the MGCC contracted with the accounting firm Deloitte & Touche LLP to assess the allegations. In October, the Minister of Finance announced that the Office of the Auditor General had been instructed to conduct a special audit. The Auditor General decided to review the governance and accountability framework to better determine how First Nations gaming was managed, make recommendations to improve gaming agreements, and improve accountability.

The Auditor General's report, released to the Legislature on 30 April 2003, indicated that the Dakota Tipi First Nation had mismanaged its books and potentially broken a number of laws by inappropriately spending approximately $14,000 in bingo profits. "As a result of an absence of effective governance," the report read, "there was virtually no accountability over the raising and spending of gaming revenues."[26] The author of the report, Jon Singleton, went on to suggest that bingo and VLT money may have been used for criminal activities as part of former Chief Pashe's battle to remain in power. Singleton also indicated that VLT proceeds had been used to influence a band member to swear a false affidavit against Pashe's enemies in January 2002 as well as to pay legal fees and travel expenses for non-band members to appear in a Winnipeg court.[27] The report recommended that the province maintain its suspension of Dakota Tipi gaming activities until a stable band council was elected.[28]

A new council had been elected the previous October in what was the community's first open vote in 24 years. Dennis Pashe was ousted from power and replaced by Cornell Pashe, who indicated his desire to see gaming re-established at Dakota Tipi, but apparently did very little about it. Two years later Dennis Pashe was re-elected, and contacted provincial officials about having the bingo reinstated and the VLTs operational. In May 2005, the MGCC issued the band a license to run bingos, but withheld permission to operate VLTs. Members of the new Sioux Valley Bingo Committee indicated their hope that the bingo would again attract the 100 people a night, as it had prior to being shut down in 2002, and that revenues could be channeled into a children's meal program and similar social programs.[29] MGCC spokesperson Susan Olynik said that the province wanted to first make sure that the band was capable of accounting for revenue before it could get its VLT machines back.[30]

The Proposed Saskatoon Casino

In 2002, First Nations leaders in Saskatchewan began working toward expanding their gaming operations. The first move in their strategy was to promote a larger casino, preferably in an urban centre, to take advantage of both tourism and static municipal populations. Saskatoon was selected as the potential site. In December 2002, the Saskatoon Tribal Council (STC) presented Saskatoon city council with a 200-page report outlining every aspect of the project. The proposed 105,000 square foot complex would comprise a casino, a showroom, and an attached six-storey parkade, while offering more than 40 table games and 700 slot machines. The STC anticipated that the $65-million downtown complex would generate $100 million in economic activity, including approximately $5 million for local charities. Property taxes in excess of $1.5 million would be paid to the City of Saskatoon. Casino employment would exceed 700 people, including 17 managers at an annual average salary of $40-75,000, 106 supervisory jobs paying $30-38,000, and 590 operational jobs tabbed at $20-29,000 annually.[31] Peripheral benefits such as casino construction would generate a further $92 million in service jobs and related industries, producing 922 person-years of employment and an estimated $32.2 million in labour income. An additional 1,800 direct and indirect jobs would be realized in the form of construction, tourism, and the resultant operational industries. It was expected that the casino's annual operating expenditures would exceed $50 million, the majority of that ending up with local suppliers for goods and services, and that the casino would attract an estimated two-million visitors to Saskatoon annually, with tourists spending more than $36-million each year — an estimate which did not account for monies spent in the casino itself. In all, SIGA's take from the casino would be in the neighbourhood of $19.4 million a year. After reviewing the proposal, city council, with the backing of a number of business owners and the Chamber of Commerce, voted six to five to allow a downtown casino to be built.

This was not the first time a Saskatoon casino had been proposed. As recently as December 1999 — notwithstanding a 1994 plebiscite showing Saskatoon residents to be opposed to a downtown casino — the STC had made a modest proposal to build a 50,000 square foot casino which would cost in the neighbourhood of $10 million and employ some 300 people. Little more was heard about the proposal until June 2000, when Saskatoon resident Pauline Ham wrote to city council outlining her opposition to the construction of additional casinos provincially. The following September, City Councillor Owen Fortosky requested "that a plebiscite be held, with question, wording and date to be determined by Council, on the development and/or expansion of casinos in Saskatoon."[32] Councillor Lenore Swystun requested additional information about "how public consultations on casino gaming in Saskatoon may be conducted," including format and cost.[33] Council members then requested that city administrators meet with key participants in the casino development project to establish dates of public consultations and time lines.[34]

All the key players — including the STC, the FSIN, and the mayor's office — were willing participate in a public consultation process, including a town hall meeting.[35] Fortosky moved "that the motion be amended to read as follows: that a binding bylaw vote be held, with question, wording and date of the vote to be determined by Council, on the development and/or expansion of casinos in Saskatoon."[36] Council abstained on the amendment vote, but resolved to defer the matter until the public consultation process had been completed. The executive committee of city council recommended that a public review, as well as Fortosky's motion, "be postponed until after the City has received a proposal for a casino."[37] Council accepted the recommendation and talk of a plebiscite was deferred until the 16 December 2002 council meeting.

In late November 2002, STC and SIGA representatives asked Saskatoon city council for permission to make a presentation "with respect of the proposed relocation of the Emerald Casino,"[38] a facility operated by the Saskatoon Prairieland

Park Corporation (SPPC) and located on the Exhibition Grounds next to the Western Development Museum in southeast Saskatoon. At the next city council meeting, STC spokesperson Lester Lafond presented the proposal for a new complex to be located in the heart of Saskatoon at 22nd St. and Pacific Ave. SIGA's Ed Bellegarde then outlined a plan to purchase the Emerald Casino and strike an agreement to hire its employees. He indicated that the project, once completed, would generate close to $70-million annually and result in 1,000 new jobs.[39] Following the presentation, Councillor Fortosky again asked the mayor and council to consider his motion and its amendment.[40]

Two weeks later, on 16 December, 49 of 172 people who petitioned city council for time to speak on the issue were heard.[41] Of those, 17 spoke against the casino while more than 30 supported it. Carmel Dodd, co-chair of the Saskatoon Anti-Poverty Coalition, requested that an impact study be commissioned to evaluate the casino's effects on the people of Saskatoon, and that a plebiscite be held during the next civic election to determine the people's position.[42] Casino supporters included Todd Brandt of Tourism Saskatoon, who spoke in glowing terms of the impact the casino could have on tourism and local businesses. Rob Jones, executive director of the Centennial Auditorium (now known as Teachers Credit Union Place), spoke in support of a destination casino in the proposed location and outlined the planned partnership involving the auditorium.[43] The majority of the 17 people who opposed the casino cited concerns ranging from a fear of gambling addiction to a philosophical discussion about the morality of gambling.

Six months later, at the 12 May 2003 council meeting, a petition for a referendum was submitted to Saskatoon Mayor Jim Maddin by the Coalition Against Gambling Expansion in Saskatoon (CAGES).[44] This followed the 17 April submission of their petition to the City Clerk's Office in accordance with Section 106 of *The Cities Act*. Having collected nearly 28,000 signatures, well in excess of the minimum 21,000 required to force a plebiscite,[45] they argued that the City of Saskatoon was legally obligated to determine the casino issue by plebiscite. They requested that the following questions be asked during the next municipal election:

1. Are you in favour of a casino to be located at 22nd Street and Pacific Avenue, Saskatoon, as described in the "2002 Saskatoon Casino Project Proposal" presented to City Council on Dec. 2, 2002?

2. Do you approve City Council acting to transfer, acquire, sell, exchange, allow or approve the use of City land, City controlled land or interests in land to provide a site for or to accommodate development of new and expanded casino gambling in Saskatoon?

When City Council met on 9 June, more than 150 people crowded the chamber to hear city council announce that it would hold a plebiscite during the fall municipal elections. An STC request to hold a summer plebiscite was ignored. Lafond announced on 21 August that plans to build the casino in Saskatoon had been rescinded and the project would be relocated to the Whitecap Reserve, 26 km southeast of Saskatoon.[46]

At the Saskatoon city council meeting of 8 September, more than two weeks after the STC announced its move to Whitecap, debate continued, fuelled in part by three of the casino's main opponents: Darwin Seed of Citizens for a Quality Saskatoon, Randy Donauer of CAGES, and MP for Saskatoon-Humboldt Jim Pankiw. Seed, clearly distrusting the STC and FSIN announcement that Saskatoon was no longer the preferred site, maintained the importance of leaving the plebiscite questions on the municipal election ballot. Pankiw supported this position, stating that it was important that the City of Saskatoon respect the wishes of the petitioners and conduct a vote on the casino. Donauer indicated that their position had not changed and he requested that city council not consider the new location until the original proposal had been withdrawn. He also asked that an additional plebiscite be held on the issue of a casino on the Whitecap Reserve. Mark Regier of the Saskatoon Prairieland Park Corporation requested that the Whitecap casino be subject to an agreement with the SPPC and SIGA, and that, in the absence of such an agreement, the SPPC's Emerald Casino not be restricted from expanding.[47]

Ed Bellegarde, president and CEO of SIGA, informed the mayor and council that he would not officially withdraw the proposal for a downtown casino, nor did he object to the upcoming referendum. He also presented the *2003 Dakota Dunes Resort Project Proposal* while outlining how other Saskatchewan communities have benefited generally from First Nations gaming. He stated that both the Rural Municipality of Dundurn and Whitecap Reserve residents were receptive to the proposal, and asked for council's formal support. Dundurn Reeve Fred Wilson and Councillor Fred Baran were on hand to declare their support for the Whitecap Reserve casino, and urged Saskatoon's mayor and council to help make the casino a reality. Councillor McPherson from the town of Outlook was also supportive. In the end, Saskatoon city council supported SIGA's proposal for a casino situated on the Whitecap Dakota First Nation. The plebiscite was held concurrently with the 22 October municipal elections. The results were: 44,307 against Resolution 1 and 35,766 for; 41,356 against Resolution 2 and 37,885 for. The City of Saskatoon was obligated to defeat resolutions 1 and 2.[48]

Conclusion

It would seem that, in most cases, First Nations are being asked not only to conform to provincial regulatory frameworks but to take into consideration the views of mainstream society and prepare for negative reactions. To facilitate reserve economies and nation building, apparently, First Nations must first conform to mainstream Canadian views and opinions. Then there is the conflict between the federal policy agenda — which stresses assimilation in the guise of participation in Canadian society — and First Nations' gaming interests. Government has mandated that First Nations participate in the Canadian economy, but when gaming is the chosen path, governments at every level try to make it impossible for them to do so. What is perhaps most frustrating for First Nations are the reasons given to halt casino projects: people are willing to forego economic growth in order to remain on the moral high ground, from which vantage point they tend to lose sight of the fact that gaming initiatives are not aimed at assisting them — the people resisting — but their neighbours who are in need of economic assistance. On the other hand, events at Dakota Tipi underscore the need for a regulatory framework to ensure that no community is given the opportunity to operate a casino until it is capable of doing so properly.

CHAPTER NINE

Recent Developments
In First Nations Gaming

The First Nations gaming industry in Canada is, if anything, fluid. It is constantly changing, and though the majority of media reports focus on major casino projects and proposed new operations, these do not represent the most recent happenings in First Nations gaming. The Mi'kmaq of Nova Scotia, for instance, have signed 11 gaming agreements with provincial authorities since 1995, and control a significant proportion of the province's VLTs. In Quebec, the Mohawks of Kahnawake have for five years managed an internet gaming operation, to the consternation of both provincial and federal officials. Labour unions have infiltrated First Nations casinos in Saskatchewan and Ontario, though not without a fight, and in British Columbia, a provincial moratorium on gaming expansion temporarily undermined plans to remodel a former residential school on the St. Mary's Reserve near Cranbrook into a destination casino. These events are examined in this chapter.

Gambling on Casinos: Notes from British Columbia

The St. Eugene Mission was founded in the heart of Ktunaxa/Kinbasket territory by the Oblates of Mary Immaculate, an order of the Roman Catholic Church. In 1910, the federal government replaced the first building with what became the first industrial and residential school in western Canada. Until its closure in 1970, the school was host to more than 5,000 children from the Shuswap, Blackfoot, Okanagan, and Ktunaxa First Nations in British Columbia and Alberta. The government originally planned to renovate the mission buildings for use as residences for the mentally handicapped, but that did not occur. The site was abandoned until June 1974, when the Canadian government awarded the five bands of the Ktunaxa/Kinbasket Tribal Council (KKTC) equal ownership over the land, some 346 acres divided into two parcels. This unique arrangement resulted in one reserve being owned by five First Nations. It also led to two decades of debate over what to do with the property. While a number of proposals were considered, the communities could agree on only one issue: they had to respect the wishes of elder Mary Paul, who in 1983 said, "Since it was within the St. Eugene Mission school that the culture of the Kootenay Indian was taken away, it should be within that building that it is returned."[1]

For a time, the issue of what to do with the mission site took a back seat to treaty and self-government discussions that absorbed the local communities. The Ktunaxa/Kinbasket filed a claim under the newly established tri-partite treaty process, then spent much of 1994 and 1995 preparing for negotiations. By 1996 a framework agreement was being finalized as the creation of the Ktunaxa/Kinbasket Tribal Council was worked out. The final agreement enabled the KKTC to begin investigating economic development initiatives. They invited Stephen Cornell, co-director of the Harvard Project on American Indian Economic Development, to the community for consultations. Cornell claimed that "investment must not be thought of as just a financial investment, but as a human investment and our youth have to believe that they need to invest their life within our communities."[2] Faced with the ongoing dilemma of what to do with the property combined with a need to secure work for the local youth, the KKTC responded to a 1997 provincial call for proposals for casino projects: its casino proposal would be the centrepiece of a larger resort complete with golf course, restaurant, and hotel.[3]

The KKTC announced its plans to devote 321 acres of the mission site to develop a world-class, $23-million destination resort. As St. Mary's First Nation Chief, KKTC administrator, and chair of the St. Eugene Mission Development Board, Sophie Pierre said that the development "will provide jobs and economic stability for the Ktunaxa/Kinbasket people and provide an avenue for them to start healing from the effects of the residential school."[4] Expected to take two years to complete, the resort would comprise an 18-hole golf course, recreational facilities, and 119 guest rooms, along with an interpretive centre and an arts and crafts centre marketing the work of local artists. It was anticipated that, in addition to the construction costs, the project would pump upwards of $2.6-million tourist dollars into the local economy annually, and employ 124 people full-time. In November 1999, the province granted final approval to begin construction on what was by now being touted as a $35-million resort. Immediately, Pierre announced that the casino, with 300 slot machines and 25 table games, would open in early Spring 2000, followed by the golf course, and the hotel a year later. Negotiations began with various hotel operators, with Delta Hotels and Resorts chain emerging as the front runner.[5]

Initially, everything appeared to proceed smoothly. A 31 March media report stated that "the floor area of the building appears to be at least as big as an average hockey rink," and that there were at least 25 workers on site.[6] In April, gambling expert Rose Van Ens was flown to Cranbrook for a number of training sessions, preparing councillors to deal with problem gamblers.[7] It soon became apparent, however, that there were problems with the project. Although the golf course opened on schedule, KKTC officials announced in April 2000 that they were pushing the casino's opening date ahead to August. When the casino was still not complete in January 2001, Pierre attributed the delays to the KKTC's failure to secure an agreement with Delta Hotels and Resorts, in spite of CEO John Johnston's public support of the project.[8] Finally, on 21 June, Pierre announced that the KKTC had reached an agreement with Delta to operate the hotel and named spring 2002 as the casino's official opening date. By this point, the five bands, along with Delta, the Royal Bank of Canada, and the Columbia Basin Trust were the project's main investors.[9] Construction began immediately and, as of January 2002, it appeared that the casino would meet its scheduled opening date of 21 June, National Aboriginal Day.

The now $42.1-million resort finally opened to the public on 21 September. The 19,000 square foot casino, managed by the BC Lottery Commission (BCLC) and operated by Lake City Casinos of Kelowna, featured 225 slot machines, 10 gaming tables, a tele-horse racing wagering area, and a restaurant and bar. Of the 110 employees, close to one dozen were of First Nations origin. It was announced to the media that 20 per cent of the casino's profits would remain with the five bands, 40 per cent would be directed to the province, and the remaining 40 per cent would be divided among the BCLC and Lake City Casinos.[10] The final stage — the former residential school transformed into a heritage hotel with original wood beams and flooring — opened on 21 January 2003 with 23 guest rooms, six meeting rooms, a restaurant, and lounge. It was here that interested community members would start training in the various aspects of the hospitality industry.[11] As Pierre proclaimed, "we created 250-plus new jobs and the resort now makes us the third largest private employer in the region. . . . Our project is creating new revenue for our communities and the economies of our neighbours. It will strengthen the BC Rockies as an international tourist destination." For her work on the development, Pierre was given the 2002 Individual Economic Developer of the Year Award by the Council for the Advancement of Native Development Officers (CANDO), was awarded the Queen's Golden Jubilee commemorative medal for outstanding contributions for the KKTC, and was a recipient of a National Aboriginal Achievement Award in 2003.[12]

As early as the following October, however, it became apparent that the St. Eugene Resort was facing significant financial challenges. The first hint came at a KKTC-called community forum with the Regional District of East Kootenay (RDEK). According to Pierre, the forum had been struck to encourage dialogue between the First Nation and non-Native communities following a decline in the tourism industry precipitated by SARS and the mad cow scares and that summer's forest fires.[13] But according *Daily Townsman* columnist Gerry Warner, who had followed the project from its inception, the resort's difficulties had more to do with the fact that "the resort never made a meaningful effort to market itself to the locals."[14] Construction delays and cost over-runs were debilitating. On 23 December, the KKTC petitioned the BC Supreme Court for protection from creditors under the *Companies' Creditors Arrangement Act*. KKTC legal counsel John Grieve informed the media that, "at the present time, due to a lack of cash flow and a consequent working capital deficit, the resort is no longer able to meet its obligations as they fall due":

> . . . in order to avoid enforcement proceedings by its secured creditors, claims from unsecured creditors, including construction contractors, and termination of its utilities and other critical supply agreements, the resort requires the protection . . . with an opportunity to further consider and implement the refinancing or restructuring opportunities available.[15]

In all, the resort's net operating losses through 31 October 2003 were $2,201,554. When added to the construction debt carried over from 2002, the sum amounted to more than $4.5 million. Of the total debt, nearly $19 million was secured by the real and personal property of the resort. A $3.6 million loan from the Royal Bank was used to maintain operations.[16] The KKTC was given until 13 February either to file its restructuring plan or apply for further extension to creditor protection.[17]

After several months of negotiations for creditor protection, the KKTC proposed selling the resort. In the meantime, court documents were released in which Pierre admitted that the KKTC had diverted federal money earmarked for health and welfare to sustain the failing resort. In a sworn affidavit, Pierre said, "There is no doubt that [the KKTC] has used some program funding in order to acquire and maintain its interest in the resort," adding that such actions were taken "with the full knowledge and acquiescence of all the bands." Former Shuswap First Nations Chief Paul Sam confirmed that $3.2 million in federal funds and $21.8 million in public money had been diverted to the failing enterprise, but he disputed the notion that "myself or anyone I know of on behalf of this band has consented to Ktunaxa Kinbasket Treaty Council diverting program money provided by the Federal Government." Even more contentious were Sam's suggestions that both Pierre and the KKTC were "making it difficult for anyone to come in and buy [the St. Eugene's Mission Resort] because we want to buy it for $11.1 million." Sam understood this to mean that "Sophie Pierre and [St. Eugene's Mission Chief Executive Officer] Helder Ponte would . . . deny water, sewage and other necessary servicing to the SEM Resort should a buyer other than KKTC take it over." During this period Pierre recanted her sworn testimony, claiming that is was "absolutely untrue" and that "no money . . . has gone in to keep the resort going. It's going on its own."[18] However, Kinbasket Group of Companies CEO Dean Martin described the project as a total failure, and said, "This result will have a dire impact on First

Nations' struggle to establish credibility and business certainty necessary to attract financial institutions and investor involvement in economic development of First Nations lands."[19]

The negative publicity did not deter the Mnjikaning of Ontario or the Samson Cree of Alberta from proposing a joint venture that would take over ownership and operation of the St. Eugene's Mission Resort. The proposal was acceptable to the BC Supreme Court, which ordered the sale of St. Eugene's Mission Resort on 18 October for $11.1 million, with a takeover date of 16 November. As a result, non-secured creditors lost their money while secured creditors such as the Royal Bank, the Columbia Basin Trust, and Lake City Casinos Ltd. received a percentage of their original investment.[20] Samson Cree member and lawyer Denise Lightning indicated that "this is a restructuring," and it "would be premature to say any specific things other than to say that we will be maintaining relationships in the best way we can coming in."[21] The new management team that was brought in to operate the resort was headed by Brian Wills of Lyn Peakes Consulting in Vancouver, but the resort's financial operations remained under the control of the court-appointed restructuring officer, Jeff Keeble, of Deloitte & Touche in Vancouver.[22] Among the strategies employed to attract customers was an aggressive marketing campaign aimed at the west coast and Alberta populations and a $600,000 health club featuring an Olympic-sized swimming pool, a fitness centre, a fully-equipped gym, a steam room, a sauna, and two hot tubs.[23] While it may appear that the resort is back on track, Pierre admitted that the fallout of cost overruns and uncontrollable factors such as the decline in tourism hurt a number of local non-Native businesses. "We have some bridges to mend," she said.[24]

The Blue Heron and the Golden Eagle

Following Premier Bob Rae's 1991 announcement promoting the construction of a casino to generate revenue for provincial First Nations, the Casino Rama proposal generated the most attention. Relegated to the background was the Mississaugas of Scugog Island proposal. Located on tiny Scugog Island, approximately 70 km northeast of Toronto, the Mississaugas were one of 14 Ontario First Nations to make a bid for the casino. Despite the need for alternate funding sources and a desire to generate employment to attract the majority of the 180 nation members back to the island, not everyone in the community was comfortable with the idea of a high-stakes casino. Prior to the final decision, community members decided against the proposal, forcing the band council to consider an alternative strategy in the event that the island was chosen as host community. The Mississaugas proposal was passed over. Soon afterward, the band's public relations manager, Gary Edgar, approached the community with a scaled-down plan for a charity casino, and the community accepted it.

At the northwestern end of the province, near Kenora, officials of the Wauzhushk Onigum (Rat Portage) First Nation were swept up in the casino frenzy as well. Determined to cash in on gaming's potential, band officials decided to approach the province about establishing a $15-million casino development in a local arena. In early 1993, the province authorized the Ministry of Consumer and Commercial Relations (MCCR) to negotiate agreements with First Nations regarding the regulation and licensing of charitable gaming on reserves. The MCCR subsequently negotiated charitable gaming agreements with the Mississaugas of Scugog Island in June, followed by the Wauzhushk Onigum in October. Both agreements provided for the creation of a gaming code defining First Nations' authority with respect to different gaming activities, and for the formation of a gaming commission to control, administer, and regulate gaming activities. Both communities soon had development plans in place.

The Wauzhushk Onigum Nation had been interested in gaming since 1985. According to a statement made by Chief George Kakeway, band members viewed a casino as a means to "increase the flow of visitors and have Lake of the Woods as a destination where we could have visitors, whether from abroad or overseas or from Manitoba."[25] Stressing that the 5,700 cottages in nearby Lake of the Woods boosted the region's summer population from 17,000 to more than 50,000, the potential customer base was promoted as "an economic stimulant in our community" that, if properly tapped, could provide "a better quality of life in terms of housing developments or renovations or improving the road infrastructure and so on."[26] In sum, Kakeway envisioned the casino as a means of enabling his people to pursue self-sufficiency.

The Great Blue Heron Casino at Lake Scugog employs close to 1,000 people. Of this total, "15 belong to Scugog First Nation, and about 100 belong to other First Nations."[27] The Mississaugas originally formed a non-profit, charitable association to oversee this process. As the host community of a 70,000 square foot charitable casino featuring 452 slot machines, 50 table games, and pull tabs, the band receives five per cent of the revenues from the slot machines; of that total, they have agreed to share 30 per cent with Scugog Township.

The Golden Eagle Charity Casino near Kenora, Ontario entered into a similar agreement with the province, permitting the community to operate table games and bingos at their casino, although there are no slot machines. Revenue from this facility must be used for charitable purposes and stay on reserve. Operated by the Washushk Onigum Foundation, the 7,500 square foot Golden Eagle casino includes a 435-seat bingo hall, two roulette tables, four blackjack tables, two "Let it Ride" tables, and Keno.

As part of the provincial/First Nations agreements permitting charitable casinos on the two reserves, the host communities have been granted a source of much-needed revenue for economic development. The casino has also enabled the Mississaugas of Scugog First Nation to operate its own housing program. The other major component of each agreement is that a portion of each complex's gaming revenues be forwarded to the province for redistribution. Through the Ontario Trillium Foundation, which receives annually $100 million from the provincial government generated by charity casinos, the funding is distributed to charities and non-profit organizations according to four categories: arts and culture, environment, sports and recreation, and human and social services.[28]

Historically, legal gambling in Canada developed as a means of generating revenue for charitable causes, but in recent years, gaming as a funding source for charity has come under fire. In 1999, a Canada West Foundation study of 400 non-profit charities across Canada concluded that "gambling revenues are an increasingly important source of funding for the non-profit sector, despite the facts that such revenues are often unstable and present ethical conflicts for a number of organizations." In Ontario, charitable organizations receive 10 per cent of their revenues from gambling. Despite concerns over the ethics of funding charitable works through gambling, the study found that the "commitment to their cause overrides their ethical concerns about gambling."[29] Fuelling the debate is a recent report by University of Lethbridge researchers Robert Williams and Rob Wood, who found that about 35 per cent of Ontario gaming revenue is derived from moderate and severe problem gamblers, with an even higher proportion for gaming machines and horse racing.[30]

Hidden in Plain Sight: The Nova Scotia First Nations Gaming Industry

The Mi'kmaq have signed 11 provincial/First Nations gaming agreements since 1995. In each case, the revenues are designated to reserve economic development. Nova Scotia has 13 Mi'kmaq First Nations, with populations ranging from 215 in the Annapolis Valley First Nation to 3,593 in the Eskasoni First Nation. Registered Indians provincially total 12,797, with 4,093 living off-reserve. Politically, 13 band councils represent the interests of the registered Indian population, along with two tribal councils: the Confederacy of Mainland Mi'kmaq and the Union of Nova Scotia Indians.[31] In recent years, the Mi'kmaq have been embroiled in a number of issues centred on natural resources, most notably the events at Burnt Church in 2001 and, more recently, timber harvesting rights. As a result, the provincial First Nations gaming industry, although modest when compared with that of Casino Rama or the Saskatchewan gaming industry, nevertheless provides the Mi'kmaq with an economic foundation from which to initiate larger initiatives to improve reserve conditions.

The government of Nova Scotia controls casino operations through the Nova Scotia Gaming Corporation (NSGC). The NSGC owns a 25 per cent share of Atlantic Lottery Corporation (ALC), thereby controlling VLT and provincial lottery operations. However, the Office of Aboriginal Affairs is responsible for First Nations gaming and for gaming agreements between the government and provincial bands. According to the Nova Scotia provincial government, "gaming on native reserve lands is not regulated in the same manner as off-reserve gaming" because the Canadian Parliament exercises "exclusive legislative authority over matters respecting First Nation members and lands." Because federal law "gives the provinces authority to license native gaming," the government of Nova Scotia in 1998 "chose to exercise this delegated authority by way of agreements with individual Band Councils." The perceived need to monitor and regulate reserve gaming motivated the province to enter into 11 separate agreements. By the end of March 1998, there were 400 VLTs on reserve lands, generating $11.7 million in total wagers.[32]

This represented a little more than one-eighth of provincial VLTs (3,170). Public concern about the growth of provincial gaming led to a moratorium on 29 June 1998, which effectively froze the number of VLTs province-wide. The resulting *Act* did not apply to VLTs on reserves, which now number 615 on the Yarmouth Reserve, the Gold Reserves, and the Wildcat Reserve. Each band council pays an administrative fee of $56 per week, per machine to be paid to the ALC, although revenues raised through the gaming agreements are retained by the First Nation community.[33] The province/First Nations agreements determine the permissible number of VLTs. As a result of these agreements, which prohibit the licensing of casinos on reserve, the Mi'kmaq band councils receive a share of the Sydney casino's profits, to be used in reserve economic development projects. The agreements can range from two months to five years, although an automatic renewal clause is activated if neither party requests renegotiation.

The agreements also require each band council to institute and maintain its own gaming commission for the purpose of licensing and regulating on-reserve gaming; they call for an annual audit of each gaming commission to be submitted for government review, while also allowing for provincial government inspections. Since the first agreements were signed in 1995, the estimated annual First Nations gaming revenue allotment has grown to $35 million, which is used to enhance existing First Nation source revenues.[34] These totals are supplemented by revenues generated by the Sydney Casino. In 2001-02, this represented an additional $2.5 million distributed to First Nations communities with gaming agreements, a total that grew to $2.7 million the following year.[35]

Even so, First Nations gaming has come under fire by the provincial government, which has informed all bands that it desires renegotiated gaming agreements. "We have been speaking with First Nations about their current gaming arrangements and moving to a more socially responsible model," officials admit.[36] Concerned with "the lack of controls afforded by a decentralized distribution model without uniform standards of social responsibility, customer service and regulatory oversight," an interdepartmental steering committee consisting of senior officials from the departments of Environment and Labour, Finance, Health, the NSGC, the Office of Aboriginal Affairs, the Office of Health Promotion, and the Treasury and Policy Board was struck and worked for several months to develop a comprehensive strategy. According to government officials, First Nations are being treated as another level of government regarding the gaming issue.[37] The forced renegotiation of gaming agreements, however, has made First Nations leaders keenly aware that they are not, in fact, another level of government.

Exacerbating existing tensions is the public desire for greater government regulation of First Nations gaming. A government-sponsored survey of 800 adults, for instance, confirmed that only 12 per cent of respondents believed that First Nations should be responsible for setting their own gaming standards, but 84 per cent indicated that the same rules and regulations that apply to gambling on First Nations Reserves should apply to gambling elsewhere in the province.[38] When asked, "Is there some other way you believe the revenues should be spent?" none of the respondents suggested that gaming profits should go toward supporting Native reserves.[39] The regional print media ran a handful of stories on these issues, while the *Globe and Mail* and the *National Post* have virtually ignored them. It is troubling that the national press has failed to highlight government attempts to rewrite gaming agreements or to expand on the public's opinion that First Nations should not be permitted to run their own gaming enterprises, and that gaming revenues should not be used to assist First Nations.

The Battle Against Labour Unions

Unions are another aspect of the gambling industry that First Nations leaders are being forced to contend with. It is an issue that has the potential to become increasingly divisive, something that SIGA has dealt with first-hand. As several researchers have reported, casinos "present workers with some unique conditions of noise, stress, violence and harassment which owners need to address but seemingly do not without pressure from workers through their unions. Union representation is important, for both non-Aboriginal and Aboriginal workers."[40]

As the Dutch Lerat affair played itself out in the media, SIGA lawyers argued before the Saskatchewan Court of Appeal that their employees should not be permitted to form a union. At the centre of the controversy was Prince Albert's Northern Lights Casino and the Canadian Auto Workers union (CAW), the largest private-sector union in Canada, whose members are by no means confined to actual auto workers, but work in a broad range of industries, including First Nations gaming facilities. Still reeling from the 1999 certification vote that resulted in CAW's legal representation of 300 casino employees, SIGA lawyers argued that the four casinos fell under federal jurisdiction and, as such, were exempt from provincial labour standards.

The Saskatchewan Court of Appeal, however, found to the contrary, ruling that the province has jurisdiction over the unionized employees at SIGA casinos. An independent mediator was appointed to produce a report which would form the basis of a collective bargaining agreement. It was expected that the final pact would raise employees' wages between $3 and $4 per hour, in addition to a one-time, $650 payment in lieu of retroactive pay. As SIGA lawyers were planning to argue against the recommendations at a provincial labour board hearing scheduled for 24 September, a casino dealer, Charmine Evans, lobbied for a new vote, and, just before Christmas 2000, CAW was decertified. SIGA refused to negotiate a collective agreement, the central issues being grievance procedures and the collection of union dues, all prior to issues of salary and working conditions being properly dealt with. According to researchers, the key motivator was SIGA's "opposition to the union movement generally," and had more to do with "First Nations leaders not wishing to have the authority of Chief and Council challenged."[41]

SIGA's victory over CAW was short lived, and by 2002, union organizing activity was once again taking place. This time, Painted Hand Casino employee Cory Delorme was actively seeking the support of the Public Service Alliance of Canada (PSAC) in Yorkton. As with Northern Lights, Bear Claw, and the Gold Eagle, the Painted Hand Casino was not a union shop, something the PSAC sought to remedy. Owing to Delorme's efforts, the PSAC applied for a certification order on 29 November 2002, albeit without majority support. A secret ballot was held on 10 January 2003, and a majority of Painted Hand employees voted against the union. The PSAC's application was dismissed. It was later revealed that, during the union drive of 2002, Delorme had received numerous official warnings and was suspended from work a number of times. Delorme attributed his suspensions to his union participation. He was fired in January 2003.

Following Delorme's dismissal, Saskatchewan Retail, Wholesale and Department Store Union (RWDSU) organizer Gord Schmidt was contacted by Painted Hand employees asking that he commence a second organizing drive. In 2001, Schmidt tried on numerous occasions to rally casino employees to form a union, to the point that he was temporarily banned from the premises. The RWDSU halted its efforts in the face of corporate resistance, but later that February, Schmidt called a meeting with interested casino employees to discuss the possibility of another organizing drive, at which point he was informed that the majority of Painted Hand workers were hesitant to become involved owing to their belief that labour activism had resulted in Delorme's sacking. Several weeks of interviews followed, at which point the RWDSU determined that it would be unable to achieve the majority support required for certification owing to workers' fears of management retribution. This ended the RWDSU recruitment and organizing drive.

Undeterred by recent events, on 1 April 2003, the Canadian Union of Public Employees (CUPE) opened a Yorkton office with the intent of initiating its own organizing drive at the Painted Hand Casino. Linda Pelletier headed the organizing drive, and her talks with employees led her to conclude that most casino workers believed that Delorme's labour activism had led to his dismissal. Pelletier assured them that they could not be fired for supporting CUPE, and the organizing drive continued for four weeks. It came to a halt following the 2 May layoff of Trevor Lyons, who had signed a CUPE support card on 29 April. Interest was rekindled after CUPE officials learned of the previous RWDSU drive, and CUPE decided to offer its support. In a deposition before the Saskatchewan Labour Relations Board, Pelletier stated that the union drive would likely be unsuccessful unless the two men were reinstated. Both reinstatement applications were denied.[42]

Casino Rama officials have faced similar union incursions in Ontario. On 10 May 2004, amid red and blue balloons, cabana-style tents, with the theme music to the film *Rocky* wafting on the breeze, International Brotherhood of Teamsters Union Canada president Robert Bouvier, Teamsters Local 938 president Larry McDonald, and union head, James P. Hoffa, son of the late union leader, were in Orillia to hold a press conference in an effort to unite Casino Rama employees endeavouring to achieve certification with the Ontario Labour Relations Board. Citing management intimidation, patron disrespect, and ongoing health and safety issues, the goal of the large group represented mostly by dealers was to install the Teamsters as their labour advocate. In an open field near the Ramara Centre, Hoffa declared before the crowd of several thousand casino workers, "This is the battle for all people. It's a battle here in Ontario about workers' rights and on-the-job dignity." With more than 1.4 million members in Canada and the United States, including thousands of North American casino workers, the Teamsters were the sixth group to attempt to unionize the casino's 3,800 employees. During the rally, Hoffa dismissed the fears of those in attendance, stating affirmatively, "This corporate giant will be brought to its knees, we're not going to take it any more."[43]

According to McDonald, a request was forwarded to the Teamsters office in the spring of 2003, requesting what he described as "a group of disgruntled workers at the casino to have us look at helping to improve their working conditions." Vowing not to "sit back and watch hard working casino workers abused by this corporate giant," McDonald initiated a 14-month union drive aimed at rallying the support of Casino Rama's 1,038 table game dealers and supervisors.[44] The Teamsters managed to generate the 40 per cent support required by Ontario legislation to allow them to file for certification. The next step was a two-day, government-supervised vote, which was called for 11-12 May 2004. Following the vote, Ontario Labour Relations Board staff notified the Teamsters and casino officials that "just under 62 per cent of about 900 votes cast were against joining one of the largest North American Unions." Casino Rama spokesperson Sherry Lawson maintained that "the size of our victory is significant," and that "we are most pleased that our staff did not let a small minority of people make such an important decision for them." Despite management assurances to improve relations with the floor workers, casino employee and union supporter Kelly Griffin maintained that he would continue to support the Teamsters.[45] As of this writing, the Teamsters were still lobbying casino workers to call another certification vote.[46]

Union mobilization in Canada's First Nations' gaming industry has gone largely unreported by the mainstream media. Also absent are any academic analyses. With SIGA's announcement that it has received approval to open two more casinos — one in Swift Current and one outside Saskatoon — and the anticipated opening of the Enoch Cree Casino west of Edmonton, First Nations casino operators can expect to face mounting labour activism. Although it has yet to occur, negotiated bargaining agreements will likely become the norm as large and well-established unions such as the Teamsters, CAW, and CUPE, to name a few, continue to make inroads into what has become a multi-million dollar industry. Events in Canada parallel recent happenings in the United States, where unions are concentrating their energies on the $18-billion tribal gaming industry following a National Labor Relations Board's (NLRB) 2004 ruling that tribally-owned casinos in California "appeared to be more like a commercial enterprise than a government function." Subsequently, unions were granted access to tribal casino employees.[47] Indian leaders had argued, unsuccessfully, that tribal sovereignty shelters tribes from the *National Labor Relations Act* which gives US workers the right to unionize. The resulting competition among California unions led Unite Here, an American labour organization, to sue the Communications Workers of America, claiming that the latter violated "an AFL-CIO mandate that restricted other unions from pursuing casino workers in the state."[48]

The Great Blue Heron Charity Casino run by the Mississaugas of Scugog Island is the only First Nations casino in Canada where unions have made headway. CAW had been the certified bargaining agent at the casino since January 2003, but all parties had to await a Ontario Labour Board decision on whether the casino was governed by the legal framework of the *Ontario Labour Relations Act*. The ruling came in December 2003, and not long afterward, more than 650 CAW casino workers voted 91 per cent in favour of a strike to support their demands for a collective agreement. The issues included wages and benefits, shift schedules, contracting out, seniority provisions, and contract language. On 17 July 2004, the two sides reached an agreement on a three-year contract that provides the 700 casino workers with wage increases ranging from $2 per hour for those at the maximum wage rate to between 15 and 30 percent for those earning below the maximum rate.[49]

The Potential for Conflict Over Internet Gaming

Recently, First Nations have initiated internet gaming operations, specifically the Kahnawake Mohawks in Quebec and the Six Nations near Brantford, Ontario. According to a report by the US-based financial management company Bear, Stearns, the global gambling industry began with legal internet gambling in Australia. By the end of 1999 there were 40 international online gambling websites, and it is estimated that there are "250 public and private companies that share in the ownership, development, and operations of more than 650 'e-gaming' web properties worldwide." Additionally, while "internet gambling operator revenues are difficult to track, internet gambling wagers are estimated at approximately $1.2 billion in 1999, which is nearly an 80 per cent increase from 1998."[50] As of 2003, the number of internet gambling sites was estimated at 1,800, generating $4.3 billion.[51] In a subsequent report, Bear, Stearns recognized that, in many countries, participating in or establishing online gaming sites is illegal, but concluded that "legislators in the US realize how difficult it would be to ban online gaming from every computer in the US. They feel that the government would be more successful at shaping a regulatory landscape."[52]

The *Criminal Code of Canada* gives provinces the authority to conduct a lottery scheme on or through an electronic device. Currently, no province is engaged in an online lottery scheme using the internet.[53] One report is quick to note, however, that "Many on-line gaming companies have situated themselves in Vancouver, Canada, which is now known within the trade as the internet gaming capital of the world. Companies strategically house servers or make Vancouver the company headquarters largely in order to dodge US authorities." The report adds that, "Because Canadian law regarding on-line gambling is as unclear as US law, groups are beginning to test authorities by setting up on both sides of the US-Canada border."[54] Of late, additional pressure has been exerted upon the Canadian government to clarify and/or expand on the current *Criminal Code* gaming provisions, for "no aspect of an online operation need be located in Canada for Canadians to access the gaming action over the internet, other than the public communications systems and the user's PC." The question, in this instance, "is whether there is sufficient connection between the gaming operation and the Canadian jurisdiction," for without this connection, "it would be difficult to apply the *Code* and enforce a ban on an online gaming operation." Finally, even if there was a clear connection, "the manner in which the *Code* will apply to online gaming is far from clear."[55]

A recent decision, *R. v. Starnet Communications International Inc.*,[56] determined that it is illegal for a Canadian-based internet gambling site to accept bets from Canadian citizens. Starnet Communications International Inc. (SCI) was incorporated in Delaware and operated from a location in Vancouver, British

Columbia. SCI is a publicly traded company that creates software for internet gambling sites. BC police became suspicious that SCI was accepting online wagers from Canadians and set up a sting operation, in the process gambling nearly $5,000 on the company's site. The company's subsidiaries were incorporated in Antigua, where online gaming is legal and where SCI had an online gaming license. However, one of their subsidiaries, located in Vancouver, was the locale responsible for website administration. Employing approximately 100 people, the Vancouver subsidiary developed the server and client software packages, which permitted customer access to gaming. Charges were laid in 1999, and a deal was struck: SCI pleaded guilty to one criminal gambling count under s. 202(1)(b), was fined $100,000 and forfeited approximately US $4 million as proceeds of crime pursuant to s. 462.37 of the *Criminal Code of Canada*. The key point in this decision is that any individual or company interested in offering online gaming in Canada must minimize or eliminate all connections to Canada. If this is not possible, banning Canadian access to the site is the prudent next move.

The emergence of online gaming means the introduction of new business opportunities that will be difficult to ignore. The Canadian government would be wise to heed Bear, Stearns conclusions regarding the difficulty in banning online gaming, and perhaps begin shaping a regulatory landscape. First Nations leaders are putting additional pressure on the federal government to clarify existing legislation as they continue to pursue internet gaming. In June 1996, for instance, the Kahnawake First Nation near Montreal established the Kahnawake Gaming Commission (KGC) pursuant to the provisions of their Kahnawake Gaming Law. The legislation dictates that Kahnawake is a sovereign nation and, as such, has jurisdiction over issuing gaming licenses for lottery schemes. The KGC's mandate is to regulate and control gaming and gaming-related activities that take place within or from Mohawk territory. By January 1999, Mohawk Internet Technologies (MIT), guided by a four-member board of directors, had been established as an e-gaming web site. It does not operate an interactive gaming site; rather, MIT is the internet service provider, hosting online gambling sites on servers located on reserve land.

The Kahnawake band council was pragmatic and recognized that the law respecting internet gaming was, at best, ambiguous. They sought to legitimize their operations in anticipation of a legal battle. In July 1999, the band council and the KGC worked toward establishing a legitimate regulatory environment, approaching the former director of the New Jersey Division of Gaming, Frank Catania, for help. With the assistance of Murray Marshall, the KGC's legal counsel, the two men developed a regulatory framework designed to ensure that all interactive gambling and gaming activities conducted within or from the Mohawk territory satisfied three basic principles:

1. The Commission must ensure that only suitable persons and entities are permitted to operate within Kahnawake;
2. All games offered must be fair to the player; and,
3. All winners are paid.

To meet the first criterion, the KGC's application process is complex, involving a rigorous investigation to eliminate high-risk candidates.[57] The KGC charges a $10,000 annual licensing fee while employing PriceWaterhouseCoopers to audit their operations to ensure fairness.

The Kahnawake band council currently plays host to about 30 cybercasinos.[58] The council maintains that, as a sovereign nation within Canada, it has the right to offer internet gaming. At the same time, they are pressuring the federal government to pass legislation designating Kahnawake an internet gaming destination. Since internet gaming is in violation of Quebec's provincial gaming provisions, the Kahnawake operations are under constant scrutiny. On more than one occasion, investigations have been initiated by both the provincial and federal governments as well as the provincial police. Quebec's Minister of Public Security, Serge Menard, has gone on record as opposing the Kahnawake online casinos in Quebec on the grounds that they are illegal. However, the province has to date taken no legal action to halt these activities, one reason being the still palpable tensions resulting from the Oka crisis in 1990.[59] While it is likely that internet gambling will eventually be made legal, operators in the meantime will need to contend with strong opposition, ranging from anti-gambling lobbyists to public and private interests threatened by its economic potential.[60]

Conclusion

Often lost in the mix due to their nature, but equally informative in terms of generating a better understanding of why First Nations leaders gravitate so willingly toward high-stakes gaming, are small projects demonstrating gaming to be a larger issue extending beyond simply establishing casinos. The case of the Ktunaxa/Kinbasket, the one casino project in Canada that lost significant money immediately, is an excellent example not of mismanagement but of the tenuous nature of the tourism industry and how global events such as SARS can ultimately spell disaster. The most important theme is gaming's adaptability as the contexts demand, specifically in terms of the gambling market and the regulatory environment. In Nova Scotia, for example, First Nations didn't simply settle on VLT casinos; they knew the market could not support a second large provincial casino, but additional studies showed that VLT casinos would be profitable. Despite its tough start, the St. Eugene's Resort fit within the provincial regulatory environment that sought casino proposals in early 1997. The Kahnawake Mohawk venture into internet gaming was necessitated by a restrictive regulatory environment in Quebec that would not permit their participation. In the tradition of maintaining territorial sovereignty at all costs, the Kahnawake gaming venture also challenges federal delegation of gaming authority to the provinces, while encouraging the alteration of provincial legislation to authorize what current statutes suggest is permissible.

On other fronts, labour unions have begun to infiltrate reserve casinos, and in both Ontario and Saskatchewan for-profit casinos have, to date, resisted their incursions. Curiously, as workers at the Blue Heron charity casino lobbied for union representation, casino operators did little to resist certification. The Blue Heron and Golden Eagle First Nation charity casinos have been quite successful, but largely ignored by the mainstream media. They are, nevertheless, casinos in the traditional sense: they house card games, game tables, and fall within Ontario's regulatory environment. A portion of the revenues generated filter back to the host communities to be used for social programming. The discussed examples illustrate the various dimensions of gaming models, and the relative effectiveness of dissimilar models at generating revenue to combat economic difficulties. They also reveal that First Nations casinos are not impervious to labour unions, collective bargaining agreements, or the decisions of tribunals established to investigate employer wrong-doing. Much is to be learned from further study of these unique models and the introduction of industry-specific issues such as labour unions.

Room for Optimism

In 1996, policy analyst Warren Skea introduced the concluding chapter of his doctoral dissertation by asserting, "At the beginning of this research it was stated that there has been relatively little work in the area of gambling policy in Canada and almost no analysis of the issue of Native casino gambling."[1] It is disturbing that, 10 years later, those very words could have been used to introduce the final chapter of this study. In that time, two charity and eight for-profit First Nations casinos have become operational in Canada, the Mi'kmaq in Nova Scotia gained considerable control over provincial VLT operations, and the Kahnawake Mohawks launched an internet gaming site. As a result of these events, hundreds of millions of dollars in gaming revenue has been realized by First Nations in Canada. More importantly, dozens of First Nation communities in Canada are now using gaming revenues to bolster faltering economies and fund social programming, while channeling a percentage of those funds into additional economic development initiatives. Academics have paid limited and inadequate attention to First Nations gaming, be it the community based decision-making processes leading to casino proposals or the development of provincial gaming policies. Even popular areas of study — such as problem gaming, the potential infiltration of organized crime, or the projected casino-driven increase in crime levels in both reserve and neighbouring non-Native communities — have gone largely ignored.

In many ways this is surprising, considering the level of attention that has historically been paid to First Nations gaming. The first missionaries and settlers to North America wrote about "Indian" games, although these games were quickly delineated into anthropological taxonomies that would influence later writers. Eventually, the missionary and Puritan influence can be discerned in writings aiming at the lack of First Nations morality resulting from participating in games, a theme that was evident in both the proposed Saskatoon casino and the Headingley urban reserve debates. By the late 1800s, salvage anthropologists were in the field cataloguing the Indians' last days and writing extensively about gaming

167

and wagering practices. Yet even in this era, writers experienced difficulty discerning gaming's significance in First Nations society. Was it for political, divinatory, economic, or spiritual purposes? Was it simply a form of entertainment? Or did gaming fit into all these categories? Contemporary First Nations leaders' reasons for embracing gaming have become more straightforward: casinos are being employed to improve reserve economies. It is the subsequent investigation into gaming's vagaries that obscures our understanding of gaming's role in contemporary First Nations society, which, in turn, forces us to broaden our range of inquiry to include the self-government debate, claims of sovereignty, reserve economic development, federal Indian policy, judicial decisions, social determinants of health, political interaction with Canadian society, federal delegation of gaming authority to the provinces, and the impact of federal gaming laws on First Nations interests, to name a few.

Had First Nations leaders interested in pursuing reserve casinos approached their investigation the same way Canadian academics have pursued the study of First Nations gaming, the industry would never have emerged. Citing the *Indian Act* as the foremost impediment to economic development and the need to begin considering alternative strategies, most First Nations leaders looked to the US tribal gaming industry. The Seminole high-stakes bingo operation and the Pequot's Foxwoods Casino were influential. First Nations leaders in both Saskatchewan and Ontario commissioned reports to determine gaming's potential; they had educated themselves about gaming long before approaching the government to establish economic and political partnerships.

With the exception of Ontario Premier Bob Rae, Canadian provincial officials expressed little enthusiasm for reserve casinos. Even had they been interested, they were reluctant to relinquish provincial gaming jurisdiction to First Nations. While this may seem curious, even callous, considering the staggering levels of reserve underdevelopment and First Nations unemployment, "Indians and lands reserved for Indians" were a federal responsibility. To provincial premiers, First Nations represented little more than one of the nation's many cultural groups seeking economic development opportunities. First Nations leaders cited the *Constitution Act, 1982*, protecting their unique status, and pointed to the 1996 final report of the Royal Commission on Aboriginal Peoples (RCAP), in which they were described as "Partners in Confederation." They also argued that "Indian reserves" were federal enclaves made up of Crown land, and thus shielded from provincial legislation. In challenging existing policies and legislation, First Nations leaders were soon confronted with federal Indian policy that was based on both political and judicial decisions. The Shawanaga and Eagle Lake First Nations became embroiled in lawsuits after establishing a reserve bingo, followed by community leaders being charged with violating the *Criminal Code*. Their contention that control over reserve gaming was an Aboriginal right protected by section 35 of the *Constitution Act, 1982*, was denied by the Supreme Court of Canada, forcing First Nations to acquiesce to provincial jurisdiction over gaming.

Prior to opening a casino, First Nations must now acquire a provincial gaming license. A provincial-First Nations gaming agreement must be negotiated as well. By the mid-1990s, accessing the required licenses was easier, owing in part to changing attitudes: many provincial politicians by now considered gaming the best means available to stimulate First Nations economic development. In Ontario, Premier Rae envisioned the profits of one central First Nations casino igniting provincial First Nations economic development. Saskatchewan Premier Roy Romanow engaged in a dialogue with provincial, municipal, and First Nations leaders which eventually led to the establishment of four provincial casinos operated by the Federation of Saskatchewan Indian Nations (FSIN) and the Saskatchewan Indian Gaming Authority (SIGA). Nova Scotia entered into agreements with 11 provincial First Nations to share VLT revenues, and 50 per cent of the profit from Casino Sydney is returned to the 11 communities. In Alberta, an eight-stage process was established to evaluate First Nations proposals to establish reserve casinos.

If this type of interaction sometimes led to moments of acrimony, it also exposed the difficulties of establishing fruitful political and economic relationships with mainstream Canadian society. Following the NDP's ouster by the Progressive Conservatives in Ontario in 1995, for example, Premier Mike Harris rescinded the Ontario-First Nations gaming agreement and imposed a 20 per cent Win Tax on Casino Rama revenues. This shut down casino construction and pitted the First Nations against the new provincial government. Even more shocking were events in Manitoba, where, of the five First Nations casino proposals selected in November 2000, only two are operational. The remaining three proposals — from Sioux Valley, Swan Lake, and Nisichawayasihk — failed to achieve provincial acceptance. In the case of the latter two, public pressure fuelled by racism proved too great for provincial politicians to ignore, and they permitted the proposals to lapse with minor resistance. In his 1992 RCAP presentation, Roseau River member Carl Roberts highlighted the fact that, when First Nations gaming is mentioned, "it all of a sudden becomes a moral issue. When it is done by governments, it is an economic venture to provide employment."[2] It is hypocritical to acquiesce to one segment of society that is demonstrably anti-gaming when it happens to be a First Nations casino proposal, while simultaneously accepting government-sanctioned gaming. In either case, opponents cite the potential for increased problem gambling. But there is little evidence to support this. There is a tremendous gap in the literature pertaining to the effects gaming could potentially have on a First Nations community, making it impossible to determine the validity of any argument.

In Canada, there have been no government-sponsored federal studies investigating the potential social impacts of gaming among First Nations people. With the exception of the Alberta Alcohol and Drug Abuse Commission on First Nations Adolescent Gambling, which demonstrated that 49 per cent of its sample were either problem gamblers or were at risk of becoming problem gamblers, little work has been done that would allow academics and policy makers to make persuasive arguments regarding the benefits and social costs of gaming in First Nation communities. The study did reveal that parents' gambling behaviour influenced their children's, but concluded that "gambling is not the result of lack of opportunity or lack of interest in other activities; thus providing more activities will not likely solve the problem." It also charged that, "given the current high levels of participation, these activities may provide the medium through which problem prevention could occur."[3]

What is often ignored in the gaming debate is the First Nation perspective of what a casino could mean to a community. At Mnjikaning, gaming revenues have been used to improve community water and sewage systems, roads, communications infrastructure, schools, and libraries. Day care, senior centres, medical services, and recreation centres are also increasingly becoming the norm in communities that have access to gaming revenues. Lower unemployment levels and improved health and education have resulted.[4] Gaming as economic empowerment is one important theme; so, too, is gaming as political and social empowerment. Even the seemingly innocuous debates over the First Nation right to establish community by-laws permitting smoking in casinos have become acts of agency and sites of empowerment and contestation, underscoring a larger trend whereby to improve reserve economies by constructing casinos one must adhere to provincial regulatory frameworks while taking into consideration its impact on outside interests. The goal to economic self-sufficiency rests in taking a holistic approach to economic development that entails investigating the most basic variables. The need for First Nations leaders to balance the myriad of conflicting pressures is paramount to their gaming success.

Interestingly, even during the most contentious negotiations, First Nations leaders have never attempted to isolate their casinos from mainstream Canadian society. In much the same way that Aboriginal self-government is promoted, First Nation leaders promote cultural interface, hopeful that the residual benefits of a casino will accrue not only to them but to neighbouring communities. Statistics demonstrate that reserve casinos need non-Native patrons, for a casino cannot be considered successful until more than 80 per cent of its customers come from outside the host community. The Aseneskak Casino in Manitoba discovered this the hard way, losing close to $1 million in its first year of operations, largely owing to limited tourist traffic. The goal is to introduce money into the community through the casino. In addition to gambling revenues, jobs will be created, resulting in greater economic stability. This, in turn, leads to diminished reliance on social programs as the community begins to take greater control over day-to-day activities. As the economy begins to grow and new business are initiated, economic stability attracts people back into the community since money is being channeled into improving infrastructure.

While Canada lacks comparable statistics, US data suggest that a successful reserve casino will be of benefit to neighbouring communities, be they First Nation or non-First Nation. Once a casino has been established, new and unique pressures come to bear. A lack of managers trained in casino operations raises accountability challenges. SIGA found out during the Dutch Lerat affair just how debilitating a perceived breach in accountability can be to economic success. Fortunately for SIGA, people continued to gamble and its four casinos remain profitable. The affair did, however, have the potential to irreparably undermine customer trust and business patronage. The Casino of the Rockies' troubles hinged on the tenuous nature of the tourism industry, which, in this case, was affected by a number of regional forest fires, the SARS crisis, and threats of mad cow disease. Casino Rama was affected by similar events, including border closures following 9/11. But unlike the Casino of the Rockies, which was dependent on tourism, Casino Rama did not rely on US tourism dollars to remain profitable.

The introduction of labour unions can be destabilizing, especially to those First Nations still promoting reserve lands as sovereign territories impervious to provincial legislation. SIGA officials understood that with casinos came unions, hence its lobby to see casinos constructed on reserve lands, where it was anticipated that provincially regulated unions would be proscribed owing to its federal reserve status. This did not stop the Canadian Auto Workers (CAW) from becoming certified in November 1999 to represent Northern Lights Casino workers in Prince Albert in negotiations with their employer. The two parties were unable to reach an agreement on a contract, the main obstacles being grievance procedures, seniority, and the collection of union dues. A legal challenge followed which resulted in the Saskatchewan Court of Appeal ruling that the province has jurisdiction over unionized employees working at SIGA casinos.[5] SIGA applied to have the union decertified, but failed. In June 2002, SIGA was ordered to respect a collective agreement awarded to the casino workers in January by the Saskatchewan Labour Relations Board, a decision it has since challenged by taking its case to the Supreme Court of Canada.

Despite the inherent difficulties in entering the gaming field, First Nations leaders still consider gaming a flexible tool of economic development, and one that can be patterned according to the local market and regulatory environment. Even with the ever-present risk of financial ruin, First Nations inevitably look to gaming first, if to only discount it following further investigation. Once again, Carl Roberts cautioned First Nation leaders and provincial and federal legislators of the need to look beyond gaming as an economic foundation, but rather to embrace it as a solid beginning of what can become a diverse and dynamic economy:

> I think people have to understand that gaming is only a kick-start to a lot of the economic viability that can be established in this community. I think it would be foolhardy on anyone to establish an economic base on one industry. There has to be diversification and so on. Gaming may last 10 or 15 years. Beyond that, there has to be other forms of economic rejuvenation or development within our communities.[6]

There are a number of different gaming models currently being used across Canada. In Saskatchewan, four full-time reserve casinos account for 70 per cent of the jobs held by Native people in a workforce now numbering more than 1,100. The Ontario model embraces one centrally located casino, Casino Rama, from which gaming revenues are distributed to 132 provincial First Nations. Manitoba and Alberta have both adopted a revenue-sharing model, whereby all provincial First Nations receive a portion of casino revenues. While this model will likely be successful in Alberta, where it is expected that seven First Nations casinos will be operational by the end of 2007, it has failed in Manitoba where two small casinos must relinquish a percentage of revenues for re-distribution to the remaining 61 First Nations. In Nova Scotia, New Brunswick, Manitoba, and Quebec, agreements are in place permitting First Nations to operate VLTs on reserve, to hold high-stakes bingos, and to sell lottery tickets, whereas similar agreements do not exist in Newfoundland/Labrador or Prince Edward Island. In British Columbia, the Casino of the Rockies was the brainchild of five First Nations, all of whom continue to benefit, albeit minimally, from gaming revenues.

There is no doubt that gaming is a risky venture. According to sociologist J. Rick Ponting, "casino gambling is an undertaking with very high stakes. The very fact that the stakes are so high — that individuals and the community as a whole stand to lose so much and hope to gain so much — could make it extremely difficult to resolve conflict around this issue."[7] Joseph Kalt, co-director of the Harvard Project on American Indian Economic Development, has expressed similar concerns. In his statement to the National Gambling Impact Study Commission in 1998, Kalt articulated his amazement at how the success of a handful of tribes had coloured the public's perception regarding Indian gaming, noting that, in 1996, "more than half of all Indian gaming revenues were generated by only eight tribes' operations."[8] Owing to the extensive history of economic depression and lack of ideas to establish strong economies, First Nation leaders often consider gaming worth the risk. There is room for optimism. According to US legal scholar Nelson Rose, the "Indian Gaming Regulatory Act was one of the greatest things that has ever happened to Native Americans . . . we have seen an economic revitalization on reservations unequalled at any time in American history."[9]

In her presentation to the RCAP in 1992, Tobacco Plains First Nations member Denise Birdstone anticipated the day when First Nations gaming can reproduce the positive effects she sees occurring in the United States:

> Even though there is some ethnical [sic] and moral questions behind gaming, I think that ultimately it is the answer for many First Nations' communities. We have seen examples in the United States where First Nations' communities were able to build schools, cultural facilities and recreational facilities solely on the revenues from gaming. It has become the employment basis, the economic base for communities that were destitute. I think the jurisdiction question has to be settled, so that's another avenue of economic potential.[10]

According to former Assembly of First Nations (AFN) Grand Chief Matthew Coon Come, First Nations leaders have a moral responsibility to rise to the challenge of becoming economically self-sufficient prior to becoming self-governing, adding that "First Nations are responsible to our constituents."[11] The implication is that First Nations principles and standards outweigh those of Canada's political elite, and that, should gaming be recognized at the community level as a legitimate economic initiative, it is the leadership's responsibility to facilitate it. According to this logic, community leaders are negligent if they acquiesce to the argument that gaming is a problematic venture bordering on the morally reprehensible. To simply desire legitimacy, however, is not sufficient, for a government must actively strive for legitimacy, and this is done by stimulating economic growth through the initiation of profitable initiatives.

Of final note, the one major theme emerging in this study was that the literature related to First Nations gaming is fundamentally silent on salient questions now challenging First Nations leaders and provincial and federal officials. For instance, what economic impact do reserve casinos have on their host communities? How have gaming revenues assisted non-host communities in revenue sharing agreements? Are there marked increases in gaming-related pathologies following the introduction of casinos to reserves? If so, how are these issues being dealt with? In what ways do First Nations casinos economically affect neighbouring non-Native communities? How has this new wealth influenced the ever-changing Aboriginal self-government debate? What gaming models are most profitable, and why? And how do we begin to measure these effects? How has the introduction of gaming affected communities that house a significant number of gaming opponents? Has political stability been affected? Has culture been compromised? These are a few of the questions that require study prior to anyone being able to assert that First Nations gaming is a negative or positive influence. This book has offered a foundation on which to examine these issues.

NOTES

Introduction — pp. 12-23

1   "Gambling oasis planned for Osoyoos," *Penticton Herald*, 13 Oct. 1993, p. 1.

2   "Nanaimo band plans big casino on reserve," *Victoria Times Colonist*, 18 Sept. 1992, p. A-1-A-2.

3   "Mohawks might set up trust fund for casino deal," *Montreal Gazette*, 5 Oct. 1993, p. A-1.

4   Canada, *For Seven Generations: An Information Legacy of the Royal Commission on Aboriginal Peoples, Vol. II* (Ottawa: Canada Publications Group, 1996), p. 775.

5   *Ibid.*, p. 775.

6   Julie Cruikshank, "Oral Traditions & Oral History: Reviewing Some Issues," *The Canadian Historical Review* 75, no. 3 (1994).

7   For a general discussion, see Arthur J. Ray, *Indians in the Fur Trade* (Toronto: University of Toronto Press, 1998); Arthur J. Ray & Donald Freeman, *'Give Us Good Measure': An Economic Analysis of Relations Between the Indians of Hudson's Bay Company Before 1763* (Toronto: University of Toronto Press, 1978); Shepherd Krech, ed., *The Subarctic Fur Trade: Native Social & Economic Adaptations* (Vancouver: UBC Press, 1984); & Frank Tough, *'As Their Natural Resources Fail': Native Peoples & the Economic History of Northern Manitoba, 1870-1930* (Vancouver: UBC Press, 1996).

8   W. Dale Mason, *Indian Gaming: Tribal Sovereignty & American Politics* (Norman: University of Oklahoma Press, 2000), p. 9.

9   John Hylton, ed., *Aboriginal Self-Government in Canada: Current Trends & Issues* (Saskatoon: Purich Publishing, 1994), p. 10.

10   Alan Maslove with Carolyn Dittburner, "The Financing of Aboriginal Self-Government" in *Aboriginal Self-Government in Canada: Current Trends & Issues*, ed. John Hylton (Saskatoon: Purich Publishing, 1994), pp. 145-62.

11   Stephen Cornell & Joseph Kalt, "Sovereignty & Nation Building: The Development Challenge in Indian Country Today," *American Indian Culture & Research Journal* 22, no. 4 (Nov. 1998).

12   See Canada, *Aboriginal Self-Government: The Government of Canada's Approach to Implementation of the Inherent Right & the Negotiation of Aboriginal Self-Government* (Ottawa: Minister of Public Works & Government Services, Canada, 1995); see also Indian & Northern Affairs, *Towards Sustainable, Successful First Nation Communities: Good Governance, the Governance Continuum & Governance Programming*, Discussion Paper (Ottawa: Self-Government Branch, Indian & Northern Affairs, 2000).

13   Menno Boldt, *Surviving as Indians: The Challenge of Self-Government* (Toronto: University of Toronto Press, 1993), p. 223.

14   L. Kiedrowski, *Native Gaming & Gambling in Canada: A report prepared for the Department of Indian & Northern Affairs* (Ottawa: Minister of Public Works & Government Services, Canada, 2001).

15   *Ibid.*

16 Marilee Janter-White, "Beyond Modernism: Anishinaabe Abstraction, Activism & Traditionalism" (Ph.D. diss., University of California, 1998), p. 6; see also Eric Hobsbawm & Terrence Ranger, eds., *The Invention of Tradition* (Cambridge: Cambridge University Press, 1983).

17 Carl A. Boger, *The Effects of Native American Gaming on Businesses within the Wisconsin Dells Area* (Wisconsin: University of Wisconsin-Stout, 1995).

18 Center for Applied Research, *The Benefits & Costs of Indian Gaming in New Mexico* (New Mexico: Center for Applied Research, 1996).

19 *Ibid.*

20 *Indian Reservations & the New Mexico Economy: Reservation-based Gaming Enterprises* (New Mexico: New Mexico Indian Reservation Economic Study Group, 1999).

21 M. K. Evans & Evans, Carroll & Associates, *The Economic Impact of the Indian Gaming Industry in Wisconsin & Potential Impact of Modified Compact Term* (Wisconsin: 2002).

22 T. M. Gabe, *The Economic Effects of Gaming on Rural Minnesota* (Minnesota: University of Minnesota, 1994).

23 Stephen A. Hoenack, G. Rens & Stephen A. Hoenack & Associates, *Effects of the Indian-owned Casinos on Self-Generating Economic Development in non-urban areas of Minnesota* (Minnesota: Stephen A. Hoenack & Associates, 1995).

24 Minnesota Indian Gaming Association, *The Economic Impact of Indian Gaming in Minnesota: A Review & Summary of the Economic Benefits of Tribal Gaming for Rural Counties & the State* (Minnesota: Minnesota Indian Gaming Association, 1998).

25 Thomas A. Garrett, *Casino Gambling in America & its Economic Impacts* (Federal Reserve Bank of St. Louis, 2003).

26 R. P. Liner, *The Impact of Three Land Based Casinos in Louisiana* (Louisiana: Universe Inc., 2004).

27 William Evans & Julie Topoleski, *The Social & Economic Impact of Native American Casinos* (Washington: Working Paper No. 9198, National Bureau of Economic Research, Sept. 2002).

28 Jonathan B. Taylor, Matthew B. Krepps & Patrick Wang, *The National Evidence on the Socioeconomic Impacts of American Indian Gaming on non-Indian Communities* (Massachusetts: Harvard Project on American Indian Economic Development, 2000).

29 Jonathon B. Taylor & Joseph P. Kalt, *American Indians on Reservations: A Databook of Socioeconomic Change Between the 1990 & 2000 Censuses* (Massachusetts: The Harvard Project on American Indian Economic Development, 2005), p. xi.

30 *Ibid.*, p. xii.

31 Dean A. Bangsund & F. Larry Leistritz, *Casinos in the upper Midwest: A Discussion of the Impacts* (North Dakota: Department of Agricultural Economics, North Dakota State University, 1997).

32 Patrick Basham & Karen White, *Gambling with our Future? The Costs & Benefits of Legalized Gambling* (British Columbia: The Fraser Institute, 2001).

33 *Update on Impacts of Tribal Economic Development Projects in San Diego County* (California: County of San Diego Board of Supervisors, 2002).

34 M. K. Duffie, "Goals for fourth world peoples & sovereignty initiatives in the United States & New Zealand," *American Indian Culture & Research Journal*, 22, no. 1 (1998), pp. 183-212.

35 For an excellent overview of this issue, see Bruce E. Johansen, *Life & Death in Mohawk Country* (Golden, CO: North American Press, 1993).

36 Sioux Harvey, "Two Models of Sovereignty: A Comparative History of the Mashantucket Pequot Tribal Nation & the Navajo Nation," *American Indian Culture & Research Journal*, 20, no. 1 (1996), pp. 147-194.

37 D. A. Korn, "Gambling expansion in Canada: Implications for health & social policy," *Canadian Medical Association Journal*, 163, no. 1 (2000), pp. 61-64.

38 Virgina McGowan, Judith Dressler, Gary Nixon & Misty Grimshaw, *Recent research in the socio-cultural domain of gaming & gambling: An annotated bibliography & critical overview* (Edmonton: Alberta Gaming Research Institute, 2000), p. 14.

39 Robin Kelley, *First Nations Gambling Policy in Canada* (Calgary: Canada West Foundation, 2001), p. 6.

40 M. Griffiths, "Pathological gambling: A review of the literature," *Journal of Psychiatric & Mental Health Nursing*, no. 3 (1996), pp. 347-353.

41 E. M. Christiansen, "Gambling & the American economy," *The Annals of the American Academy of Political & Social Science*, 556 (1998), pp. 36-52.

42 J. Ferris & T. Stirpe, *Gambling in Ontario: A Report from a General Population Survey on Gambling-Related Problems & Opinions* (Ontario: Addiction Research Foundation, 1995).

43 Jamie Wiebe, *Manitoba Youth Gambling Prevalence Study* (Manitoba: Addictions Foundation of Manitoba, 1999).

44 Lennart E. Henriksson, *Government, Gambling & Healthy Populations* (Canadian Centre on Substance Abuse, 1999). www.ccsa.ca/plweb-cgi/fastweb.exe?getdoc+view1+General+232+21++First Nations%20gambling.

45 David Hewitt, *Spirit of Bingoland: A Study of Problem Gambling among Alberta Native People* (Edmonton: Nechi Training, Research & Health Promotions Institute/AADAC, 1994).

46 *Ibid.*

47 David Hewitt & Dale Auger, *Firewatch on First Nations Adolescent Gambling* (Edmonton: Nechi Training, Research & Health Promotions Institute, 1995).

48 R. C. Bland, S. C. Newman, H. Orn & G. Stebelsky, "Epidemiology of pathological gambling in Edmonton," *Canadian Journal of Psychiatry*, 38, no. 2 (1993), pp.108-112.

49 Garry Smith & Harold Wynne, *Gambling in Canada: Triumph, Tragedy, or Tradeoff? Gambling & Crime in Western Canada: Exploring Myth & Reality* (Calgary: Canada West Foundation, 1999).

Chapter 1 — pp. 24-40

1 Margo Little, "The Moral Dilemma of High Stakes Gambling in Native Communities," (M.A. thesis, Laurentian University, 1997), p. 1.

2 Karen Campbell, "Community Life and Governance: Early Experiences of Mnjikaning First Nation with Casino Rama" (M.A. thesis, University of Manitoba, 1999), p. 14.

3   John B. Ashton, *The History of Gambling in England* (Montclair, NJ: Patterson Smith, 1969 [1896]), p. 2.

4   Kathryn Gabriel, *Gambler Way: Indian Gaming in Mythology, History, and Archaeology in North America* (Colorado: Johnson Books, 1996), p. 4.

5   Ashton, *The History of Gambling in England*, p. 3.

6   Gabriel, *Gambler Way*, p. 4.

7   Alex Blaszczynski, "A History of Gambling." Paper Presented at the National Conference on Gambling, St. Edmunds's Private Hospital and the IPS Employee Assistance, Darling Harbour, Sydney, Australia, 31 Oct. 1996.

8   Virgina McGowan, Judith Droessler, Gary Nixon & Misty Grimshaw, *Recent research in the socio-cultural domain of gaming and gambling: An annotated bibliography and critical overview* (Edmonton: Alberta Gaming Research Institute, 2000).

9   *Stewart Culin, Ethnographer*. www.ahs.uwaterloo.ca/museum/archive/culin.

10 W. H. Holmes, *Twenty-fourth Annual Report at the Bureau of American Ethnology* (Washington, DC: United States Government Printing Office, 1907), pp. 39-40.

11 Stewart Culin, *Games of the North American Indian* (Lincoln: University of Nebraska Press, 1992), p. 35.

12 Alex Whitney, *Sports and Games the Indians Gave Us* (New York: McKay, 1977), p. 51.

13 Francis Jennings, *The Invasion of America: Indians, Colonialism, and the Kant of Conquest* (New York: W.W. Norton and Company, 1976), p. 57.

14 Culin, *Games of the North American Indian.*

15 Ruben Gold Thwaites, *The Jesuit Relations and Allied Documents: Travels and Explorations of the Jesuit Missionaries in New France*, Vol. 31 (Cleveland: The Burrow Bros. Co., 1896-1901), p. 190; *Ibid.*, Vol. 32, p. 252.

16 Quoted in George Eisen, "Voyagers, Black Robes, Saints, and Indians," *Ethnohistory* 24, no. 3 (Summer 1977), pp. 191-205; original found in Zenobins Membre, "Narrative of 1680-1681," in the *Historical Collections of Louisiana*, Vol. 4, eds. Perry Miller & Thomas H. Johnson (1852), p. 151.

17 Gabriel Sagard, *The Long Journey to the Country of the Hurons*. Translated by H. H. Laughton (Toronto: The Champlain Society, 1939), p. 96.

18 Reverend J. W. Wilson, "Report on the Blackfoot Tribes," in *Report of the Fifty-seventh Meeting of the British Association for the Advancement of Science* (London: 1888), p. 192.

19 Thwaites, *The Jesuit Relations and Allied Documents*, Vol. 8, p. 143; and Vol. 10, p. 15.

20 *Ibid.*, Vol. 18, p. 151.

21 *Ibid.*

22 Yale D. Belanger, "Lacrosse Sticks," in *Native Americans and Sport*, Vol. 1., ed. C. Richard King (New York: M. E. Sharpe Inc., 2004), pp. 179-181; see also Thomas Vennum, *American Indian Lacrosse: Little Brother of War* (Washington, DC: Smithsonian Press, 1994); Janine Jones and Pam Dewey, "Little Brother of War," *Smithsonian Magazine* (Dec. 1997).

23 See Nicolas Perrot, *Histoire de l'Amerique Septentrionale par M. de Bacqueville de la Potherie, Vol. II* (Paris: 1722), p. 124.

24 Kenneth Cohen, "A Mutually Comprehensible World? Native Americans, Europeans and Play in Eighteenth-Century America," *American Indian Quarterly* 26, no. 2 (Winter 2001), pp. 67-93.

25 Thwaites, *The Jesuit Relations and Allied Documents*, Vol. 16, p. 196.

26 Virginia McGowan, Lois Frank, Gary Nixon & Misty Grimshaw, "Sacred and Secular Play in Gambling Among Blackfoot Peoples of Southwest Alberta," in *Culture and the Gambling Phenomenon*, ed. A. Blaszyczinski (Sydney, National Association for Gambling Studies, 2002), pp. 241-255.

27 Stewart Culin, "American Indian Games," *American Anthropologist* 5, no. 1 (Jan.-Mar. 1903), pp. 58-64.

28 Thwaites, *The Jesuit Relations and Allied Documents*, Vol. 38, pp. 146-147.

29 Andrew McFarland David, *Indian Games*, www.authorama.com/indian-games.html.

30 Pierre Boucher, *Canada to the Seventeenth Century* (Montreal: 1883), p. 57; Paul Charlevoix, "Histoire de la Nouvelle France: Journal d'un Voyage etc, par P. de Charlevoix," *Histoire de la Nouvelle France*, Vol. III (Paris: 1744), p. 188.

31 P. Latitau, *Mœurs des Sauvages Ameriquains*, Vol. II (Paris: 1724), p. 351.

32 Vine Deloria, *Red Earth, White Lies: Native Americans and the Myth of Scientific Fact* (New York: Scribner, 1995), p. 58.

33 Alanson Skinner, "Notes on the Plains Cree," *American Anthropologist* 16, no. 1 (Jan.-Mar. 1914), pp. 68-87; and Albert B. Reagan & F. W. Waugh, "Some Games of the Bois Fort Ojibwa," *American Anthropologist* 21, no. 3 (July-Sept. 1919), pp. 264-278.

34 See Little, "The Moral Dilemma of High Stakes Gambling in Native Communities," specifically chap. 1.

35 See, for example, Erica Hallebone, "Women and the New Gambling Culture in Australia," *Society and Leisure* 22, no. 1 (1999), pp. 101-125.

36 Culin, *Games of the North American Indian*, p. 110.

37 *Ibid.*, p. 183.

38 Thwaites, *The Jesuit Relations and Allied Documents*, Vol. 14, p. 79.

39 *Ibid.*, Vol. 10, p. 129.

40 *Ibid.*, Vol. 14, p. 46.

41 *Ibid.*, Vol. 55, p. 135.

42 *Ibid.*, Vol. 62, p. 199.

43 Little, "The Moral Dilemma of High Stakes Gambling in Native Communities," p. 19.

44 John Ewers, *The Horse in Blackfoot Indian Culture* (Washington, DC: Smithsonian Press, 1955).

45 Little, "The Moral Dilemma of High Stakes Gambling in Native Communities," p. 23.

46 Francis R. Guth, *Western Values Comparison in Gambling: With a Comparison to North American Aboriginal Views* (Sault Ste. Marie, ON: Algoma, 1994), p. 5.

47 Thwaites, *The Jesuit Relations and Allied Documents*, Vol. 16, p. 201.

48 *Ibid.*, Vol. 10, p. 81.

49 *Ibid.*, Vol. 10, p. 79.

50   Edward Winslow, "Relation," in *Chronicles of the Pilgrim Fathers of the Colony of Plymouth*, ed. Alexander Young (Boston: Charles C. Little and James Brown, 1841), pp. 307-308.

51   *Ibid.*

52   W. M. Beauchamps, "Iroquois Games," *The Journal of American Folklore* 9, no. 35 (Oct.-Dec. 1896), pp. 269-277.

53   See George A. Dorsey, "Certain Gambling Games of the Klamath Indians," *American Anthropologist* 3, no. 1 (Jan.-Mar. 1901), pp. 14-27; & Alan P. Merriam, "The Hand Game of the Flathead Indians," *Journal of American Folklore* 68, no. 269 (July-Sept. 1955), pp. 313-324.

54   Paul Du Ru, *Journal*. Translated by R. L. Butler (Chicago: The Caxton Club, 1934), p. 52.

55   Chrestien Le Clercq, SJ, *New Relations in Gaspesia*. Translated by W. F. Ganong (New York: Greenwood Press, 1968), pp. 294-295.

56   Culin, *Games of the North American Indian*, p. 176.

57   Le Clercq, *New Relations in Gaspesia*, p. 97.

58   See J. R. Miller, *Skyscrapers Hide the Heavens: A History of Indian-White Relations in Canada*, 3rd Ed. (Toronto: University of Toronto Press, 2001).

59   Robert Berkhofer, *The White Man's Indian: Images of the American Indian from Columbus to the Present* (New York: Knopf, 1978), p. 119.

60   *Ibid.*

61   See Robert Hardy, *Longbow: A Social and Military History* (London: Bois d'Arc Press, Distributed by Lyons & Burford, 1992).

62   Barry Ferguson, "Gamex '93 Gaming Law Review," in *Successful First Nations Gaming in Canada II*. Proceedings of the First Nations Gamexpo '93 (Vancouver: 1993, May 10-11).

63   Ashton, *The History of Gambling in England*.

64   Ferguson, "Gamex '93 Gaming Law Review."

65   Ashton, *The History of Gambling in England*, p. 15.

66   Blaszczynski, "A History of Gambling."

67   *Ibid.*

68   Ashton, *The History of Gambling in England*.

69   Ferguson, "Gamex '93 Gaming Law Review."

70   Thwaites, *The Jesuit Relations and Allied Documents*, Vol. 22, pp. 94-95.

71   *Ibid.*

72   *Ibid.*, p. 14.

73   *Ibid.*, Vol. 53, pp. 13-14.

74   *Ibid.*

75   *Ibid.*

76   John Milloy, "The Early Indian Acts: Developmental Strategy and Constitutional Change," in *As Long as the Sun Shines and Water Flows: A Reader in Canadian Native Studies*, eds. Antoine S. Lussier and Ian A.L. Getty (Vancouver: UBC Press, 1983), pp. 56-64.

77 See Robert A. Williams, *The American Indian in Western Legal Thought: The Discourses of Conquest* (Oxford: Oxford University Press, 1990), p. 229.

78 John Leslie, *Commissions of Inquiry into Indian Affairs in the Canadas, 1828-1858: Evolving a corporate memory for the Indian Department* (Ottawa: Treaties and Historical Research Centre, DIAND, 1985), p. 185.

79 See Darlene Johnston, "First Nations and Canadian Citizenship," in *Belonging: The Meaning and Future of Canadian Citizenship,* ed. William Kaplan (Montreal: McGill-Queen's University Press, 1993), p. 353.

80 Mark Larrimore, "Sublime Waste: Kant and the Destiny of the 'Races'," in *Civilization and Oppression*, ed. Catherine Wilson (Calgary: University of Calgary Press, 1999).

81 John F. Leslie, "Assimilation, Integration, or Termination? The Development of Canadian Indian Policy, 1943-1963" (Ph. D. diss., Carleton University, 1999).

82 See, for example, John S. Milloy, *"A National Crime": The Canadian Government and the Residential School System, 1879 to 1986* (Winnipeg: University of Manitoba Press, 1999); and J. R. Miller, *Shingwauk's Vision: A History of Native Residential Schools* (Toronto: University of Toronto Press, 1996).

83 Mark S. Dockstator, "Toward an Understanding of Aboriginal Self-Government: A Proposed Theoretical Model and Illustrative Factual Analysis" (Ph. D. diss., York University, 1993); and A. H. Mawhiney, *Towards Aboriginal Self-Government* (New York: Garland Publishing, 1994).

84 Sarah Carter, *Lost Harvests: Prairie Indian Reserve Farmers and Government Policy* (Montreal & Kingston: McGill-Queen's University Press, 1990); see also Robin Brownlie, *A Fatherly Eye: Indian Agents, Government Power, and Aboriginal Resistance in Ontario, 1918-1939* (Don Mills: Oxford University Press, 2003).

85 Noel Dyck, *"What is the Indian Problem": Tutelage and Resistance in Canadian Indian Administration* (St. John's, Newfoundland: Institute of Social and Economic Research, 1991), p. 91.

86 Katherine Pettipas, *Severing the Ties that Bind: Government Repression of Indigenous Religious Ceremonies on the Prairies* (Winnipeg: University of Manitoba Press, 1994), p. 3.

87 Allison Fuss Mellis, *Riding Buffaloes and Broncos: Rodeo and Native Traditions in the Northern Great Plains* (Norman: University of Oklahoma Press, 2003).

88 See for example Tina Loo "Dan Cranmer's Potlatch: Law as Coercion, Symbol, and Rhetoric in British Columbia, 1884-1951," *Canadian Historical Review* 73, no. 2 (1992), pp. 125-165; Elizabeth Furniss, "The Carrier Indians and the Politics of History," in *Native Peoples: The Canadian Experience,* ed. R. Bruce Morrison and C. Roderick Wilson (Toronto: Oxford University Press, 1995), pp. 508-545; Douglas Hudson. "The Okanagan Indians," in *Indian Peoples: The Canadian Experience*, ed. R. Bruce Morrison and C. Roderick Wilson (Toronto: Oxford University Press, 1995), pp. 484-507.

89 See generally Yale D. Belanger, "Seeking a Seat at the Table: A Brief History of Indian Political Organizing in Canada, 1870-1951" (Ph.D. diss., Trent University, 2005); and Leslie, "Assimilation, Integration, or Termination?"

90 http://www.ravenstrick.com/games.htm. Accessed 5 Jan., 2005.

1   Bradford Morse, "Permafrost Rights: Aboriginal Self-Government and the Supreme Court in *R. v. Pamajewon*," *McGill Law Journal* 42 (1997), p. 1020.

2   Colin S. Campbell & Garry Smith, "Gambling in Canada: From Vice to Disease to Responsibility: A Negotiated History," *Canadian Bulletin of Medical History* 20, no. 1 (2003), pp. 121-149.

3   Morse, "Permafrost Rights."

4   Christine Carberry, "When Times are Tight: Lotteries, Casinos and Revenue Policy in the American States and Canadian Provinces," (M.A. thesis, University of Western Ontario), p. 20.

5   M. Maclean, "Gaming and Criminal Law regulation," *Gaming in British Columbia* (Vancouver: Pacific Business and Law Institute, 1996), p. 5.

6   John M. Findlay, *People of Chance* (New York: Oxford University Press, 1986), p. 15.

7   Charles Clotfelter & Philip Cook, *Selling Hope: State Lotteries in America* (Cambridge, MA: Harvard University Press, 1989), p. 20.

8   Brian Hutchinson, *Betting the House: Winners, Losers, and the Politics of Canada's Gambling Obsession* (Toronto: Viking, 1999), p. 57.

9   *Ibid.*, p. 57

10 Suzanne Morton, *At Odds: Gambling and Canadians, 1919-1969* (Toronto: University of Toronto Press, 2003), p. 8.

11 Carberry, "When Times are Tight," p. 20.

12 Colin S. Campbell, "Canadian Gambling Legislation: The Social Origins of Legalization" (Ph.D. diss., Simon Fraser University, 1995), p. 25

13 National Archives of Canada (NAC), Record Group (RG) 2, Series A-1-a, Volume (Vol.) 494 (n/d) Royal Colonization Lottery: Colonial Office.

14 *Ibid.*

15 *Ibid.*

16 *Ibid.*

17 *Ibid.*

18 NAC, RG 2, Series A-1-a, Vol. 494 (24 Sept. 1886), letter Chas. R. Rowe to Jas. G. Cowles, High Commissioner for Canada.

19 NAC, RG 2, Series A-1-a, Vol. 494 (30 Nov. 1886), letter Charles Tupper to the Secretary of the State.

20 NAC, RG 2, Series A-1-a, Vol. 494 (5 Nov. 1886), letter Lieutenant Governor L. R. Masson to Office of Secretary of State.

21 NAC, RG 2, Series A-1-a, Vol. 494 (11 Nov. 1886), letter Deputy Minister of Justice George Burbridge to Under Secretary of State Grant Vowell.

22 NAC, RG 2, Series A-1-a, Vol. 494 (16 Nov. 1886), letter G. White to Under Secretary of State Grant Vowell.

23 Quoted in Michael Seelig & Julie Seelig, "'Place Your Bets!' On Gambling, Government and Society," *Canadian Public Policy* 24, no. 1 (1998), p. 92.

24 Morton, *At Odds*, p. 10.

25 *Ibid.*

26 Hal Pruden, "An Overview of the Gambling Provisions in Canadian Criminal Law and First Nations Gambling," *Journal of Aboriginal Economic Development* 2, no. 2 (2002), p. 37.

27 Morton, *At Odds*, p. 11.

28 J. A. Osborne, "The Legal Status of Lottery Schemes in Canada: Changing the Rules of the Game" (LL.M. thesis, University of British Columbia, 1989), pp. 38-39.

29 For this discussion see Campbell, "Canadian Gambling Legislation," specifically chapter 4, Gambling in the Moral Cauldron.

30 Campbell, "Canadian Gambling Legislation," p. 181.

31 NAC, RG 2, Vol. 1170 (7 June 1917), Order in Council — Suspension of federal gambling activities.

32 Morton, *At Odds*, pp. 144-146.

33 Chris Hosgood, "Poker and the Police in Early Twentieth Century Alberta." Paper presented at the Western Social Science Association Annual Conference, Las Vegas, NV, 10 April 2003.

34 *Ibid.*

35 *Ibid.*

36 Quoted in Hosgood, "Poker and the Police in Early Twentieth Century Alberta."

37 Morton, *At Odds*, p. 51.

38 *Ibid.*, pp. 51-52.

39 Campbell & Smith, "Gambling in Canada," p. 126.

40 Veronique Mandal & Chris Vander Doelen, *Chasing Lightning: Gambling in Canada* (Toronto: United Church Publishing House, 1999), p. 16.

41 Quoted in Campbell & Smith, "Gambling in Canada," p. 127.

42 Osborne, "The Legal Status of Lottery Schemes in Canada: Changing the Rules of the Game" p. 41; and Morton, *At Odds*, p. 11.

43 Campbell, "Canadian Gambling Legislation," p. 214.

44 *Ibid.*, p. 218.

45 *Ibid.*, p. 225.

46 See Papers of the Privy Council Office, NAC, RG 2, Series A-5-a, Vol. 2642 (20 May 1948), Post Office; use of mails for lotteries, pp. 5-6.

47 Osborne, "The Legal Status of Lottery Schemes in Canada: Changing the Rules of the Game" p. 47.

48 Morton, *At Odds*.

49 Campbell, "Canadian Gambling Legislation."

50 NAC, RG 2, Series A-5-a, Vol. 2642 (14 March 1959), Legislation — Amendments to the Criminal Code: Gambling, pp. 10-11.

51 NAC, RG 2, Series A-5-a, Vol. 2642 (17 Nov. 1959), Legislation — Plans for next session, p. 5.

52 *Ibid.*

53 *Ibid.*

54 NAC, RG 2, Series A-5-a, Vol. 2642 (26 May 1961), Criminal Code Amendment— Lotteries and gambling.

55 *Ibid.*, pp. 4-5.

56 *Ibid.*

57 NAC, RG 2, Series A-5-a, Vol. 2642 (22 Jan. 1963), Provincial Lotteries,

58 NAC, RG 2, Series A-5-a, Vol. 2642 (30 Jan. 1963), Provincial Lotteries—Tabling of Correspondence, p. 10.

59 Osborne, "The Legal Status of Lottery Schemes in Canada: Changing the Rules of the Game," pp. 55-56.

60 New Hampshire Lottery Commission (NHLC), *History of the New Hampshire Lottery.* www.nhlottery.org/about-us/history.asp. Accessed 31 Jan. 2006.

61 Osborne, "The Legal Status of Lottery Schemes in Canada: Changing the Rules of the Game," p. 59.

62 Pruden, "An Overview of the Gambling Provisions in Canadian Criminal Law and First Nations Gambling," p. 37.

63 *Ibid.*

64 See Manitoba Gaming Control Commission (MGCC), "History." www.mgcc.mb.ca/history.html. Accessed 31 Jan. 2006.

65 *Ibid.*

66 Ontario Lottery and Gaming Corporation (OLGC), "History" http://corporate.olgc.ca/corp_about_history.jsp. Accessed 31 Jan. 2006.

67 Pruden, "An Overview of the Gambling Provisions in Canadian Criminal Law and First Nations Gambling," p. 38.

68 *Ibid.*

69 Campbell, "Canadian Gambling Legislation," p. 247.

70 Pruden, "An Overview of the Gambling Provisions in Canadian Criminal Law and First Nations Gambling," p. 38.

71 *Ibid.*, p. 38.

72 Michel Labrosse, *The Lottery . . . From Jacques Cartier's Day to Modern Times* (Montreal: Stanke, 1985) p. 199.

73 Pruden, "An Overview of the Gambling Provisions in Canadian Criminal Law and First Nations Gambling," p. 38.

74 Carberry, "When Times are Tight," p. 29.

75 Campbell, "Canadian Gambling Legislation," p. 240.

76 Rhys Stevens, *Casinos in Alberta* (Lethbridge: Alberta Gaming Research Institute, 2004); also Colin S. Campbell, "Parasites & Paradoxes: Legalized casino gambling in Alberta, Canada," in *Gambling Papers: Proceedings of the Fifth National Conference on Gambling and Risk Taking,* ed. W. R. Eadington (Reno, NV: University of Nevada, Reno, 1981), pp. 186-207.

77 See Campbell & Smith, "Gambling in Canada."

78 Alberta Gaming and Liquor Commission (AGLC), "Casino Gaming: Table Games" (2001). www.aglc.gov.ab.ca/pdf/lpr/LPR_Report_09-Casino.pdf. Accessed 31 Jan. 2006.

79 AGLC, "Casino Gaming: Table Games."

80 See Stevens, *Casinos in Alberta*, p. 3.

81 *Government of Alberta News Release.* Quoting Alberta Minister of Gaming Ron Stevens, "Government approves policies to effectively manage growth of gaming: Community support required for new casinos; VLT cap to remain." 22 Oct. 2001. www.gaming.gov.ab.ca/news/20011022.asp. Accessed 2 June 2005.

82 Campbell, "Canadian Gambling Legislation," p. 250.

Chapter 3 — pp. 55-69

1 Canada, *For Seven Generations: An Information Legacy of the Royal Commission on Aboriginal Peoples,* Vol. II (Ottawa: Canada Publications Group, 1996), p. 775.

2 Quoted in Warren Skea, "Time to Deal: A Comparison of the Native Casino Gambling Policy in Alberta and Saskatchewan" (Ph.D. diss., University of Calgary, 1997), p. 102.

3 J. Rick Ponting, "Historical Overview and Background, Part II: 1970-96," in *First Nations in Canada: Perspectives on Opportunity, Empowerment, and Self-Determination,* ed. J. Rick Ponting (Toronto: McGraw-Hill Ryerson, 1997), p. 29.

4 Canada, *The Report of the Joint Parliamentary-Senate Committee Hearings on Indian Affairs in Canada* (Ottawa: Queen's Printer, 1961), p. 605.

5 Harry Hawthorn, *Survey of the Contemporary Indians of Canada,* vol. 1&2 (Ottawa: Department of Indian Affairs and Northern Development, Indian Affairs Branch, 1966 & 1967).

6 Alan Cairns, *Citizen's Plus: Aboriginal Peoples and the Canadian State* (Vancouver: UBC Press, 2000), p. 8.

7 David Newhouse, "Hidden in Plain Sight: Aboriginal Contributions to Canada and Canadian Identity: Creating a New Indian Problem." Paper delivered before the Thirtieth Anniversary Canadian Studies Conference, *First Nations – First Thoughts,* University of Edinburgh, Scotland (5-7 July 2001).

8 Ponting, "Historical Overview and Background," p. 31.

9 Canada, *Statement of the Government of Canada on Indian Policy,* 1969. www.fcpp.org/publications/worth_a_look/spr/native.html. (Accessed 3/10/2000), p. 3.

10 *Ibid.,* p. 5.

11 Expressed succinctly in the National Indian Brotherhood's *Red Paper:* "We view this as a policy designed to divest us of our Aboriginal, residual, and statutory rights. If we accept this policy we lose our rights and our lands, we become willing partners in cultural genocide. This we cannot do."

12 Noel Dyck, "Representation and Leadership of a Provincial Indian Association," in *The Politics of Indianness: Case Studies and Ethnopolitics in Canada,* ed. Adrian Tanner (St. John's, NF: Institute of Social and Economic Research, Memorial University, 1983), pp. 197-305.

13 Indian Chiefs of Alberta, *Citizen's Plus* (Edmonton: Indian Association of Alberta, 1970), p. 4.

14 See David R. Newhouse, Kevin Fitzmaurice & Yale D. Belanger, *Creating a Seat at the Table: Aboriginal Programming at Canadian Heritage* (Ottawa: Canadian Heritage, 2005).

15 For example, see Will Kymlicka, *Immigration, Citizenship, Multiculturalism: Exploring the Links* (Malden, Mass.: Blackwell Publishing, 2003); *Multicultural Citizenship* (New York: Columbia University Press, 2000); *Finding our Way: Rethinking Ethnocultural Relations in Canada* (New York: Oxford University Press, 1998); *Ethnic Associations and Democratic Citizenship* (Princeton, NJ: Princeton University Press, 1997); *Multicultural Citizenship: A Theory of Minority Rights* (New York: Oxford University Press 1995); Patrick Macklem, *Indigenous Difference and the Constitution of Canada* (Toronto: University of Toronto Press, 2001); and Charles Taylor, *Multiculturalism and the Politics of Recognition* (Princeton, NJ: Princeton University Press, 1994); and *Reconciling the Solitudes: Essays on Canadian Federalism and Nationalism* (Montreal & Kingston: McGill-Queen's University Press, 1993)

16 Quoted in Newhouse, Fitzmaurice & Belanger, *Creating a Seat at the Table*, p. 5.

17 *Calder v. The Attorney General of British Columbia*. (1973), 34 *D.L.R.* (3d) at 145 (also reported: [1973] *S.C.R.* at 313, [1973] 4 *W.W.R.* at 1)

18 Yvonne Pompana, "Devolution to Indigenization: The Final Path to Assimilation of First Nations" (M.A. thesis, University of Manitoba, 1997).

19 Quoted in Newhouse, Fitzmaurice & Belanger, *Creating a Seat at the Table*, p. 9.

20 See Douglas Sanders, "The Indian Lobby," in *And No One Cheered. Federalism, Democracy and the Constitution Act*, eds. K. Banting and R. Simeon (Toronto: Methuen, 1983).

21 See Indian Tribes of Manitoba (Manitoba Indian Brotherhood), *Whabung — Our Tomorrows* (Manitoba, 1971).

22 See Cam Mackie, "Some reflections on Indian Economic Development," in *Arduous Journey: Canadian Indians and Decolonization*, ed. J. Rick Ponting (Toronto: McClelland & Stewart, 1986).

23 Indian Tribes of Manitoba, *Whabung — Our Tomorrows.*

24 J. Rick Ponting & Roger Gibbins, *Out of Irrelevance* (Toronto: Butterworths, 1980), p. 32.

25 NAC, Manuscript Group (MG) 26, J13 (23 Aug. and 20 Sept. 1945), Diaries of Prime Minister William Lyon Mackenzie King.

26 T. R. L. MacInnes, "History of Indian Administration in Canada," *Canadian Journal of Economics and Political Science* 12, no. 3 (Aug. 1946), p. 393.

27 MacInnes, "The History of Indian Administration in Canada," pp. 393-394.

28 Canada, *House of Commons, Debates*, (13 May 1946), p. 1446.

29 *Ibid.*, p. 1492.

30 NAC, RG10, vol. 6810, file 470-2-3, Pt. 1. Indian Association of Alberta *Memorial*, submitted to the Special Joint Parliamentary Committee (SJC) investigating the *Indian Act*, p. 19.

31 Canada, Parliament, *Special Joint Parliamentary Committee of the Senate and the House of Commons appointed to examine and consider the Indian Act* (hereinafter referred to as the SJC), Minutes of Proceedings and Evidence, No. 30 (5 June 1947), p. 1567.

32 Native Brotherhood of British Columbia Brief, submitted to the Special Joint Parliamentary Committee (SJC) investigating the *Indian Act*, 1947, p. 8.

33 SJC, Minutes of Proceedings and Evidence No. 16 (1 May 1947), p. 771.

34 NAC, RG10, vol. 6810, file 470-2-3, Pt. 1. IAA *Memorial*, p. 13.

35 SJC, Minutes of Proceedings and Evidence, No. 30 (5 June 1947), p. 1614.

36 Royal Commission on Aboriginal Peoples (RCAP), *For Seven Generations: An Information Legacy of the Royal Commission on Aboriginal Peoples* [CD-ROM] (Ottawa: Canada Communications Group, 1996).

37 Ponting & Gibbins, *Out of Irrelevance*, p. 32.

38 Andrew J. Siggner, "The Socio-Demographic Conditions of Registered Indians," in *Arduous Journey: Canadian Indians and Decolonization*, ed. J. Rick Ponting (Toronto: McClelland & Stewart, 1986), p. 58.

39 *Ibid.*, p. 42.

40 *Ibid.*, p. 34.

41 Ponting, "Historical Overview and Background," p. 47.

42 Ponting & Gibbins, *Out of Irrelevance*, p. 43.

43 *Ibid.*, p. 36.

44 Siggner, "The Socio-Demographic Conditions of Registered Indians," p. 60.

45 Andrew J. Siggner, "A Socio-Demographic Profile of Indians in Canada," in *Out of Irrelevance*, Ponting & Gibbins, p. 61.

46 Siggner, "The Socio-Demographic Conditions of Registered Indians," p. 70.

47 *Ibid.*, p. 63.

48 Ponting, "Historical Overview and Background," p. 52.

49 Siggner, "The Socio-Demographic Conditions of Registered Indians," p. 74.

50 Ponting, "Historical Overview and Background," p. 61.

51 Siggner, "The Socio-Demographic Conditions of Registered Indians," p. 67.

52 Ponting, "Historical Overview and Background," p. 62.

53 Siggner, "The Socio-Demographic Conditions of Registered Indians," p. 72.

54 Royal Commission on Aboriginal Peoples (RCAP), *For Seven Generations*.

55 *Ibid.*, research reports record number 48002.

56 Siggner, "The Socio-Demographic Conditions of Registered Indians," p. 71.

57 Menno Boldt, *Surviving as Indians: The Challenge of Self-Government* (Toronto: University of Toronto Press, 1993).

58 David Hawkes, *The Search for Accommodation* (Kingston, ON.: Institute of Intergovernmental Relations, 1987), p. 1.

59 J. Anthony Long, Leroy Little Bear & Menno Boldt, "Federal Indian Policy and Indian Self-Government in Canada: An Analysis of a Current Proposal," *Canadian Public Policy* 8, no. 2 (1982), pp. 192-194.

60 Quoted in Olive P. Dickason, *Canada's First Nations: A History of Founding Peoples from Earliest Times* (Toronto: McClelland Stewart, 1994), p. 408.

61 Boldt, *Surviving as Indians*, p. 88.

62 Canada, *Special Committee on Indian Self-Government* (Task Force) (Ottawa: Queen's Printer, 1983), p. 39.

63 Keith Penner, "Their Own Place: The Case for a Distinct Order of Indian First Nation Government in Canada," in *Governments in Conflict? Provinces and Indian Nations in Canada*, eds. J. Anthony Long & Menno Boldt (Toronto: University of Toronto Press, 1988), p. 141.

64 Canada, *Special Committee on Indian Self-Government*, pp. 39-40; see also Penner, "Their Own Place."

65 Mackie, "Some reflections on Indian Economic Development," p. 219.

66 J. Rick Ponting, "Economic Development Provisions of the New Claims Settlements," in *Arduous Journey: Canadian Indians and Decolonization*, ed. J. Rick Ponting (Toronto: McClelland & Stewart, 1986), p. 90.

67 *Ibid.*

68 Response of federal government quoted in Yale D. Belanger & David R. Newhouse, "Emerging From the Shadows: The Pursuit of Aboriginal Self-Government to Promote Aboriginal Well-Being," *Canadian Journal of Native Studies* 24, no. 1 (2004), pp. 129-222.

69 A. M. Mawhiney, *Toward Aboriginal Self-Government: Relations Between Status Indian Peoples and the Government of Canada, 1969-1984* (New York: Garland Publishing, Inc., 1994), pp. 125-126.

70 *Ibid.*

71 Evelyn Peters, *Aboriginal Self-Government in Canada: A Bibliography, 1986* (Kingston: Institute of Intergovernmental Relations, Queen's University, 1986), p. 23.

72 David Hawkes, *Negotiating Aboriginal Self-Government: Developments Surrounding the 1985 First Ministers' Conference,* (Kingston: Institute of Intergovernmental Relations, Queen's University, 1985), p. 10.

73 Garry Smith & Harold Wynne, *VLT Gambling: A Preliminary Analysis, Final report* (Edmonton: Alberta Gaming Research Institute, 2004).

74 Colin S. Campbell, Timothy Hartnagel & Garry Smith, *The Legalization of Gambling in Canada* (Ottawa: The Law Commission of Canada, 2005), p. 29.

Chapter 4 — pp. 70-82

1 Federal Bureau of Investigation (FBI), "Indian Gaming Investigations/The Indian Gaming Working Group (IGWG)." www.fbi.gov/hq/cid/indian/indgaming.htm. Last accessed 31 Jan. 2006.

2 See generally Warren Skea, "Time to Deal: A Comparison of the Native Casino Gambling Policy in Alberta and Saskatchewan" (Ph.D. diss., University of Calgary, 1997).

3 US Supreme Court, *California v. Cabazon Band of Mission Indians*, 480 U.S. 202 (1987).

4 Information for this paragraph was gleaned from the American Gaming Association. www.americangaming.org/industry/index.cfm. Last accessed 2 Feb. 2006.

5 FBI, "Indian Country Crime." www.fbi.gov/hq/cid/indian/indgaming.htm. Accessed 28 Nov. 2005.

6 See Jessica R. Cattelino, "High Stakes: Seminole Sovereignty in the Casino Era" (Ph.D. diss., New York University, 2004); and Daniel Twetten, "Public Law 280 and the Indian Gaming Regulatory Act: Could Two Wrongs Ever Be Made Into a Right?" *The Journal of Criminal Law and Criminology* 90, no. 4 (Summer 2000), pp. 1317-1352.

7 Cattelino, "High Stakes."

8   US Supreme Court, *Seminole Tribe of Florida v. Florida* (1996) 517 U.S. 44.

9   *Johnson v. Mcintosh* (1823) 8 Wheaton, 543; *Cherokee Nation v. Georgia* (1831) 30 U.S. 1; *Worcester v. Georgia* (1832) 6 Peters 515, 31 U.S. 530.

10 *Cherokee Nation v. Georgia*, 16.

11 Leigh Gardner, Joseph P. Kalt & Katherine A. Spilde, *Cabazon, The Indian Gaming Regulatory Act, and the Socioeconomic Consequences of American Indian Governmental Gaming: A Ten-Year Review* (Cambridge, MA.: The Harvard Project on American Indian Economic Development, 2005), p. iii.

12 Kim Isaac Eisler, *Revenge of the Pequots: How a Small Native American Tribe Created the World's Most Profitable Casino* (New York: Simon & Shuster, 2001).

13 Eduardo Cordiero, "The Economics of Bingo: Factors Influencing the Success of Bingo Operations on American Indian Reservations" (Harvard Project on American Indian Economic Development, 1989), p.1.

14 Carole Goldberg & Duane Champagne, "Ramona Redeemed: The Rise of Tribal Political Power in California," *Wicazo Sa Review* 17, no. 1 (2002), p. 46.

15 Dave Desbrisay, "The Gaming Industry in Aboriginal Communities," in *For Seven Generations: An Information Legacy of the Royal Commission on Aboriginal Peoples* [CD-ROM] (Ottawa: Libraxus, 1996).

16 James David & Sam Otterstrom, "Growth of Indian gaming in the United States," in *Casino Gambling in America: Origins, Trends, and Impacts*, eds. Klaus J. Meyer-Arendt & Rudi Hartmann (New York: Cognizant Communication Corporation, 1998).

17 *Indian Gaming Regulatory Act*, 25 USC. §2701 (1988) http://www.nigc.gov/nigc/laws/igra/igra_index.jsp.

18 *Ibid.*, s. 11.

19 Penny Coleman, Deputy General Counsel, National Indian Gaming Commission, testimony before the National Gambling Impact Study Commission, Tempe, AZ (30 July, 1998).

20 These statistics were provided by the National Indian Gaming Association (NIGA). www.tribal-institute.org/lists/gaming.htm. Last accessed 2 Feb. 2006.

21 "Dispelling the Myths about Indian Gaming." www.onenationoklies.com/NDNgaming.html. Last accessed 2 Feb. 2006.

22 Menno Boldt, *Surviving as Indians: The Challenge of Self-Government* (Toronto: University of Toronto Press, 1993), p. 196.

23 *Ibid.*, p. 198.

24 *Ibid.*, p. 141.

25 See Steven A. Light & Kathryn R. L. Rand, *Indian Gaming and Tribal Sovereignty: The Casino Compromise* (Kansas: University of Kansas, 2005), p. 106.

26 Fergus M. Bordewich, *Killing the White Man's Indian: Reinventing Native Americans at the End of the Twentieth Century* (Toronto: Doubleday, 1997), p. 111.

27 John J. Bodinger de Uriarte, "Imagining the Nation with House Odds: Representing American Indian Identity at Mashantucket," *Ethnohistory* 50, no. 3 (2003), pp. 549-565.

28 Jack Campisi, "The Emergence of the Mashantucket Pequot Tribe, 1637-1975," in *The Pequots in Southern New England*, eds. Laurence M. Hauptman & James D. Wherry (Norman: University of Oklahoma Press, 1990), p. 139.

29 David E. Wilkins, *American Indian Politics and the American Legal System* (Lanham, MD: Rowman & Littlefield, 2002), p. 13.

30 *Ibid.*, p. 14.

31 *Ibid.*

32 Wilkins, *American Indian Politics and the American Legal System*, p. 24.

33 Cohen, *Handbook of Federal Indian Law*, p. 2.

34 Quoted in de Uriarte, "Imagining the Nation with House Odds," p. 657.

35 Sioux Harvey, "Two Models to Sovereignty: A Comparative History of the Mashantucket Pequot Tribal Nation and the Navajo Nation," *American Indian and Culture Research Journal* 20, no. 1 (1996), p. 181.

36 Cathy H. C. Hsu (Ed.). *Legalized Casino Gambling in the United States: The Economic and Social Impact* (Binghampton, NY: Haworth, 1999).

37 Lincoln S. Dyer, "Southeastern Connecticut Economic Secrets revealed," *The Connecticut Economic Digest* 2, no. 5 (May 1997), pp. 1-4.

38 Ann-Marie d'Hauteserre, "Foxwoods Casino Resort: An Unusual Experiment in Economic Development," *Economic Geography* (1998), pp. 112-121.

39 Harvey, "Two Models to Sovereignty," p. 181.

40 Quoted in de Uriarte, "Imagining the Nation with House Odds."

41 Carl A. Boger, Jr., Daniel Spears, Karen Wolfe & Li-chun Lin, "Economic Impacts of Native American Casino Gaming," in *Legalized Casino Gambling in the United States*, p. 141.

42 Fred Carstensen, William Lott, Stan McMillen, Bobour Alimov, Na Li Dawson, & Tapas Ray, *The Economic Impact of the Mashantucket Pequot Tribal Nation Operations in Connecticut* (Storrs, CT.: University of Connecticut, 2000).

43 Rick Green, "Hunting for Foxwoods: Foes of Expansion Take Aim at $100 Million Plan," *The Hartford Courant* (26 Aug. 2003). www.gamblingproblem.net/gambling_makes_the_news.htm.

44 Joseph Kalt, *Statement Before National Gambling Impact Study Commission* (16 March 1996), p. 1.

Chapter 5 — pp. 83-100

1 Colin S. Campbell, "Canadian Gambling Legislation: The Social Origins of Legalization" (Ph.D. diss. Simon Fraser University, 1995); *cf* also Suzanne Morton, *At Odds: Gambling and Canadians, 1919-1969* (Toronto: University of Toronto, 2003).

2 Quoted in Robin Kelley, "First Nations Gambling: Policy In Canada," *Journal of Aboriginal Economic Development* 2, no. 2 (2002), p. 43.

3 Shawanaga First Nations, Ojibway Territory, Home Page. http://www.shawanaga.com. Last accessed 26 March 2004.

4 Hal Pruden, "An Overview of the Gambling Provisions in Canadian Criminal Law and First Nations Gambling," *Journal of Aboriginal Economic Development* 2, no. 2 (2002), p. 40.

5 The Shawanaga and Eagle Lake First Nations unilaterally decided to design and implement gaming by-laws without provincial consent.

6   Barry Ferguson, "Gamex (93 Gaming Law Review)," in *Successful First Nations Gaming in Canada II. Proceedings of the First Nations Gamexpo '93* (Vancouver: 1993, May 10-11), p. 5.

7   See www.landclaimsdocs.com/court/pdf/rvjones.PDF. Last accessed 25 March 2004.

8   *Ibid.*

9   Ross Skoggard, "Severe shortage of native art is being blamed on bingo," *Toronto Star* (10 Sept. 1989), p. E-4

10 "Native bingo illegal, court rules," *Toronto Star* (27 Sept. 1991), p. A-12.

11 Bradford Morse, "Permafrost Rights: Aboriginal Self-Government and the Supreme Court in *R. v. Pamajewon*" 47 *McGill Law Journal* (1997), pp. 1011-1042.

12 "Gaming laws unfair, natives say," *Kitchener-Waterloo Record* (15 Oct. 1993), p. C-6

13 *R. v. Furtney* [1991] 3 S.C.R., p. 89. See also Paul K. Frits, "Aboriginal Gaming — Law and Policy," in *Aboriginal Issues Today: A Legal and Business Guide*, eds. Stephen B. Smart & Michael Coyle (Vancouver: Self-Counsel Press, 1997), pp. 228-229.

14 *R. v. Furtney*, p. 91.

15 *Ibid.*

16 *R. v. Gladue and Kirby* (1986) 30 CCC (3d) (Alta. Prov. Ct.) 308; and *R. v. Furtney*.

17 Frits, "Aboriginal Gaming — Law and Policy," p. 229.

18 *Ibid.*

19 Chief Roger Jones. Presentation made before the Royal Commission on Aboriginal Peoples, public consultation process (1 June 1993). Record 7/142.

20 Information for this paragraph was gleaned from www.landclaimsdocs.com/court/pdf/rvjones.PDF.

21 *Criminal Code of Canada* (Toronto: Canada Law Book, 1996). Accordingly, "every one who keeps a common gaming house or common betting house is guilty of an indictable offence and liable to imprisonment for a term not exceeding two years."

22 "Native bingo illegal, court rules," *Toronto Star*, 27 Sept. 1991, p. A-12.

23 "Native bands need license to run bingos, Supreme Court rules," *Kitchener Waterloo Record*, 27 Sept. 1991, p. B-4.

24 "Reserve's unlicensed bingo illegal," *Ottawa Citizen* (27 Sept. 1991), p. A-4.

25 Ontario, *Debates and Proceedings*, Mr. Miskokomon, 3rd Session, 35th Legislature, 24 Aug. 1993.

26 Coopers and Lybrand Consulting Group, *Report to the Ontario Casino Project: Ontario Casino Market and Economic Impact Study* (Aug. 12, 1993), p. v.

27 Ed Buller, "Community Healing Processes: Investments and Benefits." Paper presented at *Best Practice Interventions in Corrections for Indigenous People Conference* convened by the Australian Institute of Criminology, Sydney, Australia (8-9 Oct. 2001).

28 See Karen Campbell, "Community Life and Governance: Early Experiences of Mnjikaning First Nation with Casino Rama" (M.A. thesis, University of Manitoba, 1999), pp. 19-20.

29 "Government, casino squabble over revenue," *The Ottawa Citizen* (13 Feb. 1996), p. A-3.

30 "Natives say Tories have reneged on new casino deal," *The Hamilton Spectator* (13 Feb. 1996), p. A-8.

31 "Native chief angry after Tories demand cut of casino profits," *The Calgary Herald* (13 Feb. 1996), p. A-11.

32 "300 builders laid off as Indian casino talks stall," *Toronto Star* (18 Feb. 1996), p. A-12.

33 William Walker & Bruce DeMara, "Casino construction resumes, but without deal, Indians say," *Toronto Star* (9 March 1996), p. A-17.

34 *Ibid.*

35 Union of Ontario Indians (UOI), *Maintain, Protect, Enhance: A Discussion Paper on Casino Rama.* www.anishinabek.ca/uoi/pdf/FINAL-Casino%20Rama.pdf, , p. 6.

36 *R. v. Pamajewon* [1996] 2 S.C.R. 821.

37 Ontario Court of Appeal (1994), 21 O.R. (3d) 385.

38 *R. v. Pamajewon*, p. 11.

39 Thomas Isaac, *Aboriginal Law: Cases, Materials and Commentary* (Saskatoon: Purich, 1999), p. 526.

40 Morse, "Permafrost Rights," pp. 1011-1042.

41 *R. v. Pamajewon*, p. 825.

42 *Ibid.*, p. 826.

43 *Ibid.*

44 *Ibid.*, p. 824.

45 *Ibid.*, p. 825.

46 *Lovelace v. Ontario* [2000] 1 S.C.R. 950.

47 See the factum of the intervenor, Congress of Aboriginal Peoples (CAP), *Lovelace v. Ontario and the Chiefs of Ontario.* Court File No.: 26165.

48 "Aboriginals ask court for share of casino profits: $100 million from Rama project sought," *Toronto Star* (24 July 1996), p. A-5.

49 *Lovelace v. Ontario* [1998] 2 C.N.L.R. 36; (1997) 33 O.R. (3d) 735.

50 *Ibid.*, para. 49.

51 *Ibid.*

52 Richard Foot, "Supreme Court ruling on casino profits could dramatically alter native rights: Status v. Non-status: Not just millions of dollars, but a way of life at stake," *National Post* (20 July 2000), p. A-9.

53 Rick Mofina, "Non-status Indians don't have right to casino profits, top court rules: Group claimed exclusion violated constitutional rights," *The Ottawa Citizen* (21 July 2000), p. A-4.

54 *Ibid.*

55 *R. v. Powley* [2003] S.C.C. 43.

56 Jim Rankin, "The fast first days of Casino Rama," *Toronto Star* (13 Oct. 1996), p. A-1.

57 Michelle Mandel, "Waiting on Lady Luck: Reserve residents hope to see returns from Casino Rama's success," *Toronto Sun* (10 Dec. 2001), pp. 38-41.

58 See Yale D. Belanger, "The Morality of Aboriginal Gaming: A Concept in the Process of Definition," *Journal of Aboriginal Economic Development* 2, no. 2 (2002).

59 "Chippewas sue province over casino taxes," *The Hamilton Spectator* (1 Nov. 2001), p. B-7.

60 Colin McKim, "Province didn't grab casino profits, document states," *Barrie Examiner* (2 Jan. 2002), p. A-3.

61 *Ibid.*

62 Colin McKim, "Band will fight for casino share," *Orillia Packet and Times* (5 July, 2001), p. 1.

63 Shannon Kari, "Progress made in casino row, natives say: Seven-year fight over $1-billion from Casino Rama," *National Post* (14 Feb. 2005), p. A-8.

64 *Ibid.*

65 Lauren Carter, "Diversifying Rama: Sharon Stinson Henry says it's time for a new plan," *Orillia Packet and Times* (24 Aug. 2004), p. A-3.

66 *Ibid.*

67 "Casinos aim to overcome setbacks," *St. Catharines Standard* (21 Apr, 2005), p. A-4.

68 Colin McKim, "Mnjikaning eyes new partner for casino deal," *Orillia Packet and Times* (8 Sept. 2005), p. A-1.

69 Lauren Carter, "Diversifying Rama," p. A-3.

70 "Peterson leads talks on gaming revenues," *North Bay Nugget* (19 Feb. 2005), p. A-1.

71 *Ibid.*

Chapter 6 — pp. 101-122

1 "The next throw," *The Economist* 334 (18 Mar 1995), pp. 27-29.

2 Statistics Canada Catalogue no. 75-001-XPE, p. 8.

3 Dave DesBrisay, "The Gaming Industry in Aboriginal Communities," in *For Seven Generations: An Information Legacy of the Royal Commission on Aboriginal Peoples* [CD-ROM] (Ottawa: Libraxus, 1996).

4 "A gamble," *The Economist* 331 (18 June 1994), p. 54.

5 E. L. Grinols, "Incentives explain gambling's growth," *Forum for Applied Research and Public Policy* 11 (1996), pp. 119-124.

6 Colin S. Campbell & Garry J. Smith, "Canadian gambling: trends and public policy issues," *The Annals of the American Academy of Political and Social Science* 556 (1998), pp. 22-35.

7 Loleen Y. Berdahl & Canada West Foundation, *The Impact of Gaming upon Canadian non-profits: A 1999 Survey of Gaming Grant Recipients* (Calgary: Canada West Foundation, 1999).

8 Office of the Treaty Commissioner, *Statement of Treaty Issues: Treaties as a Bridge to the Future* (Saskatoon: OTC, 1998), p. 64.

9 Federation of Saskatchewan Indian Nations, *Indian Government* (1977).

10 Kathryn Gabriel, *Gambler Way: Indian Gaming in Mythology, History, and Archaeology in North America* (Colorado: Johnson Books, 1996), p. 215.

11 N. Ribis & M. Traymar, "Raising the Stakes: Raises the Issues," *Cultural Survival Quarterly* 19, no. 4 (1996), p. 11

12 The statistics used to this point in the paragraph can be found in Katherine Marshall, "The gambling industry: Raising the stakes," *Perspectives* (Winter 1998). Statistics Canada Catalogue no. 75-001-XPE. p. 8.

13 Terry Wotherspoon & Vic Satchewich, *First Nations: Race, Class, and Gender Relations* (Scarborough: Nelson, 1993).

14 Warren Skea, "Time to Deal: A Comparison of the Native Casino Gambling Policy in Alberta and Saskatchewan" (Ph.D. diss., University of Calgary, 1997), p. 103.

15 Saskatchewan Government, "Casino Expansion Policy Paper," Feb. 1993.

16 *Ibid.*

17 Skea, "Time to Deal," p. 110.

18 *Ibid.*, p. 114.

19 *Harker v. Regina (City),* 1995, CanLII 3906.

20 *Ibid.*, p. 127

21 Saskatchewan, *Debates and Proceedings*, Mr. Laudermilch, 32nd Legislature, 1 June 1993, p. 2134.

22 Federation of Saskatchewan Indian Nations, *Saskatchewan Aboriginal Peoples in the 21st Century: Social, Economic and Political Changes and Challenges* (Regina: PrintWest Publishing Services, 1997), pp. 45, 49, 88.

23 *Ibid.*, p. 78.

24 "Natives open a casino despite Saskatchewan government opposition," *Globe and Mail* (27 Feb. 1993), p. A-4.

25 Casinoman, "Memories of casino raid remain vivid." www.casinoman.net/gambling-news/article/memories-of-casino-raid-remain-vivid.1200.asp.

26 C. Fox, *Economic Feasibility of Casino Gaming in the Province of Saskatchewan* (Reno: Fox Consulting, 1993), p. 38.

27 *Ibid.*

28 Saskatchewan, *Debates and Proceedings*, Ms. Haverstock, 23rd Legislature, May 1994, p. 2681.

29 For en excellent overview of events, see Skea, "Time to Deal," chap. 6, pp. 97-165.

30 The information for this paragraph was gleaned from Cathy Nilson, "The FSIN-Province of Saskatchewan Gaming Partnership: 1995 to 2002" (M.A. thesis, University of Saskatchewan, 2004), pp. 49-50.

31 See Lorna Wenger & Beth Mckechnie, *FastFacts on Gambling* (Manitoba: The Awareness and Information Unit of the Addictions Foundation of Manitoba, 1999), p. 22.

32 Jason Warick, "Casino books opened: FSIN takes audit process one step further," *Saskatoon StarPhoenix* (31 May 2000), p. A-1.

33 Murray Mandryk, "Nothing learned in SIGA affair," *Saskatoon StarPhoenix* (17 Nov. 2000), p. A-14.

34 *Ibid.*

35 *Ibid.*

36 *2002 Framework Agreement*, p. 23. www.igr.ca/pub_docs/2002_Gaming_Framework_Agreement.pdf.

37 *Ibid.*, p. 17.

38 *Ibid.*

39   Dan Zakreski, "Manitoba First Nation drops SIGA as partner," *Saskatoon StarPhoenix*
      (27 June 2000), p. A-4; and "Enoch bets on American firm," *Edmonton Sun* (3 Dec.
      2003), p. 1.

40   Yale D. Belanger, "Building the Opakwayak Cree Nation (OCN) Economy," *Journal
      of Aboriginal Economic Development* 4, no. 1 (2005), p. 77.

41   Murray C. Sinclair, "Presentation to the Federal Task Force on Indian Gaming," in
      Gaming on Reserves: Discussion Paper Prepared by a Departmental Task Force. (Ottawa:
      Department of Indian Affairs and Northern Development, 1987), Annex 4-A.

42   Chuck Koppang, "Native Gaming in Manitoba," paper Presented at the Conference
      on First Nations Gambling in British Columbia, Duncan, BC, 30 Sept. and 1 Oct.
      1992, p. 1-2.

43   *Ibid.*

44   Manitoba, Office of the Auditor General, *Dakota Tipi First Nation Gaming
      Commission and First Nation Gaming Accountability in Manitoba* (Winnipeg: Manitoba
      Office of the Auditor General, 2003).

45   DesBrisay, "The Gaming Industry in Aboriginal Communities."

46   Koppang, "Native Gaming in Manitoba," p. 3.

47   Kathy Brock, "Relations with Canadian Governments: Manitoba," in *For Seven
      Generations: An Information Legacy of the Royal Commission on Aboriginal Peoples* [CD-
      ROM] (Ottawa: Libraxus, 1996).

48   Manitoba Lotteries Foundation, *Fact Sheet: Native Gaming Commissions*; and *Fact
      Sheet: Video Lottery Terminal Siteholder Agreements*; and *Lottery Licences for Reserves*.

49   Manitoba, *Debates and Proceedings*, Fourth Session, 35th Legislature, 28 June 1993, p.
      4838.

50   Brock, "Relations with Canadian Governments: Manitoba."

51   Quoted in DesBrisay, "The Gaming Industry in Aboriginal Communities."

52   *Ibid.*, record 41446.

53   *Ibid.*; original found at *Winnipeg Free Press* (20 Jan. 1993), pp. A-1, B-2.

54   Angus Reid Group, Inc., Canadians' *Attitudes Toward Aboriginal Gaming — Final
      Report* (1993), p. 21.

55   *Ibid.*, p. 14.

56   *Ibid.*, p. 21.

57   Assembly of Manitoba Chiefs (AMC), "Planning Change," brief submitted to the
      Royal Commission on Aboriginal Peoples (1993), p. 32.

58   Assembly of Manitoba Chiefs (AMC), *Protocol and Structural Plan for First Nations
      Gaming Commission in Manitoba*. Submission to the Honourable Bonnie Mitchelson,
      Minister of Lotteries, and the Honourable Jim Downey, Minister of Northern Affairs
      (Winnipeg: 1993).

59   Manitoba, *First Nations Gaming Policy Review Report* (Bostrom Report) (1997).

60   *Ibid.*

61   "First native casino to open next summer in Manitoba," *Alberni Valley Times* (18 Dec.
      2000), p. B-2.

62   "OCN casino gets pole position: Province gives gaming operation at The Pas the go-
      ahead," *The Drum* (16 Nov. 2001).

63 *Paskwayak Business Development Corporation*. www.opaskwayak.mb.ca/pbdc.php. Accessed 15 May 2005.

64 *History of the Opaskwayak Cree Nation*. www.opaskwayak.mb.ca/history.php. Accessed 13 May 2005.

65 Helen Buckley, *From Wooden Ploughs to Welfare: Why Indian Policy Failed in the Prairie Provinces* (Montreal and Kingston: McGill-Queen's University Press, 1992), p. 70.

66 Belanger, "Building the Opaskwayak Cree Nation (OCN) Economy," p. 76.

67 *Kikiwak Inn*. www.opaskwayak.mb.ca/kikiwakinn.php. Accessed 18 May 2005.

68 *The Pas Food Town*. www.opaskwayak.mb.ca/foodtown.php. Accessed 18 May 2005.

69 *OCN Shell Gas Bar*. www.opaskwayak.mb.ca/ocnshell.php. Accessed 17 May 2005.

70 *Your Dollar Store With More*. www.opaskwayak.mb.ca/dollarstore.php. Accessed 17 May 2005.

71 "OCN casino gets pole position," *The Drum* (16 Nov. 2001).

72 Manitoba Office of the Auditor General, *Dakota Tipi First Nation Gaming Commission*, 2003, p. 13.

73 Manitoba Government, *Employment Opportunities Result from Casino Training Program* (15 Feb. 2002). www.gov.mb.ca/ana/pdf/employment.html. Accessed 16 June 2003.

74 Bill Redekop, "First aboriginal casino tries harder: The Pas's Aseneskak experiences growing pains," *Assembly of Manitoba Chiefs News Brief* (17 Feb. 2002). www.manitobachiefs.com/news/2003/nbfeb03/02170305.html. Accessed 17 June 2003.

75 "Native-run casino loses almost $1 million," *CBC News Online* (12 Sept. 2003). http://winnipeg.cbc.ca/regional/servlet/View?filename=mb_aseneskak20030912. Accessed 13 March 2005.

76 Redekop, "First aboriginal casino tries harder."

77 See, for example, http://providence.areaconnect.com/statistics.htm; http://hartford.areaconnect.com/statistics.htm; http://boston.areaconnect.com/statistics.htm; www.citypopulation.de/USA-NewYork.html. Accessed 6 Feb. 2005.

78 The Greater Toronto Area, www.greater.toronto.on.ca/ataglance/mapprofile.html. Accessed 6 Feb., 2005.

79 See www.citypopulation.de/Canada-Manitoba.html; also Inky Mark (M.P.) www.inkymark.com/dauphin_swan_river_communities_pop.htm. Both accessed 6 Feb. 2005.

80 "Brokenhead reserve gets tentative casino approval," *Grassroots* 8, no. 4 (21 July 2004), p. 6.

81 Carol Sanders, "Smokers hit casino jackpot: ban doesn't apply to reserve's facility," *Winnipeg Free Press* (30 May 2005).

82 Manitoba, *Debates and Proceedings*, Mr. Doer, 2nd Session, 38th Legislature, 4 March 2004, p. 611.

83 Manitoba, *Debates and Proceedings*, Mr. Sale, 2nd Session, 38th Legislature, 24 May 2005.

84 *Ibid.*

85 Manitoba, *Debates and Proceedings*, Mr. Chomiak, 3rd Session, 38th Legislature, 25 May 2005.

Chapter 7 — pp. 123-137

1   Tsuu T'ina First Nation Chief Sanford Big Plume, Speech to the Calgary Chamber of Commerce (19 Nov. 2004). www.calgarychamber.com/abcalcoc/doc.nsf/files/9658DA B9ADB8C9AC87256F55007BD291/$file/Chief%20Big%20Plume%20Speech%20(P DF).pdf. Accessed 1 Feb. 2006.

2   Alberta Gaming Research Institute (AGRI), *Research Reveals … An Update on Gambling Research in Alberta*, 4, no. 2 (Dec. 2004), p. 4.

3   Alberta Gaming and Liquor Commission (AGLC), Casino Licensing Process — 8-Step Process. www.aglc.gov.ab.ca/gaming/charitable_gaming/casino/8_step_process.asp. Accessed 1 Feb. 2006.

4   Alberta, *Achieving a Balance: Gaming Licensing Policy Review* (Alberta: Alberta Gaming and Liquor Commission, 30 July, 2001), para. 6-31.

5   Warren Skea, "Time to Deal: A Comparison of the Native Casino Gambling Policy in Alberta and Saskatchewan" (Ph.D. diss., University of Calgary, 1997), p. 170.

6   Wendy Dudley, "Big buck bingo set for reserve," *Calgary Herald* (24 July 1993), p. B-1.

7   Monte Stewart, "Natives seeking own gaming commission," *Calgary Herald* (29 Aug. 1993), p. A-4.

8   Skea, "Time to Deal," p. 174.

9   It would be 1996 before the Pamajewon decision undermined First Nations sovereignty arguments.

10 Lotteries Review Committee, *New Directions for Lotteries and Gaming*, Chair — Judy Gordon, MLA Stettler Lacombe (Aug. 1995).

11 "Klein nod given to reserve casinos already, says MLA," *Edmonton Journal* (17 March 1995).

12 Jim Cunningham, "Natives told to be patient," *Calgary Herald* (27 Aug. 1995), p. A-1.

13 "Tsuu T'ina open to some changes," *Calgary Herald* (30 Jan. 1996), p. A-6.

14 *Ibid.*

15 MLA Committee on Native Gaming, *Final Report* (1996), p. 16.

16 *Ibid.*

17 Alberta Gaming and Liquor Commission (AGLC), *Annual Report: Protecting the Integrity of Alberta's Gaming and Liquor Industries* (Alberta: Alberta Gaming and Liquor Commission, 2002-03)

18 Alberta Gaming and Liquor Commission (AGLC), *Benefiting Albertans* (Alberta: Alberta Gaming and Liquor Commission, 2003).

19 AGLC, *Annual Report 2002-03.*

20 Enoch Community Profile. www.enochecdev.ca/community.html. Accessed 1 Feb. 2006.

21 Debora Steele, "Past wrong at Enoch put right for $52 million," *Sweetgrass*, Vol. 11, No. 9, p. 2 (22 Aug. 2004). www.ammsa.com/sweetgrass/topnews-Aug-2004.html. Accessed 1 Feb. 2006.

22 Indian and Northern Affairs Canada, *Message from the Confederacy of Treaty Six First Nations.* www.ainc-inac.gc.ca/ab/ayr04/ayrty6_e.html. Accessed 27 Nov. 2005.

23 Alberta Gaming and Liquor Commission (AGLC), *Annual Report: Protecting the Integrity of Alberta's Gaming and Liquor Industries* (Alberta Gaming and Liquor Commission, 2001-02), p. 19.

24 Debora Steele, "Enoch's future full of hope and promise," *Sweetgrass* (18 Oct. 2004).

25 Laura Severs, "Casino project coming up aces for Enoch: proposed resort predicted to be an economic boom," *Business Edge* 4, no. 26 (8 Aug. 2004).

26 Steele, "Enoch's future full of hope and promise."

27 *Ibid.*

28 City of Edmonton, *Report of the executive committee* (Edmonton, 1 May 2002).

29 "Edmonton Mayor Fights Casino Plan," *Gambling Magazine* (7 Nov. 2002). 216.239.63.104/search?q=cache:FqGd8xsGnLIJ:www.gamblingmagazine.com/managearticle.asp%3Fc%3D360%26a%3D1127+%22enoch+cree%22+casino&hl=en

30 *Report of the executive committee.*

31 "Council accused of racism in casino debate," CBC Edmonton (9 July 2003). edmonton.cbc.ca/regional/servlet/View?filename=ed_casino20030709. Accessed 1 Feb. 2006.

32 *Ibid.*

33 "Enoch casino can't be stopped, city told," *Edmonton Journal* (21 Nov. 2003), p. B-3.

34 *Ibid.*

35 "Enoch will go it alone on casino," *Gambling Magazine* (24 June 2003). 216.239.63.104/search?q=cache:N7mArVERIcoJ:www.gamingmagazine.com/managearticle.asp%3Fc%3D420%26a%3D2947+%22enoch+cree%22+casino&hl=en. Accessed 1 Feb. 2006.

36 "Alberta Tribe makes offer for casino services," CBC News (28 June 2004).

37 "First native-run casino gets go ahead," CBC Calgary (16 April 2004). http://calgary.cbc.ca/regional/servlet/View?filename=ca_enoch20040416. Accessed 1 Feb. 2006.

38 "Proposed Native-owned casino may move," *Indian Country Today* (13 Aug. 2003). www.indiancountry.com/content.cfm?id=1060799797. Accessed 1 Feb. 2006.

39 Cinda Chavich, "Native band bets on ambitious development: A casino is just the first phase of what the Tsuu T'ina Nation has planned," *The Globe and Mail* (26 Oct. 2004), B-12.

40 David Parker, "Whatever Happened to . . ." *Calgary Real Estate News* 22, no. 17 (22 April 2004). http://www.cren.ca/content_view2?CONTENT_ID=1445. Accessed 1 Feb. 2006.

41 Chavich, "Native band bets on ambitious development: A casino is just the first phase of what the Tsuu T'ina Nation has planned," p. B-12.

42 Elizabeth Churchill, "Tsuu T'ina: A History of a First Nation's Community, 1890-1940" (Ph.D. diss., University of Calgary, 2000), p. 80.

43 For a more detailed discussion of the history and events leading up to the 1970s, see Churchill "Tsuu T'ina"; and P. Whitney Lackenbauer, "Vanishing Indian, Vanishing Military: Military Training and Aboriginal Lands in the Twentieth Century" (Ph.D. diss., University of Calgary, 2004).

44 Canadian Environmental Assessment *Registry*, CEA Registry Reference Number: *04-01-4572. www.ceaaacee.gc.ca/050/Viewer_e.cfm?SrchPg=3&CEAR_ID=4572.* Accessed 1 Feb. 2006.

45 Amy Steele, "Gambling on independence: Tsuu T'ina Nation sees benefits to casino, developments — but some residents have doubts," *FFWD* (8 July 2004). www.ffwdweekly.com/Issues/2004/0708/news1.htm. Accessed 1 Feb. 2006.

46 *Ibid.*

47 *Ibid.*

48 *Ibid.*

49 "Tsuu T'ina OK casino," CBC Edmonton (2 July 2004). edmonton.cbc.ca/regional/servlet/View?filename=ed_casino20040702. Accessed 1 Feb. 2006.

50 "Calgary ring road to be built," *C-News* (13 March 2005). cnews.canoe.ca/CNEWS/Canada/2005/03/13/959502-cp.html. Accessed 1 Feb. 2006.

51 Parker, "What Ever Happened to . . . "

52 *Dominion of Canada Annual Report of the Department of Indian Affairs for the Year Ended 31st Dec. 1885*, p. xlviii.

53 Information for this paragraph can be found at Stoney Nakoda Nation, "History." www.stoney-nation.com/history.htm.

54 Joan Black, "Judge lays blame in teen suicide," *Windspeaker* (1999). www.ammsa.com/windspeaker/WINDNEWSNOV99.html. Accessed 2 Feb. 2006.

55 Joan Black, "Judge lays blame," *Sweetgrass* (11 Oct. 1999). www.ammsa.com/sweetgrass/OCT99.html#anchor81431. Accessed 2 Feb. 2006.

56 "Accounts call for RCMP investigation of Stoney reserve," CBC News, 3 Dec. 1998.

57 Jason Fekete, "Stoney casino slated for Highway 1: $27M project could draw 400,000 a year," *Calgary Herald* (22 June 2005).

58 *Ibid.*

59 Jeff Gailus, "Valley of Ghosts," *Alberta Venture* 9, no. 3 (2005). www.albertaventure.com/abventure_4126.html. Accessed 2 Feb. 2006.

60 Shawn Logan, "Stoney casino bid nears fruition," *Cochrane Eagle* (24 Aug. 2005).

61 Gailus, "Valley of Ghosts."

Chapter 8 — pp. 138-150

1 Bruce E. Johansen, *Life and Death in Mohawk Country* (Golden, CO: North American Press, 1993); and Oren C. Lyons and John C. Mohawk, "Sovereignty and Common Sense," *Cultural Survival Quarterly* 17, no. 4 (1994), pp. 58-60.

2 Manitoba Treaty Land Entitlement Overview. Aboriginal and Northern Affairs. www.gov.mb.ca/ana/tle_overview.html. Accessed 8 Dec. 2004. Canada entered into various treaties with bands in Manitoba between 1871 and 1910. These seven treaties provided that Canada would set aside a certain amount of land as reserve land based on band populations at the time of the original surveys. Not all bands received their full allocation. Treaty Land Entitlement (TLE) refers to land Canada owes specific bands under the terms of the treaties.

3   "Manitoba Picks Five Sites For Aboriginal Casinos," *Gambling Magazine* (1999). www.gamblingmagazine.com/articles/27/27-514.htm. Accessed 9 Dec. 2004.

4   Manitoba, *First Nations Gaming Policy Review Report* (1997), p. 21.

5   Dan Le Moal, "Headingley residents reject Swan Lake casino bid for second time," *The Drum: Manitoba's Source for Aboriginal News* (nd). http://epe.lac-bac.gc.ca/100/201/300/first_perspective/2001/01-04/drum4.html.

6   Tom Brodbeck, "Doer gov't craps out as gambling czar: Sole native casino losing cash," *Winnipeg Sun* (16 Dec. 2003). www.canoe.ca/NewsStand/WinnipegSun/News/2003/12/16/pf-288395.html.

7   Manitoba, *Debates and Proceedings*, Mr. Ashton, 2nd session, 37th Legislature (7 Dec. 2000). www.gov.mb.ca/legislature/hansard/2nd-37th/vol_03/h03.html.

8   *Ibid.*, Mr. Doer (6 June 2000). www.gov.mb.ca/legislature/hansard/1st-37th/vol_041/h041.html.

9   *Ibid.*, Mr Ashton (7 Dec. 2000).

10 *Ibid.*

11 "Suzuki chided by aboriginal casino promoter: CBC star urges natives to make bread, coffins," *Edmonton Journal* (19 May 2000), p. A-9.

12 "Manitoba: Casino idea saddens Suzuki," *National Post* (19 May 2000), p. A-4.

13 Dan LeMoal, "Swan Lake casino faces an uphill battle," *The Drum*, 16 Oct. 2000.

14 *First Nations Gaming Policy Review Report*, p. 15.

15 *Ibid.*, p. 28.

16 Swan Lake First Nation. www.swanlakefirstnation.ca/slfnent.html. Accessed 7 Dec., 2004.

17 "Natives promise protests over Manitoba casino decision," *North Bay Nugget* (10 July 1999), p. A-7.

18 *Ibid.*

19 "Native Indians protest at Games opening: Winnipeg demonstrators criticize 'Third World living conditions' of Manitoba's native Indians," *The Vancouver Sun*, 24 July 1999, p. A-21.

20 "Police nab one-armed bandits from unlicensed casino," CBC News (16 Aug. 1999). www.cbc.ca/story/news/national/1999/08/16/casino990816.html.

21 ROC Archives, *Canada Calling* (Oct. 1999). www.trainweb.org/canadianrailways/CanadaCalling/Oct.1999.html.

22 Lori Culbert, "Filmon has a tough day on the campaign trail as Tuesday vote looms: Manitoba's first poll results to be released today in tight race," *National Post* (17 Sept. 1999), p. A-10.

23 "Feud on Manitoba reserve results in gunfire over Christmas holidays," *Sudbury Star* (6 Jan. 2002), p. A-4.

24 Krista Foss, "Native band split by row over chief," *The Globe & Mail* (5 Dec. 2001), p. A-7.

25 Paul Barnsley, "Minister's decision angers two bands in Manitoba," *Windspeaker* 20, no. 1 (May 2002).

26 Manitoba, Office of the Auditor General, *Dakota Tipi First Nation Gaming Commission and First Nation Gaming Accountability in Manitoba* (Winnipeg: Manitoba Office of the Auditor General, 2003), p. 1.

27 *Ibid.*, p. 22.

28 *Ibid.*, p. 7.

29 David Kuxhaus, "Bingo returns to Dakota Tipi," *Winnipeg Free Press* (2 May 2005), p. B-7.

30 *Ibid.*

31 See Darren Bernhardt, "Casino showdown at council: Mayor expects casino question will dominate tonight's meeting," *Saskatoon StarPhoenix* (16 Dec. 2002), p. A-1; and "Most councillors want Oct. casino vote," *Saskatoon StarPhoenix* (30 May 2003), p. A-1.

32 City of Saskatoon, *Minutes of the Regular Meeting of City Council* (24 Sept. 2001), pp. 11-13; see also Kim McNairn, "Slot in a plebiscite: councillor Fortosky to present a motion to force a civic vote on casino expansion in Saskatoon," *Saskatoon StarPhoenix* (22 Sept. 2001), p. A-3.

33 City of Saskatoon, *Minutes of the Regular Meeting of City Council* (9 Oct. 2001), p. 58.

34 *Ibid.*, pp. 59-60.

35 Kim McNairn, "Council favours town hall meeting on casino issue," *Saskatoon StarPhoenix* (24 Oct. 2001), p. A-6.

36 City of Saskatoon, *Minutes of the Regular Meeting of City Council* (19 Nov. 2001), p. 9.

37 City of Saskatoon, *Minutes of the Regular Meeting of City Council* (11 Feb. 2002), p. 56.

38 City of Saskatoon, *Minutes of the Regular Meeting of City Council* (2 Dec. 2002), p. 21.

39 *Ibid.*

40 *Ibid.*, p. 92.

41 City of Saskatoon, *Minutes of the Regular Meeting of City Council* (16 Dec. 2002).

42 *Ibid.*, p. 73.

43 *Ibid.*; see pp. 70-75 for commentary.

44 City of Saskatoon, *Minutes of the Regular Meeting of City Council* (5 and 12 May 2003), pp. 93-99.

45 James Parker, "Councillors threaten to boycott casino vote," Saskatoon *StarPhoenix* (23 Aug. 2003), p. A-1.

46 *Ibid.*

47 City of Saskatoon, *Minutes of the Regular Meeting of City Council* (8 Sept. 2003), pp. 13-15.

48 City of Saskatoon, *Minutes of the Regular Meeting of City Council* (3 Nov. 2003), pp. 49-50.

Chapter 9 — pp. 151-166

1 Jolayne Madden-Marsh, "All Roads Lead to the Mission," *Dreamspeaker* (Spring 1998).

2 Sophie Pierre, "Self Government — The Ktunaxa/Kinbasket Experience," talk delivered before Speaking Truth to Power, III: Self Government: Options and Opportunities, sponsored by the BC Treaty Commission, 14-15 March 2002, p. 3.

3 Troy Hunter, "Casino of the Rockies approved by province," *Raven's Eye* (Dec. 1999).

4   *Ibid.*

5   Gerry Warner, "Casino gets approval from the provincial government; Resort development will also contain hotel, pool, banquet facilities, aboriginal interpretive centre and 18-hole golf course," *Daily Townsman* (12 Nov. 1999), p. A-1; see also Hunter, "Casino of the Rockies."

6   Gerry Warner, "Workers busy at large construction project on casino site," *Daily Townsman* (31 March 2000), p. A-1.

7   Gerry Warner, "Gambling expert giving workshop on dangers: KKTC wellness group invites institute director to train counselors," *Daily Townsman* (13 April 2000), p. A-1.

8   Gerry Warner, "Band still optimistic about St. Eugene project," *Daily Townsman* (29 Jan. 2001), p. A-1.

9   Gerry Warner, "St. Eugene hotel, casino a go-ahead, chief says: Lake City Casinos of Kelowna coming in as operator, Sophie Pierre tells guests at Aboriginal Golf Tournament," *Daily Townsman* (22 June 2001), p. A-1.

10 Gerry Warner, "Casino opens Saturday: Only Aboriginal-owned Casino in B.C. ready to welcome the public," *Daily Townsman* (19 Sept. 2002), p. A-1.

11 Derrick Penner, "Residential school now a resort," *The Vancouver Sun* (8 March 2003), p. F-3.

12 Richard Landis, "Ktunaxa Kinbasket Tribal Council: Luxury Resort Leads to Economic Growth," in *Building Aboriginal and Northern Economies,* Ottawa: Indian and Northern Affairs Canada, 2003, p. 3.

13 Gerry Warner, "Forum strives for dialogue between Ktunaxa, non-aboriginal neighbours," *Daily Townsman* (20 Oct. 2003), p. A-3.

14 Gerry Warner, "Was resort the right project?" *Daily Bulletin* (16 July 2004), p. A-4.

15 Dean Bassett, "St. Eugene needs protection: Mission Hotel and Golf Course file for protection from creditors under CCAA; cite lack of cash flow and need to restructure debt," *Daily Bulletin* (30 Dec. 2003), p. A-1.

16 *Ibid.*

17 Dean Bassett, "St. Eugene gets extension," *Daily Bulletin* (3 Feb. 2004), p. A-1.

18 "Chief admits to diverting money," *Lethbridge Herald* (27 Aug. 2004), p. A-5.

19 *Ibid.*, see also "Shuswap Band members swear court documents on St. Eugene," *The Lake Windermere Valley Echo* (29 Sept. 2004), p. 6.

20 Gerry Warner, "New deal for resort," *Daily Bulletin* (31 Dec. 2004), p. 13.

21 Gerry Warner, "New resort owners prepare for takeover: Mnjikaning and Samson Cree First Nations reps bring proven casino track record, plan to target new markets," *Daily Townsman* (28 Oct. 2004), p. A-1.

22 Gerry Warner, "Ontario band buys stake in struggling Cranbrook resort," *Trail Times* (28 Oct. 2004), p. 3.

23 Gerry Warner, "The spa at St. Eugene Resort: Latest renovation stage see swimming pool, health spa opening today," *Daily Townsman* (20 May 2005), p. A-1; see also Warner, "New resort owners prepare for takeover."

24 Don Cayo, "Residential schools redux; An amazing transformation Series: Transition to Independence: Natives in the BC economy," *The Vancouver Sun* (9 July 2005), p. G-3.

25 Darcy Henton, "Taking a gamble changing an arena," *Toronto Star* (29 Sept. 1994), p. A-1.

26 *Ibid.*

27 Kathleen Orth, "Mississauga's enact a labour code," *Ontario Birchbark* (Sept. 2003). www.ammsa.com/birchbark/topnews-Sep-2003.html#anchor9056364/. Accessed 31 Jan. 2006.

28 See Ontario Trillium Foundation. www.trilliumfoundation.org. Accessed 31 Jan. 2006.

29 Loleen Y. Berdahl & Canada West Foundation, *The Impact of Gaming upon Canadian non-profits: A 1999 Survey of Gaming Grant Recipients* (Calgary: Canada West Foundation, 1999).

30 Robert Williams & Robert Woods, *Final Report: The Demographic Sources of Ontario Gaming Revenue* (Toronto: Ontario Problem Gaming Research Centre, 2004).

31 Nova Scotia, Office of Aboriginal Affairs, *Business Plan, 2005-06*, p. 3. The Union of Nova Scotia Indians tribal council represents the five First Nation communities within Cape Breton (We'koqma'q, Wagmatcook, Membertou, Eskasoni, and Chapel Island First Nations) along with two First Nations located in mainland Nova Scotia (Indian Brook and Acadia First Nations). The remaining six communities are represented by the Confederacy of Mainland Mi'kmaq (Bear River, Annapolis Valley, Glooscap, Millbrook, Paq'tnkek, and Pictou Landing First Nations). www.gov.ns.ca/abor/pubs/200506%20OAA%20BP%20Final%20Draft%20mar.pdf.

32 Auditor General of Nova Scotia, *Crown Agencies and Corporations*, Halifax: 1998, p. 14.

33 Grant Thornton Chartered Accountants, *Review of First Nation Gaming Commissions: Sources and Uses of Funds*, Halifax: 2002, p. 2.

34 Jill Sullivan-Corney, *Office of Aboriginal Affairs: Business Plan, 2005-06*, Halifax: 2005, p. 9.

35 Office of Aboriginal Affairs, *Annual Accountability Report, 2001-02*, Halifax: 2002, p. 10.

36 Government of Nova Scotia, *Gaming Strategy: Backgrounder.* www.gov.ns.ca/govt/gamingstrategy/#back. Accessed 31 Jan. 2006.

37 Government of Nova Scotia, *Better Balance: Nova Scotia's First Gaming Strategy.* www.gov.ns.ca/govt/gamingstrategy/BetterBalance.pdf/. Accessed 31 Jan. 2006.

38 Omnifacts Bristol Research, *Public Attitudes on Gaming in Nova Scotia*, Halifax: 2005, p. 60.

39 *Ibid.* p. 37.

40 Alison Dubois, Wanda Wuttunee & John Loxley, "Gambling on Casinos," *Journal of Aboriginal Economic Development* 2, no. 2 (2002), p. 58.

41 *Ibid.*, p. 58.

42 The Labour Relations Board, Saskatchewan, *Saskatchewan Joint Board, Retail, Wholesale and Department Store Union* v. *Saskatchewan Indian Gaming Authority Inc. carrying on business as the Painted Hand Casino.* LRB File Nos. 067-03, 068-03 and 069-03 (29 Aug., 2003). www.sasklabourrelationsboard.com/recent-board-decisions/2003/067-03.pdf. Accessed 31 Jan. 2006.

43 See Monique Beech, "Hoffa's son pays a visit to Ramara: Says Teamsters would hold dealers' interests high," *Orillia Packet and Times*, 11 May 2004, p. A-1.

44 See *Teamsters Canada Online: Local Union 938*, "Local Union 938: Teamsters organizing employees at Casino Rama." news.teamsters-canada.org/news.php?id=240. Accessed 1 May 2005; and Jim Purnell, "Casino dealers spurn union embrace: 14-month unionizing drive falls flat; about 62% of voters said no to joining Teamsters," *Orillia Packet and Times* (14 May 2004), p. A-1.

45 See Purnell, "Casino dealers spurn union embrace."

46 Colin McKim, "Union drive not stalled: Teamsters," *Orillia Packet and Times* (29 July 2004), p. A-3.

47 Randi Hicks Rowe, "Targeted: Unions set their sights on tribal casinos," *American Indian Report* (March 2005), p. 12.

48 Chris Nguyen, "One union sues another over California tribal casino workers," *Associated Press* (4 May 2005). www.sfgate.com/cgi-bin/article.cgi?f=/n/a/2005/05/04/state/n 200856D83.DTL.

49 *UNI Global Union*, "Casino workers ratify first contract and Great Blue Heron." www.union-network.org/ UNICasinos.nsf/0/ 4077ec5be6caa599c1256ee50024d66d? OpenDocument. Accessed 1 June 2005.

50 Alberta Gaming and Liquor Commission (AGLC), *The Use of the Internet for Gaming*. www.aglc.gov.ab.ca/pdf/lpr/LPR_Report_15-internet_Gaming.pdf. Accessed 25 March 2004.

51 Testimony of Frank Catania before the US Senate Banking Committee on Banking, Housing and Urban Affairs, 18 March 2003. banking.senate.gov/03_03hrg/031803/catania.htm. Accessed 16 Sept. 2004.

52 AGLC, *The Use of the Internet for Gaming*.

53 *Ibid.*

54 Bear, Stearns & Co. Inc., *E-Gaming Revisited — At Odds With The World*, New York: 2000.

55 See C. Ian Kyer & Danielle Hough, "Is internet Gaming Legal in Canada: A Look at Starnet," *Canadian Journal of Law and Technology* 1, no. 1. http://cjit.dal.ca. Accessed 22 Nov. 2003.

56 *R. v. Starnet Communications International Inc..* Vancouver 125795-1 (B.C.S.C.), 17 Aug. 2001.

57 Frank Catania, *Internet Gaming Regulation: The Kahnawake Experience.* www.cataniaconsulting.com/kahnawake.pdf. Accessed 22 March 2004.

58 Michael D. Lipton, "Internet Gaming in Canada," presentation made before Global Gaming Exposition. Las Vegas, Nevada, 17 Sept. 2003. www.gaminglawmasters.com/jurisdictions/canada/internet.Gaming-Speech.htm. Accessed 27 March 2004.

59 *Ibid.*

60 T. W. Bell and Cato Institute, *Internet gambling: popular, inexorable, and (eventually) legal* (Washington DC: Cato Institute, 1999).

Conclusion — pp. 167-173

1   Warren Skea, "Time to Deal: A Comparison of the Native Casino Gambling Policy in Alberta and Saskatchewan" (Ph.D. diss., University of Calgary, 1997), p. 273.

2   Carl Roberts, "Community Presentation," in For Seven Generations: An Information Legacy of the Royal Commission on Aboriginal Peoples [CD-ROM] (Ottawa: Libraxus, 1996), record no. 5444.

3   Nechi Training, Firewatch on Aboriginal Adolescent Gambling (Edmonton: Research and Health Promotions Institute, 1995), p. 28.

4   J. Antell, A. Blevins & K. Jensen, "American Indian Casino Gambling: Issues of Tribal Sovereignty and Economic Development," Journal of Community Development Society, 31, no. 1 (2000), pp. 1-18.

5   The Saskatchewan Indian Gaming Authority Inc. v. the National Automobile, Aerospace, Transportation and General Workers Union of Canada and the Saskatchewan Labour Relations Board [2000] SKCA 138.

6   Roberts, "Community Presentation," record no. 5444.

7   J. Rick Ponting, "The Paradox of On-Reserve Casino Gambling: Musings of a Nervous Sociologist," revised version of a paper prepared for the Gambling in Canada: The Bottom Line conference, Second National Symposium on Gambling, Simon Fraser University Gambling Studies Program, Vancouver, BC, 27-30 Oct. 1993, p. 8.

8   Joseph Kalt, Statement Before National Gambling Impact Study Commission, 16 March 1996.

9   Nelson Rose, "The Future of Indian Gaming," Journal of Gambling Studies, 8 (1992), p. 398.

10   Denise Birdstone, "Community Presentation," in For Seven Generations: An Information Legacy of the Royal Commission on Aboriginal Peoples [CD-ROM] (Ottawa: Libraxus, 1996).

11   Assembly of First Nations, "AFN National Chief Addresses First Nations Gaming," (2000). www.afn.ca/Press%20Realeases%20and%20...ches/afn_national_chief_addresses_fir.htm.

REFERENCES

Primary Sources

Library and Archives of Canada, Ottawa
Department of Indian Affairs, RG10.
Diaries of the Hon. W. L. Mackenzie King, MG26, J13.
Records of the Privy Council Office, RG2.

Jesuit Relations
Thwaites, Ruben Gold. *The Jesuit Relations and Allied Documents: Travels and Explorations of the Jesuit Missionaries in New France.* Cleveland: The Burrow Bros. Co., 1896-1901, vols. 10, 14, 16, 18, 22, 38, 53, 55 and 62.

Government Documents
Alberta Gaming and Liquor Commission. *Achieving a Balance: Gaming Licensing Policy Review,* 30 July 2001.

_____. *Annual Report: Protecting the Integrity of Alberta's Gaming and Liquor Industries,* 2001-02.

_____. *Annual Report: Protecting the Integrity of Alberta's Gaming and Liquor Industries,* 2002-03.

_____. *Benefiting Albertans,* 2003.

_____. *The Use of the Internet for Gaming,* 2002.

Alberta Lotteries Review Committee. *New Directions for Lotteries and Gaming.* Chair: Judy Gordon, MLA (Stettler-Lacombe), Aug. 1995.

Canada. *Aboriginal Self-Government: The Government of Canada's Approach to Implementation of the Inherent Right and the Negotiation of Aboriginal Self-Government.* Ottawa: Minister of Public Works and Government Services, 1995.

_____. *Dominion of Canada Annual Report of the Department of Indian Affairs for the Year Ended 31st Dec. 1885.*

_____. *For Seven Generations: An Information Legacy of the Royal Commission on Aboriginal Peoples,* Vol. II. Ottawa: Canada Publications Group, 1996.

_____. *Special Committee on Indian Self-Government.* Ottawa: Queen's Printer, 1983.

_____. *Special Joint Parliamentary Committee of the Senate and the House of Commons appointed to examine and consider the Indian Act, 1946-1948.*

_____. *The Report of the Joint Parliamentary-Senate Committee Hearings on Indian Affairs in Canada.* Ottawa: Queen's Printer, 1961.

_____. *Towards Sustainable, Successful First Nation Communities: Good Governance, the Governance Continuum and Governance Programming Discussion Paper.* Ottawa: Self-Government Branch, Indian and Northern Affairs, 2000.

Center for Applied Research. *The Benefits and Costs of Indian Gaming in New Mexico.* New Mexico: Center for Applied Research, 1996.

Edmonton. *Report of the Executive Committee, Edmonton,* 1 May 2002.

Federation of Saskatchewan Indian Nations. *Saskatchewan Aboriginal Peoples in the 21st Century: Social, Economic and Political Changes and Challenges.* Regina: Print-West Publishing Services, 1997.

_____. *Indian Government.* 1977.

Manitoba Lotteries Foundation. *Fact Sheet: Native Gaming Commissions,* 2000.

_____. *Fact Sheet: Video Lottery Terminal Siteholder Agreements,* 2006.

_____. *Lottery Licenses for Reserves,* 2006.

Manitoba Office of the Auditor General. *Dakota Tipi First Nation Gaming Commission and First Nation Gaming Accountability in Manitoba.* Winnipeg, 2003.

Manitoba. *Debates and Proceedings,* June 1993, June 2000, March 2004, May 2005.

_____. *First Nations Gaming Policy Review Report* (Bostrom Report). Winnipeg, 1997.

Minnesota Indian Gaming Association. *The Economic Impact of Indian Gaming in Minnesota: A Review and Summary of the Economic Benefits of Tribal Gaming for Rural Counties and the State.* Minnesota, 1998.

New Mexico Indian Reservation Economic Study Group. *Indian Reservations & the New Mexico Economy: Reservation-based Gaming Enterprises,* 1999.

Nova Scotia Auditor General. *Crown Agencies and Corporations.* Halifax, 1998.

Nova Scotia Office of Aboriginal Affairs. *Business Plan, 2005-06* (Halifax: 2005).

Office of the Treaty Commissioner. *Statement of Treaty Issues: Treaties as a Bridge to the Future.* Saskatoon, 1998.

Ontario. *Debates and Proceedings,* 24 Aug. 1993.

San Diego Board of Supervisors. *Update on Impacts of Tribal Economic Development Projects in San Diego County.* California, 2002.

Saskatchewan. *Debates and Proceedings,* June 1993, May 1994.

Saskatoon City Council. *Minutes of Regular Meeting of City Council.* 9 and 24 Oct. 2001, 19 Nov. 2001, 2 and 16 Dec. 2002, 5 and 12 May 2003, 23 Aug. 2003, 8 Sept. 2003, 3 Nov. 2003.

Government, Industry, and Aboriginal Reports

Angus Reid Group, Inc. *Canadians' Attitudes Toward Aboriginal Gaming—Final Report* (1993).

Assembly of Manitoba Chiefs. "Planning Change," brief submitted to the Royal Commission on Aboriginal Peoples (1993).

_____. *Protocol and Structural Plan for First Nations Gaming Commission in Manitoba.* Submission to the Honourable Bonnie Mitchelson, Minister of Lotteries, and the Honourable Jim Downey, Minister of Northern Affairs. Winnipeg: 1993.

Bangsund, Dean A. and F. Leistritz. *Casinos in the Upper Midwest: A Discussion of the Impacts.* North Dakota: Department of Agricultural Economics, North Dakota State University, 1997.

Bear, Stearns and Co. Inc. *E-Gaming Revisited—At Odds With The World*. New York, 2000.

Coopers and Lybrand Consulting Group. *Report to the Ontario Casino Project: Ontario Casino Market and Economic Impact Study* (12 Aug. 1993).

Evans, M. K., and Evans, Carroll and Associates. *The Economic Impact of the Indian Gaming Industry in Wisconsin and Potential Impact of Modified Compact Term*. Wisconsin, 2002.

Evans, William, and Julie Topoleski. *The Social and Economic Impact of Native American Casinos*. Washington: Working Paper No. 9198, National Bureau of Economic Research, Sept. 2002.

Ferris, J., and T. Stirpe. *Gambling in Ontario: A report from a general population survey on gambling-related problems and opinions*. Ontario: Addiction Research Foundation, 1995.

Garrett, Thomas A. *Casino Gambling in America and its Economic Impacts*. Federal Reserve Bank of St. Louis, 2003.

Grant Thornton Chartered Accountants. *Review of First Nation Gaming Commissions: Sources and Uses of Funds*. Halifax: 2002.

Hawthorn, Harry. *Survey of the Contemporary Indians of Canada*, Vols. 1 and 2. Ottawa: Department of Indian Affairs and Northern Development, Indian Affairs Branch, 1966 and 1967.

Hewitt, David, and Dale Auger. *Firewatch on First Nations adolescent gambling*. Edmonton: Nechi Training, Research and Health Promotions Institute, 1995.

Hewitt, David. *Spirit of Bingoland: A study of problem gambling among Alberta Native people*. Edmonton: Nechi Training and Research and Health Promotions Institute/AADAC, 1994.

Hoenack, Stephen, A. G. Rens, and Stephen Hoenack and Associates. *Effects of the Indian-owned Casinos on Self-Generating Economic Development in non-urban areas of Minnesota*. Minnesota: Stephen A. Hoenack and Associates, 1995.

Holmes, W. H. *Twenty-fourth Annual Report at the Bureau of American Ethnology*. Washington, DC: US Government Printing Office, 1907.

Indian Tribes of Manitoba (Manitoba Indian Brotherhood). *Whabung — Our Tomorrows*. Manitoba, 1971.

Kiedrowski, L. *Native Gaming and Gambling in Canada. A report prepared for the Department of Indian and Northern Affairs*. Ottawa: Minister of Public Works and Government Services, 2001.

Leslie, John. *Commissions of Inquiry into Indian Affairs in the Canadas, 1828-1858: Evolving a corporate memory for the Indian Department*. Ottawa: Treaties and Historical Research Centre, DIAND, 1985.

Omnifacts Bristol Research. *Public Attitudes on Gaming in Nova Scotia*. Halifax, 2005.

Research and Health Promotions Institute. *Firewatch on Aboriginal Adolescent Gambling*. Edmonton, 1995.

Smith, Garry, and Harold Wynne. *VLT Gambling: A Preliminary Analysis, Final Report*. Edmonton: Alberta Gaming Research Institute, 2004.

T. W. Bell and Cato Institute. *Internet gambling: popular, inexorable, and (eventually) legal*. Washington, DC: Cato Institute, 1999.

Taylor, Jonathan B., Matthew B. Krepps, and Patrick Wang. *The National Evidence on the Socioeconomic Impacts of American Indian Gaming on non-Indian Communities.* Massachusetts: Harvard Project on American Indian Economic Development, 2000.

Taylor, Jonathon B., and Joseph P. Kalt. *American Indians on Reservations: A Databook of Socioeconomic Change Between the 1990 and 2000 Censuses.* Massachusetts: Harvard Project on American Indian Economic Development, 2005.

Thornton, Grant. "Review of First Nations Gaming Commissions: Sources and Uses of Funds Analysis." Prepared for the Province of Nova Scotia, Office of Aboriginal Affairs, Sept. 2000.

Wenger, Lorna, and Beth Mckechnie. *Fast Facts on Gambling.* Manitoba: Awareness and Information Unit of the Addictions Foundation of Manitoba, 1999.

Wiebe, Jamie. *Manitoba youth gambling prevalence study.* Manitoba: Addictions Foundation of Manitoba, 1999.

Secondary Sources

Books, Monographs, and Reports

Ashton, John B. *The History of Gambling in England.* Montclair, NJ: Patterson Smith, 1969.

Basham, Patrick, and Karen White. *Gambling with our Future? The Costs and Benefits of Legalized Gambling.* British Columbia. Fraser Institute, 2001.

Berdahl, Loleen Y. *The Impact of Gaming upon Canadian non-profits: A 1999 Survey of Gaming Grant Recipients.* Calgary: Canada West Foundation, 1999.

Berkhofer, Robert. *The White Man's Indian: Images of the American Indian from Columbus to the Present.* New York: Knopf, 1978.

Boger, Carl A. *The Effects of Native American Gaming on Businesses within the Wisconsin Dells Area.* Wisconsin: University of Wisconsin-Stout, 1995.

Boldt, Menno. *Surviving as Indians: The Challenge of Self-Government.* Toronto: University of Toronto, 1993.

Bordewich, Fergus M. *Killing the White Man's Indian: Reinventing Native Americans at the End of the Twentieth Century.* Toronto: Doubleday, 1997.

Boucher, Pierre. *Canada to the Seventeenth Century.* Montreal: 1883.

Brownlie, Robin. *A Fatherly Eye: Indian Agents, Government Power, and Aboriginal Resistance in Ontario, 1918-1939.* Don Mills, ON: Oxford, 2003.

Buckley, Helen. *From Wooden Ploughs to Welfare: Why Indian Policy Failed in the Prairie Provinces.* Montreal and Kingston: McGill-Queen's, 1992.

Cairns, Alan. *Citizens Plus: Aboriginal Peoples and the Canadian State.* Vancouver: UBC, 2000.

Campbell, Colin, Timothy Hartnagel, and Garry Smith. *The Legalization of Gambling in Canada.* Ottawa: Law Commission of Canada, 2005.

Carstensen, Fred, William Lott, Stan McMillen, Bobour Alimov, Na Li Dawson, and Tapas Ray. *The Economic Impact of the Mashantucket Pequot Tribal Nation Operations in Connecticut*. Storrs: University of Connecticut, 2000.

Carter, Sarah. *Lost Harvests: Prairie Indian Reserve Farmers and Government Policy*. Montreal and Kingston: McGill-Queen's, 1990.

Charlevoix, Paul. *Histoire de la Nouvelle France: Journal d'un Voyage etc., par P. de Charlevoix (Histoire de la Nouvelle France, Vol. III.)* Paris: 1744.

Clotfelter, Charles, and Philip Cook. *Selling Hope: State Lotteries in America*. Cambridge, MA: Harvard, 1989.

Culin, Stewart. *Games of the North American Indian*. Lincoln: University of Nebraska, 1992.

Deloria, Vine. *Red Earth, White Lies: Native Americans and the Myth of Scientific Fact*. New York: Scribners, 1995.

Dickason, Olive P. *Canada's First Nations: A History of Founding Peoples from Earliest Times*. Toronto: McClelland Stewart, 1994.

Du Ru, Paul. *Journal*. Translated by R. L. Butler. Chicago: Caxton Club, 1934.

Dyck, Noel. *What is the Indian Problem? Tutelage and Resistance in Canadian Indian Administration*. St. John's: Institute of Social and Economic Research, 1991.

Eisler, Kim Isaac. *Revenge of the Pequots: How a Small Native American Tribe Created the World's Most Profitable Casino*. New York: Simon and Shuster, 2001.

Ewers, John. *The Horse in Blackfoot Indian Culture*. Washington, DC: Smithsonian, 1955.

Findlay, John M. *People of Chance*. New York: Oxford, 1986.

Fox, C. *Economic Feasibility of Casino Gaming in the Province of Saskatchewan*. Reno: Fox Consulting, 1993.

Gabe, T. M. *The Economic Effects of Gaming on Rural Minnesota*. Minnesota: University of Minnesota, 1994.

Gabriel, Kathryn. *Gambler Way: Indian Gaming in Mythology, History, and Archaeology in North America*. Colorado: Johnson Books, 1996.

Gardner, Leigh, Joseph P. Kalt, and Katherine A. Spilde. *Cabazon, The Indian Gaming Regulatory Act, and the Socioeconomic Consequences of American Indian Governmental Gaming: A Ten-Year Review*. Cambridge, MA: Harvard Project on American Indian Economic Development, 2005.

Guth, Francis R. *Western Values Comparison in Gambling: With a Comparison to North American Aboriginal Views*. Sault Ste. Marie: Algoma, 1994.

Hardy, Robert. *Longbow: A Social and Military History*. London: Bois d'Arc, 1992.

Hawkes, David. *Negotiating Aboriginal Self-Government: Developments Surrounding the 1985 First Ministers' Conference*. Kingston: Institute of Intergovernmental Relations, Queen's University, 1985.

_____. *The Search for Accommodation*. Kingston: Institute of Intergovernmental Relations, 1987.

Hobsbawm, Eric, and Terrence Ranger (Eds.). *The Invention of Tradition*. Cambridge: Cambridge, 1983.

Hsu, Cathy H. C. *Legalized Casino Gambling in the United States: The Economic and Social Impact*. New York: Haworth Hospitality, 1999.

Hutchinson, Brian. *Betting the House: Winners, Losers, and the Politics of Canada's Gambling Obsession*. Toronto: Viking, 1999.

Hylton, John (Ed.). *Aboriginal Self-Government in Canada: Current Trends and Issues*. Saskatoon: Purich, 1994.

Isaac, Thomas. *Aboriginal Law: Cases, Materials and Commentary*. Saskatoon: Purich, 1999.

Jennings, Francis. *The Invasion of America: Indians, Colonialism, and the Kant of Conquest*. New York: W. W. Norton, 1976.

Johansen, Bruce E. *Life and Death in Mohawk Country*. Golden: North American, 1993.

Kelley, Robin. *First Nations Gambling Policy in Canada*. Calgary: Canada West Foundation, 2001.

Krech, Shepherd (Ed.). *The Subarctic Fur Trade: Native Social and Economic Adaptations*. Vancouver: UBC, 1984.

Kymlicka, Will. *Ethnic Associations and Democratic Citizenship*. Princeton: Princeton, 1997.

_____. *Finding our Way: Rethinking Ethnocultural Relations in Canada*. New York: Oxford, 1998.

_____. *Immigration, Citizenship, Multiculturalism: Exploring the Links*. Malden: Blackwell, 2003.

_____. *Multicultural Citizenship*. New York: Columbia, 2000.

_____. *Multicultural Citizenship: A Theory of Minority Rights*. New York: Oxford, 1995.

Labrosse, Michel. *The Lottery . . . From Jacques Cartier's Day to Modern Times*. Montreal: Stanke, 1985.

Le Clercq, Father Chrestien. *New Relations in Gaspesia*. Translated by W. F. Ganong. New York: Greenwood, 1968.

Light, Steven A., and Kathryn R. L. Rand. *Indian Gaming and Tribal Sovereignty: The Casino Compromise*. Kansas: University of Kansas, 2005.

Liner, R. P. *The Impact of Three Land Based Casinos in Louisiana*. Louisiana: Universe Inc., 2004.

Macklem, Patrick. *Indigenous Difference and the Constitution of Canada*. Toronto: University of Toronto, 2001.

Mandal, Veronique and Chris Vander Doelen. *Chasing Lightning: Gambling in Canada*. Toronto: United Church, 1999.

Mason, W. Dale. *Indian Gaming: Tribal Sovereignty and American Politics*. Norman: University of Oklahoma, 2000.

Mawhiney, A. M. *Toward Aboriginal Self-Government: Relations Between Status Indian Peoples and the Government of Canada, 1969-1984*. New York: Garland, 1994.

McGowan, Virgina, Judith Dressler, Gary Nixon & Misty Grimshaw, *Recent Research in the Socio-Cultural Domain of Gaming & Gambling: An Annotated Bibliography & Critical Overview*. Edmonton: Alberta Gaming Research Institute, 2000.

Mellis, Allison Fuss. *Riding Buffaloes and Broncos: Rodeo and Native Traditions in the Northern Great Plains*. Norman: University of Oklahoma, 2003.

Miller, J. R. *Shingwauk's Vision: A History of Native Residential Schools*. Toronto: University of Toronto, 1996.

Milloy, John S. *"A National Crime": The Canadian Government and the Residential School System, 1879 to 1986.* Winnipeg: University of Manitoba, 1999.

Morton, Suzanne. *At Odds: Gambling and Canadians, 1919-1969.* Toronto: University of Toronto, 2003.

Newhouse, David R., Kevin Fitzmaurice, and Yale D. Belanger. *Creating a Seat at the Table: Aboriginal Programming at Canadian Heritage.* Ottawa: Canadian Heritage, 2005.

Perrot, Nicolas. *Histoire de l'Amerique Septentrionale par M. de Bacqueville de la Potherie,* Vol. II. Paris, 1722.

Peters, Evelyn. *Aboriginal Self-Government in Canada: A Bibliography, 1986.* Kingston: Institute of Intergovernmental Relations, Queen's University, 1986.

Pettipas, Katherine. *Severing the Ties that Bind: Government Repression of Indigenous Religious Ceremonies on the Prairies.* Winnipeg: University of Manitoba, 1994.

Ponting, J. Rick, and Roger Gibbins. *Out of Irrelevance.* Toronto: Butterworths, 1980.

Ray, Arthur J. *Indians in the Fur Trade.* Toronto: University of Toronto, 1998.

Ray, Arthur J., and Donald Freeman. *"Give Us Good Measure": An Economic Analysis of Relations Between the Indians of Hudson's Bay Company Before 1763.* Toronto: University of Toronto, 1978.

Sagard, Gabriel. *The Long Journey to the Country of the Hurons.* Translated by H. H. Laughton. Toronto: The Champlain Society, 1939.

Smith, Garry, and Harold Wynne. *Gambling in Canada: Triumph, tragedy, or tradeoff? Gambling and crime in Western Canada: Exploring myth and reality.* Calgary: Canada West Foundation, 1999.

Stevens, Rhys. *Casinos in Alberta.* Lethbridge: Alberta Gaming Research Institute, 2004.

Taylor, Charles. *Multiculturalism and the Politics of Recognition.* Princeton: Princeton University, 1994.

_____. *Reconciling the Solitudes: Essays on Canadian Federalism and Nationalism.* Montreal and Kingston: McGill-Queen's, 1993.

Tough, Frank. *'As Their Natural Resources Fail': Native Peoples and the Economic History of Northern Manitoba, 1870-1930.* Vancouver: UBC, 1996.

Vennum, Thomas. *American Indian Lacrosse: Little Brother of War.* Washington, DC: Smithsonian, 1994.

Whitney, Alex. *Sports and Games the Indians Gave Us.* New York: McKay, 1977.

Wilkins, David E. *American Indian Politics and the American Legal System.* Lanham: Rowman and Littlefield, 2002.

Williams, Robert A. *The American Indian in Western Legal Thought: The Discourses of Conquest.* Oxford: Oxford, 1990.

Wotherspoon, Terry, and Vic Satchewich. *First Nations: Race, Class, and Gender Relations.* Scarborough: Nelson, 1993.

Articles and Book Chapters

Alberta Gaming Research Institute. *Research Reveals . . . An Update on Gambling Research in Alberta*, 4, No. 2. (Dec. 2004.)

Anders, Gary C. "The Indian Gaming Regulatory Act and Native American Development." *International Policy Review* 6, No. 1 (1996): 84-90.

Antell, J., A. Blevins, and K. Jensen. "American Indian Casino Gambling: Issues of Tribal Sovereignty and Economic Development." *Journal of Community Development Society* 31, No. 1 (2000): 1-18.

Belanger, Yale D. "Building the Opaskwayak Cree Nation (OCN) Economy: A Case Study in Resilience." *Journal of Aboriginal Economic Development*, 4, No. 2 (2005): 69-82.

_____. "Lacrosse Sticks." In *Native Americans and Sport*, Vol. 1. C. Richard King (Ed.), 179-181. New York: M. E. Sharpe, 2004.

_____. "The Morality of Aboriginal Gaming: A Concept in the Process of Definition." *Journal of Aboriginal Economic Development*, 2, No. 2 (2002): 25-36.

Belanger, Yale D., and David R. Newhouse. "Emerging From the Shadows: The Pursuit of Aboriginal Self-Government to Promote Aboriginal Well-Being." *Canadian Journal of Native Studies*, 24, No. 1 (2004): 129-222.

Bland, R. C., S. C. Newman, H. Orn, and G. Stebelsky. "Epidemiology of Pathological Gambling in Edmonton." *Canadian Journal of Psychiatry*, 38, No. 2 (1993): 108-112.

Boger, Carl. A., Daniel Spears, Karen Wolfe, and Li-chun Lin. "Economic Impacts of Native American Casino Gaming." In *Legalized Casino Gambling in the United States: The Economic and Social Impact*. Cathy H. C. Hsu (Ed). New York: Haworth, 1999.

Brock, Cathy. "Relations with Canadian Governments: Manitoba." In *For Seven Generations: An Information Legacy of the Royal Commission on Aboriginal Peoples* (CD-ROM). Ottawa: Libraxus, 1996.

Campbell, Colin S., "Parasites and Paradoxes: Legalized Casino Gambling in Alberta, Canada." In *Gambling papers: Proceedings of the Fifth National Conference on Gambling and Risk Taking*. W. R. Eadington (Ed.): 186-207. Reno: University of Nevada, 1981.

Campbell, Colin, and Garry Smith. "Canadian Gambling: Trends and Public Policy Issues." *The Annals of the American Academy of Political and Social Science*, 556 (1998): 22-35.

_____. "Gambling in Canada: From Vice to Disease to Responsibility: A Negotiated History." *Canadian Bulletin of Medical History*, 20, No. 1 (2003): 121-149.

Campisi, Jack. "The Emergence of the Mashantuket Pequot Tribe, 1637-1975." In *The Pequots in Southern New England*. Laurence M. Hauptman and James D. Wherry (Eds.). Norman: University of Oklahoma, 1990.

Christiansen, E. M. "Gambling and the American economy." *The Annals of the American Academy of Political and Social Science*, 556 (1998): 36-52.

Cohen, Kenneth. "A Mutually Comprehensible World? Native Americans, Europeans and Play in Eighteenth-Century America." *American Indian Quarterly*, 26, No. 2 (Winter 2001): 67-93.

Cordeiro, Eduardo E. "The Economics of Bingo: Factors Influencing the Success of Bingo Operations on American Indian Reservations." Harvard Project on American Indian Economic Development, 1989.

Cornell, Stephen, and Joseph Kalt. "Sovereignty and Nation Building: The Development Challenge in Indian Country Today." *American Indian Culture and Research Journal, 22,* No. 4 (Nov. 1998): 187-214.

Cruikshank, Julie. "Oral Traditions and Oral History: Reviewing Some Issues." *The Canadian Historical Review*, 75, No. 3 (1994): 403-418.

Culin, Stewart. "American Indian Games." *American Anthropologist*, 5, No. 1 (Jan.-Mar. 1903): 58-64.

d'Hauteserre, Ann-Marie. "Foxwoods Casino Resort: An Unusual Experiment in Economic Development." *Economic Geography* (1998): 112-121.

David, James, and Sam Otterstrom. "Growth of Indian Gaming in the United States." In *Casino Gambling in America: Origins, Trends, and Impact.* Klaus J. Meyer Arendt and Rudi Hartmann (Eds.). New York: Cognizant Communication Corp., 1998.

de Uriarte, John J. Bodinger. "Imagining the Nation with House Odds: Representing American Indian Identity at Mashantucket." *Ethnohistory,* 50, No. 3 (2003): 549-565.

Desbrisay, Dave. "The Gaming Industry in Aboriginal Communities." In *For Seven Generations: An Information Legacy of the Royal Commission on Aboriginal Peoples* (CD-ROM). Ottawa: Libraxus, 1996.

Dorsey, George A. "Certain Gambling Games of the Klamath Indians." *American Anthropologist,* 3, No. 1 (Jan.-Mar. 1901):14-27.

Duffie, M. K. "Goals for Fourth World Peoples and Sovereignty Initiatives in the United States and New Zealand." *American Indian Culture and Research Journal,* 22, No. 1 (1998): 183-212.

Dyck, Noel. "Representation and Leadership of a Provincial Indian Association." In *The Politics of Indianness: Case Studies and Ethnopolitics in Canada.* Adrian Tanner (Ed.). St. John's: Institute of Social and Economic Research, Memorial University, 1983.

Dyer, Lincoln S. "Southeastern Connecticut Economic Secrets Revealed." *The Connecticut Economic Digest,* 2, No. 5 (May 1997): 1-4.

Frits, Paul K. "Aboriginal Gaming — Law and Policy." In *Aboriginal Issues Today: A Legal and Business Guide.* Stephen B. Smart and Michael Coyle (Eds.). Vancouver: Self-Counsel, 1997.

Furniss, Elizabeth. "The Carrier Indians and the Politics of History." In *Native Peoples: The Canadian Experience.* R. Bruce Morrison and C. Roderick Wilson (Eds.). Toronto: Oxford, 1995.

Gailus, Jeff. "Valley of Ghosts." *Alberta Venture,* 9, No. 3 (April 2005).

Goldberg, Carole, and Duane Champagne. "Ramona Redeemed: The Rise of Tribal Political Power in California." *Wicazo Sa Review,* 17, No. 1 (2002).

Griffiths, M. "Pathological Gambling: A Review of the Literature." *Journal of Psychiatric and Mental Health Nursing,* No. 3 (1996): 347-353.

Grinols, E. L., "Incentives Explain Gambling's Growth." *Forum for Applied Research and Public Policy,* 11 (1996): 119-124.

Hallebone, Erica. "Women and the New Gambling Culture in Australia." *Society and Leisure*, 22, No. 1 (1999): 101-125.

Harvey, Sioux. "Two Models of Sovereignty: A Comparative History of the Mashantucket Pequot Tribal Nation and the Navajo Nation." *American Indian Culture and Research Journal*, 20, No. 1 (1996): 147-194.

Henriksson, Lennart E., and R. G. Lipsey. "Should Provinces Expand Gambling?" *Canadian Public Policy*, 25, No. 2 (1999): 259-275.

Hudson, Douglas. "The Okanagan Indians." In *Indian Peoples: The Canadian Experience*. R. Bruce Morrison and C. Roderick Wilson (Eds.). Toronto: Oxford, 1995.

Johnston, Darlene. "First Nations and Canadian Citizenship." In *Belonging: The Meaning and Future of Canadian Citizenship*. William Kaplan (Ed.). Montreal: McGill Queen's, 1993.

Jones, Janine, and Pam Dewey. "Little Brother of War." *Smithsonian Magazine*. (Dec. 1997).

Kelley, Robin. "First Nations Gambling Policy in Canada." *Gambling in Canada Research Report*, No. 12 (Calgary: Canada West Foundation, June 2001).

Korn, D. A. "Gambling Expansion in Canada: Implications for Health and Social Policy." *Canadian Medical Association Journal*, 163, No. 1 (2000): 61-64.

Landis, Richard. "Ktunaxa Kinbasket Tribal Council: Luxury Resort Leads to Economic Growth." In *Building Aboriginal and Northern Economies*. Ottawa: Indian and Northern Affairs Canada, 2003.

Larrimore, Mark. "Sublime Waste: Kant and the Destiny of the 'Races'." In *Civilization and Oppression*. Catherine Wilson (Ed). Calgary: University of Calgary, 1999.

Long, J. Anthony, Leroy Little Bear, and Menno Boldt. "Federal Indian Policy and Indian Self Government in Canada: An Analysis of a Current Proposal." *Canadian Public Policy*, 8, No. 2 (1982): 192-194.

Loo, Tina. "Dan Cranmer's Potlatch: Law as Coercion, Symbol, and Rhetoric in British Columbia, 1884-1951." *Canadian Historical Review*, 73, No. 2 (1992): 125-165.

Lyons, Oren C., and John C. Mohawk. "Sovereignty and Common Sense." *Cultural Survival Quarterly*, 17, No. 4 (1994): 58-60.

MacInnes, T. R. L. "History of Indian Administration in Canada." *Canadian Journal of Economics and Political Science*, 12, No. 3 (Aug. 1946): 387-394.

Mackie, Cam. "Some Reflections on Indian Economic Development." In *Arduous Journey: Canadian Indians and Decolonization*. J. Rick Ponting (Ed.). Toronto: McClelland and Stewart, 1986.

Maclean, M. "Gaming and Criminal Law Regulation." In *Gaming in British Columbia*. Vancouver: Pacific Business and Law Institute, 1996.

Marshall, Katherine. "The Gambling Industry: Raising the Stakes." *Perspectives* (Winter 1998): 7-11.

Maslove, Alan, with Carolyn Dittburner. "The Financing of Aboriginal Self-Government." In *Aboriginal Self-Government in Canada: Current Trends and Issues*. John Hylton (Ed.): 145-162. Saskatoon: Purich, 1994.

McGowan, Virginia, Lois Frank, Gary Nixon, and Misty Grimshaw. "Sacred and Secular Play in Gambling among Blackfoot Peoples of Southwest Alberta." In *Culture and the Gambling Phenomenon*. A. Blaszcyzcinski (Ed.). Sydney, Australia: National Association for Gambling Studies, 2002.

Merriam, Alan P. "The Hand Game of the Flathead Indians." *Journal of American Folklore*, 68, No. 269 (July-Sept. 1955): 313-324.

Milloy, John. "The Early Indian Acts: Developmental Strategy and Constitutional Change." In *As Long as the Sun Shines and Water Flows: A Reader in Canadian Native Studies*. A. S. Lussier and A. L. Getty (Eds.): 56-64. Vancouver: UBC Press, 1983.

Morse, Bradford. "Permafrost Rights: Aboriginal Self-Government and the Supreme Court in R. v. Pamajewon." *McGill Law Journal*, 47 (1997): 1011-1042.

Penner, Keith. "Their Own Place: The Case for a Distinct Order of Indian First Nation Government in Canada." In *Governments in Conflict? Provinces and Indian Nations in Canada*. Anthony J. Long and Menno Boldt (Eds.). Toronto: University of Toronto, 1988.

Ponting, J. Rick. "Economic Development Provisions of the New Claims Settlements." In *Arduous Journey: Canadian Indians and Decolonization*. J. Rick Ponting (Ed.). Toronto: McClelland and Stewart, 1986.

_____. "Historical Overview and Background, Part II: 1970-96." In *First Nations in Canada: Perspectives on Opportunity, Empowerment, and Self-Determination*. J. Rick Ponting (Ed.). Toronto: McGraw-Hill Ryerson, 1997.

Pruden, Hal. "An Overview of the Gambling Provisions in Canadian Criminal Law and First Nations Gambling." *Journal of Aboriginal Economic Development*, 2, No. 2 (2002).

Reagan, Albert B., and F. W. Waugh. "Some Games of the Bois Fort Ojibwa." *American Anthropologist*, 21, No. 3 (July-Sept. 1919): 264-278.

Ribis, N., and M. Traymar. "Raising the Stakes: Raises the Issues." *Cultural Survival Quarterly*, 19, No. 4 (1996): 11.

Rose, Nelson. "The Future of Indian Gaming." *Journal of Gambling Studies*, 8 (1992): 383-399.

Sanders, Douglas. "The Indian Lobby." In *And No One Cheered. Federalism, Democracy and the Constitution Act*. K. Banting and R. Simeon (Eds.). Toronto: Methuen, 1983.

Seelig, Michael, and Julie Seelig. "'Place Your Bets!' On Gambling, Government and Society." *Canadian Public Policy*, 24, No. 1 (1998): 91-106.

Severs, Laura. "Casino Project Coming up Aces for Enoch: Proposed Resort Predicted to be an Economic Boom." *Business Edge*, 4, No. 26 (8 Aug. 2004).

Siggner, Andrew J. "A Socio-Demographic Profile of Indians in Canada." In *Out of Irrelevance*. J. Rick Ponting and Roger Gibbins (Eds.). Toronto: Butterworths, 1980.

_____. "The Socio-Demographic Conditions of Registered Indians." In *Arduous Journey: Canadian Indians and Decolonization*. J. Rick Ponting (Ed.). Toronto: McClelland and Stewart, 1986.

Skinner, Alanson. "Notes on the Plains Cree." *American Anthropologist*, 16, No. 1 (Jan. Mar. 1914): 68-87.

Steele, Debora. "Enoch's Future Full of Hope and Promise." *Sweetgrass*, 18 Oct. 2004.

Twetten, Daniel. "Public Law 280 and the Indian Gaming Regulatory Act: Could Two Wrongs Ever Be Made into a Right?" *Journal of Criminal Law and Criminology*, 90, No. 4 (Summer 2000): 1317-1352.

Wilson, Rev. J. W. "Report on the Blackfoot Tribes." In *Report of the Fifty-seventh Meeting of the British Association for the Advancement of Science*. London: 1888.

Dissertations and Theses

Belanger, Yale D. "Seeking a Seat at the Table: A Brief History of Indian Political Organizing in Canada, 1870-1951." Ph.D. diss. Trent University, 2005.

Campbell, Colin S. "Canadian Gambling Legislation: The Social Origins of Legalization." Ph.D. diss. Simon Fraser University, 1995.

Campbell, Karen. "Community Life and Governance: Early Experiences of Mnjikaning First Nation with Casino Rama." M.A. thesis. University of Manitoba, 1999.

Carberry, Christine. "When Times are Tight: Lotteries, Casinos and Revenue Policy in the American States and Canadian Provinces." M.A. thesis. University of Western Ontario, 1995.

Cattelino, Jessica R. "High Stakes: Seminole Sovereignty in the Casino Era." Ph.D. diss. New York University, 2004.

Churchill, Elizabeth, "Tsuu T'ina: A History of a First Nation's Community, 1890- 1940." Ph.D. diss. University of Calgary, 2000.

Dockstator, Mark S. "Toward an Understanding of Aboriginal Self-Government: A Proposed Theoretical Model and Illustrative Factual Analysis." LL.D. York University, 1993.

Janter-White, Marilee. "Beyond Modernism: Anishinaabe Abstraction, Activism, and Traditionalism." Ph.D. diss. University of California, 1998.

Lackenbauer, P. Whitney. "Vanishing Indian, Vanishing Military: Military Training and Aboriginal Lands in the Twentieth Century." Ph.D. diss. University of Calgary, 2004.

Leslie, John F. "Assimilation, Integration, or Termination? The Development of Canadian Indian Policy, 1943-1963." Ph.D. diss. Carleton University, 1999.

Little, Margo. "The Moral Dilemma of High Stakes Gambling in Native Communities." M.A. thesis. Laurentian University, 1997.

Nilson, Cathy, "The FSIN-Province of Saskatchewan Gaming Partnership: 1995 to 2002." M.A. thesis. University of Saskatchewan, 2004.

Osborne, J. A. "The Legal Status of Lottery Schemes in Canada: Changing the Rules of the Game." LL.M. thesis, University of British Columbia, 1989.

Pompana, Yvonne. "Devolution to Indigenization: The Final Path to Assimilation of First Nations." M.A. thesis. University of Manitoba, 1997.

Skea, Warren. "Time to Deal: A Comparison of the Native Casino Gambling Policy in Alberta and Saskatchewan." Ph.D. diss. University of Calgary, 1997.

Newspapers and Periodicals

Alberni Valley Times

Alberta Venture

Associated Press

Barrie Examiner

Calgary Herald

Calgary Real Estate News

Canadian Press

Cochrane Eagle

Cranbrook Daily Townsman

Daily Bulletin

Dreamspeaker

Drum

The Economist

Edmonton Journal

Edmonton Sun

Gambling Magazine

The Globe and Mail

Grassroots

The Hamilton Spectator

The Hartford Courant

Indian Country Today

Kitchener Waterloo Record

Lake Windermere Valley Echo

Lethbridge Herald

The Montreal Gazette

The National Post

North Bay Nugget

Ontario Birch Bark

Orillia Packet and Times

The Ottawa Citizen

Penticton Herald

Raven's Eye

Saskatoon StarPhoenix

St. Catharines Standard

Sudbury Star

Sweetgrass

Toronto Star

Toronto Sun

Trail Times

Vancouver Sun

Victoria Times Colonist

Windspeaker

Winnipeg Free Press

Winnipeg Sun

Presentations

Birdstone, Denise. "Community Presentation." In *For Seven Generations: An Information Legacy of the Royal Commission on Aboriginal Peoples* (CD-ROM). Libraxus, Ottawa, 1996.

Blaszczynski, Alex. "A History of Gambling." Paper Presented at the National Conference on Gambling, St. Edmunds's Private Hospital and IPS Employee Assistance, Darling Harbour. Sydney, Australia, 31 Oct. 1996.

Buller, Ed. "Community Healing Processes: Investments and Benefits." Paper presented at Best Practice Interventions in Corrections for Indigenous People Conference convened by the Australian Institute of Criminology. Sydney, Australia, 8-9 Oct. 2001.

Hosgood, Chris. "Poker and the Police in Early Twentieth Century Alberta." Paper presented at the Western Social Science Association Annual Conference. Las Vegas, NV, 10 April 2003.

Jones, Chief Roger. Presentation made before the Royal Commission on Aboriginal Peoples. Public Consultation Process. 1 June 1993. Record 7/142.

Kalt, Joseph. Statement Before National Gambling Impact Study Commission. 16 March 1996.

Koppang, Chuck. "Native Gaming in Manitoba." Paper Presented at the Conference on First Nations Gambling in British Columbia. Duncan, BC, 30 Sept. and 1 Oct. 1992.

Newhouse, David R. "Hidden in Plain Sight: Aboriginal Contributions to Canada and Canadian Identity: Creating a New Indian Problem." Paper delivered before the 30th Anniversary Canadian Studies Conference. First Nations — First Thoughts. University of Edinburgh, Scotland, 5-7 July 2001.

Pierre, Sophie "Self Government — The Ktunaxa/Kinbasket Experience." Talk delivered before Speaking Truth to Power, III: Self Government: Options and Opportunities, sponsored by the BC Treaty Commission, 14-15 March 2002.

Ponting, J. Rick. "The Paradox of On-Reserve Casino Gambling: Musings of a Nervous Sociologist." Revised version of a paper prepared for the Gambling in Canada: The Bottom Line Conference, 2nd National Symposium on Gambling, Simon Fraser University Gambling Studies Program. Vancouver, BC, Oct. 27-30, 1993.

Roberts, Carl. "Community Presentation." In *For Seven Generations: An Information Legacy of the Royal Commission on Aboriginal Peoples* (CD-ROM). Libraxus, Ottawa, 1996, record No. 5444.

Sinclair, Murray C. "Presentation to the Federal Task Force on Indian Gaming." In *Gaming on Reserves: Discussion Paper Prepared by a Departmental Task Force*. Ottawa: Department of Indian Affairs and Northern Development, 1987.

Tsuu T'ina First Nation Chief Sanford Big Plume's Speech to the Calgary Chamber of Commerce (19 Nov. 2004). www.calgarychamber.com/abcalcoc/doc.nsf/files/ 9658DAB9ADB8C9AC 7256F55007BD291/$file/Chief%20Big%20Plume%20Speech %20(PDF).pdf.

Case Law

Calder v. The Attorney General of British Columbia [1973] 34 D.L.R. (3d) 145 (also reported: [1973] S.C.R 313).

California v. Cabazon Band of Mission Indians 480 U.S. 202 (1987).

Cherokee Nation v. Georgia (1831) 30 U.S. 1.

Factum of the Intervenor, Congress of Aboriginal Peoples, *Lovelace v. Ontario and the Chiefs of Ontario*. Court File No. 26165.

Harker v. Regina (City). [1995], CanLII 3906.

Johnson v. Mcintosh (1823) 8 Wheaton, 543.

Labour Relations Board, Saskatchewan. *Saskatchewan Joint Board, Retail, Wholesale and Department Store Union v. Saskatchewan Indian Gaming Authority Inc. carrying on business as the Painted Hand Casino*. LRB File Nos. 067-03, 068-03 and 069-03 (29 Aug., 2003).

Lovelace v. Ontario [1998] 2 C.N.L.R. 36; [1997] 33 O.R. (3D) 735 (Ont. C.A.).

Lovelace v. Ontario [2000] 1 S.C.R 950 (S.C.C.)

R. v. Furtney [1991] 3 S.C.R 91.

R. v. Gladue & Kirby [1999] 30 C.C.C. (Alta. Prov. Ct.) 308.

R. v. Pamajewon, [1996] 2 S.C.R. 821.

R. v. Powley [2003] S.C.C. 43.

R. v. Starnet Communications International, Inc., [2001] (B.C.S.C.) 125795-1.

Saskatchewan Indian Gaming Authority Inc. v. the National Automobile, Aerospace, Transportation and General Workers Union of Canada and the Saskatchewan Labour Relations Board [2000] SKCA 138.

Seminole Tribe of Florida v. Florida (1996) 517 U.S. 44.

Worcester v. Georgia (1832) 6 Peters 515, 31 U.S. 530.

Internet and Multi-Media Sources

Aboriginal and Northern Affairs. "Manitoba Treaty Land Entitlement Overview." www.gov.mb.ca/ana/tle_overview.html. Accessed 8 Dec. 2004.

Alberta Gaming and Liquor Commission. "The Use of the Internet for Gaming." www.aglc.gov.ab.ca/pdf/lpr/LPR_Report_15-Internet_Gaming.pdf. Accessed 25 March 2004.

Arctic Games. www.ravenstrick.com/games.htm. Accessed 5 Jan. 2005.

Assembly of First Nations. "AFN National Chief Addresses First Nations Gaming, (2000)." www.afn.ca/Press%20Realeases%20and%20. . . ches/afn_national_chief_ad-dresses_fir.htm.

Canada. Statement of the Government of Canada on Indian Policy, 1969. www.fcpp.org/publications/worth_a_look/spr/native.html. Accessed 3 Oct. 2000.

Canadian Environmental Assessment Registry. www.ceaaacee.gc.ca/050/Viewer_e.cfm?SrchPg=3andCEAR_ID=4572. Accessed 30 Jan. 2006.

Catania, Frank. "Internet Gaming Regulation: The Kahnawake Experience." www.cataniaconsulting.com/kahnawake.pdf. Accessed 22 March 2004.

CBC News Online. "Accounts Call for RCMP Investigation of Stoney Reserve." www.cbc.ca/story/canada/national/1998/12/04/stoney981204.html. Accessed 30 Jan. 2006.

_____. "Calgary Ring Road to be Built." 13 March 2005. cnews.canoe.ca/CNEWS/Canada/2005/03/13/959502-cp.html.

_____. "Casino Decision Put off for Six Weeks." http://edmonton.cbc.ca/regional/servlet/View?filename=ed_casino20030710.

_____. "Council Accused of Racism in Casino Debate." 9 July 2003. http://edmonton.cbc.ca/regional/servlet/View?filename=ed_casino20030709.

_____. "Enoch Casino Decision Delayed Again." 20 Aug. 2003. edmonton.cbc.ca/regional/servlet/View?filename=ed_enoch20030820.

_____. "First Native-run Casino Gets Go Ahead." 16 April 2004. calgary.cbc.ca/regional/servlet/View?filename=ca_enoch20040416.

_____. "Headingley Council Says No to Casino." 28 June 2000. www.cbc.ca/story/news/national/2000/06/28/mb-casino.html. Accessed 7 Feb. 2005.

_____. "Tsuu T'ina OK Casino." 2 July 2004. http://edmonton.cbc.ca/regional/servlet/View?filename=ed_casino20040702.

Culin, Stewart. www.ahs.uwaterloo.ca/museum/archive/culin. Accessed 22 Dec. 2003.

Greater Toronto Area. www.greater.toronto.on.ca/ataglance/mapprofile.html. Accessed 6 Feb. 2005.

Hartford Connecticut Population and Demographics Resources. http://hartford.areaconnect.com/statistics.htm. Accessed 27 Jan. 2006.

Henriksson, Lennart E. "Government, Gambling and Healthy Populations." Canadian Centre on Substance Abuse. 1999. www.ccsa.ca/plweb-cgi/fastweb.exe?getdoc+view1+General+232+21++First Nations%20gambling.

Indian and Northern Affairs Canada. "Message from the Confederacy of Treaty Six First Nations." www.ainc-inac.gc.ca/ab/ayr04/ayrty6_e.html. Accessed 27 Jan. 2006.

Indian Association of Alberta. "Indian Chiefs of Alberta, Citizens Plus." 1970. www.transcanadas.ca/fee.shtml. Accessed 27 Jan. 2006.

Kyer, C. Ian, and Danielle Hough. "Is Internet Gaming Legal in Canada? A Look at Starnet." *Canadian Journal of Law and Technology* 1, No. 1. http://cjit.dal.ca. Accessed 22 Nov. 2003.

Lee, Bryce. "Canada Calling." ROC Archives. Oct. 1999. www.trainweb.org/canadianrailways/CanadaCalling/October1999.html.

Lipton, Michael D. "Internet Gaming in Canada." Presentation made before Global Gaming Exposition. Las Vegas, Nevada (17 Sept. 2003). www.gaminglawmasters.com/jurisdictions/canada/Internet.Gaming-Speech.htm.

Manitoba. "City Population." www.citypopulation.de/Canada-Manitoba.html. Accessed 27 Jan. 2006.

Manitoba. "Employment Opportunities Result from Casino Training Program." 15 Feb. 2002. www.gov.mb.ca/ana/pdf/employment.html. Accessed 16 June 2005.

Massachusetts Statistics and Demographics (US Census 2000). boston.areaconnect.com/statistics.htm. Accessed 27 Jan. 2006.

McFarland, Andrew David. "Indian Games." www.authorama.com/indian-games.html. Accessed 30 Dec. 2003.

New York Population and Demographics Resources. newyork.areaconnect.com/statistics.htm. Accessed 6 Feb. 2005.

Nova Scotia. "Better Balance: Nova Scotia's First Gaming Strategy." www.gov.ns.ca/govt/gamingstrategy/BetterBalance.pdf/. Accessed 31 Jan. 2006.

Nova Scotia. "Gaming Strategy: Backgrounder." www.gov.ns.ca/govt/gamingstrategy/#back. Accessed 31 Jan. 2006.

Ontario Trillium Foundation. www.trilliumfoundation.org/.

Opaskwayak Cree Nation. "History of the Opaskwayak Cree Nation." www.opaskwayak.mb.ca/history.php. Accessed 13 May 2005.

Rhode Island Population and Demographics Resources. Providence. http://providence.areaconnect.com/statistics.htm. Accessed 27 Jan. 2006.

Shawanaga First Nations. "Ojibway Territory." www.shawanaga.com.

Swan Lake First Nation. www.swanlakefirstnation.ca/. Accessed 7 Dec. 2004.

Swan Lake Reserve Profile. http://sdiprod2.inac.gc.ca/FNProfiles/FNProfiles_PrintForm.asp?BAND_NUMBER=293andBAND NAME=Swan+LakeandES=AC TandQ=3. Accessed 8 Dec. 2004.

Teamsters Canada Online. Local 938. "Teamsters organizing employees at Casino Rama." http://news.teamsters canada.org/news.php?id=240. Accessed 1 May 2005.

UNI Global Union. "Casino workers ratify first contract at Great Blue Heron." www.union-network.org/UNICasinos.nsf/0/4077ec5be6caa599c1256ee50024d66d?OpenDocument. Accessed 1 June 2005.

Union of Nova Scotia Indians. www.gov.ns.ca/abor/pubs/200506%20OAA%20BP%20Final%20Draft%20mar.pdf.

Union of Ontario Indians. "Maintain, Protect, Enhance: A Discussion Paper on Casino Rama," p. 6. www.anishinabek.ca/uoi/pdf/FINAL Casino%20Rama.pdf.

INDEX

D

Dakota Tipi Nation 143-46, 150

de Brébeuf, Jean 27, 32

Delta Hotels and Resorts 152-53

Delorme, Cory 160-61

Department of Indian Affairs (DIA) 37, 63, 113, 134

Department of Indian Affairs and Northern Development (DIAND) 113

Depression, the 47

dice games, historically, 25, 29, 34, 35-36, 45

discrimination 56, 64, 95-96

Doer, Gary 120, 140-42, 144

Du Ru, Paul 33

Dutch Lerat affair 110-12, 122, 159, 171

E

Eagle Lake First Nation 86, 87, 93-94, 168

economic development, Aboriginal 90, 114, 116, 118, 136, 139, 142, 155, 156, 167, 170; gaming as a mechanism for 12, 13, 23, 24, 68, 72, 69, 103, 106, 122, 169, 171; and inadequate government help 12-13, 22, 67, 104; on reserves 14, 15, 55, 56, 60-61, 63, 71, 74, 75, 77, 88, 101, 109, 117, 121, 129, 132, 157-58, 168. See further Harvard Project

economic stability 13, 77, 82, 108, 152, 171

Edmonton, AB 21, 52, 53, 123, 126, 129-32, 139, 162. See also Enoch

education 19, 44, 46, 71, 106, 110, 112, 135, 170; services and programs 14, 38, 59, 60, 68, 76, 79, 99, 101, 109, 129, 133

Emerald Casino 147-148, 149

employment 18, 56, 63, 84, 89, 101, 155, 173; off reserve 12, 63-64, 133. Compare unemployment, which see

English influence on gaming and gaming laws 35-36, 42, 43, 44

Enoch Cree First Nation 113, 124, 125, 126-27, 129-32; Casino, AB 21, 123, 137, 139, 162

Ewers, John 32

F

factionalism 19, 98, 100, 13 8, 145

failed/ failing gaming initiatives 17, 119, 123, 137, 150, 142-42, 154-55, 169

fairs and gambling 44, 46-47, 52, 53

federal jurisdiction over gaming 21, 48, 52, 74, 86, 99, 120, 159

Federal Bureau of Investigation (FBI) 75

Federation of Saskatchewan Indian Nations (FSIN) 55-56, 60, 70-71, 103-7, 108-9, 110, 121, 147, 149, 169

financial benefits of gaming. See for-profit gaming.

First Nations Gaming Commission (FNGC) 113, 115, 126

First Nations Casino Project (FNCP) 116

First Nations Development Fund 129

First Nations' jurisdiction over gaming 84-85, 91, 94, 108, 109, 115, 120-22, 142, 164

First Nations people, as one ethnicity among many 57-59, 168. Compare assimilation

fishing rights 13, 62, 101

for-profit gaming 49, 50, 51, 52-53, 54, 56, 66, 105, 115, 123, 128, 130, 157; First Nations' 16, 23, 66, 71, 75-77, 82, 83-84, 85, 87, 88-89, 108, 132, 136, 145-46, 153, 155, 156-57, 159, 167, 170; historic uses 42, 45, 47. Compare charitable gaming, which see

Fox Consulting 108

Foxwoods Resort Casino 70, 81, 91, 119, 126, 143, 168

G

Gabriel, Kathryn 25, 32

gambling: *see* gaming; wagering

games of chance 25, 27-29, 30-31, 32, 33, 34, 39-40, 41, 43, 44-46, 50, 52, 74, 75, 113; versus games of skill 25, 29, 30, 35-36, 50. *See separately* archery; bingo; bowl games; card games; counting games; dice games; horse racing; lacrosse; "snow snake"; straw games.

gaming: as cultural interaction 22, 29, 31, 33, 34; as a disease 47; as an economic development tool 12, 13, 23, 24, 68, 72, 69, 103, 106, 121-22, 169, 171; as entertainment 18, 24, 27, 35, 38, 52, 53, 168; as immoral/ amoral 28, 36, 38, 42, 44, 45, 47, 106,167; impact of 17, 19, 53, 81, 102, 108, 116, 127, 132, 137, 148, 170, 173; and murder 32, 33, 36; negative image of 27-28, 36, 42; negative reaction to 16, 17, 22, 45, 51, 52, 74, 102, 111, 139, 150, 154-55, 159, 169; as a pastime 25, 26, 27, 30; and political stability 12-13, 173; as a religious rite 26, 27, 31, 32, 39; as self-sufficiency 12, 60, 156; social views of 53, 68, 81; spiritual role of 31, 32, 38, 168; as a vice 35, 36, 42, 50; as wealth distribution mechanism, historically 31, 33, 38. *See also* casinos; charitable gaming; fairs; economic development; failed gaming initiatives; for-profit gaming; games of chance; jurisdiction; lotteries; problem gaming; resistance to gaming; revenue sharing; social issues; slot machines; support for gaming; urban reserves; wagering

Gaming Act of 1802: 44

gaming agreements 84, 92, 93, 100, 108, 109, 110, 112, 114, 115, 14345, 151, 156, 157-59, 169, 172

Gaming Framework Agreement (GFA) 109, 112, 152

Gaming Control Act 121, 141

gaming legislation 44, 46, 47, 86, 128; federal 41-42, 48-49, 50-52, 53, 125, 164-65; provincial 41, 87, 93, 95, 122, 125; US 71, 72, 81, 82. *See also* jurisdiction

gaming policy 21, 22, 71, 84, 102, 118; provincial 16, 52-53, 85, 104-5, 108, 114, 115-16, 124, 125, 126-28, 129, 140, 143, 144, 167. *See also* legislation. *See specifically* Bostrom Report

Gardner, Arnold and Allan 86-87

Gibbins, Roger 64

Glen, J. A. 61

Gold Eagle Casino, SK 12, 109, 160

Golden Eagle First Nation Charitable Casino, ON 156, 166

Gordon, Judy, 127-28

Great Blue Heron Charity Casino, ON 155-56, 162, 166

Greater Toronto Area (GTA) 119

H

Hamilton, Doreen 110-11

hand games 17, 33

Harris, Mike 84, 92-93, 97, 100, 169

Harvard Project on American Indian Economic Development 18, 77. *See further* Cornell, Stephen

Hawthorn-Tremblay Report 57, 58, 60

Hayward, Richard (Skip) 78-81

Headingley, MB 139-41, 167

health 13, 14, 85, 99, 109, 129, 135, 161, 168, 170; of the community 34, 68

Henry VIII and gaming 25, 36

Hewitt, David 20-21

Holmes, W. H. 26-27

horse racing/ equestrian events 21, 25, 28, 35, 39, 40, 44-45, 47, 153, 157

Hosgood, Chris 45-46

housing, on-reserve 38, 64, 65, 78, 80, 85-86, 133, 143, 144, 156, 157

hunting 13, 14, 34, 62, 89-90, 96, 101, 134

Huron Nation, historically 28, 31, 36, 89

resistance/opposition to gaming: political resistance 12, 17, 47, 51, 53, 102, 105, 106, 127, 165, 169. *See further* Miller Bill; moratorium on gaming

social resistance 12, 16, 17, 24, 42, 44-45, 46, 51, 68, 104, 115, 128, 131, 139, 141-42, 147-49, 159, 165

Retail, Wholesale and Department Store Union – Saskatchewan Joint Board (RWDSU) 160-161

revenue-sharing 16, 91-92, 97-98, 99-100, 101, 109, 112, 128-29, 169, 172; agreements 95, 96, 98, 116, 173. *See further* gaming

rights, Aboriginal 37-38, 59, 84, 87, 93-95, 95-97, 100, 127, 169. *See further* self government; sovereignty

Roberts, Carl 169, 171-72

Romanow, Roy 104-5, 107, 108, 109, 169

Royal Bank of Canada 153, 154, 155

Royal Colonization Lottery 43

Royal Commission 45, 48

Royal Commission on Aboriginal Peoples (RCAP) 13, 55, 87, 101, 168, 169, 173

Royal Canadian Mounted Police (RCMP) 115, 138; and Dakota Tipi 144; and OCN 113; and Stoney 135; and White Bear 107, 108

Royal North West Mounted Police (RNWMP) 46

S

Sagard, Gabriel 28

Sanderson, Sol 56

Saskatchewan Indian Gaming Authority (SIGA) 16, 110-13, 147-48, 149, 169, 171; and unions 159-60, 162

Saskatchewan Liquor and Gaming Authority (SLGA) 105-6, 110-12

Saskatoon Tribal Council (STC) 146-47, 149

Secretary of the Interior (US) 76

self-government 13-16, 18, 22, 55-56, 56-60, 63, 66-69, 71, 73, 77, 87-88, 93, 94-95, 103, 104, 106, 108, 152, 168, 170, 173

self-sufficiency 60-61, 156, 170, 173

Seminole Tribe 70-71, 72, 74, 77, 80, 168

settlements 16, 80, 130

Severe Acute Respiratory Syndrome (SARS) 98, 153, 165, 171

Shawanaga First Nation 84-85, 87-88, 93-95, 100, 168

Shepherd, Bernie 107-8

Siggner, Andrew 64

Skea, Warren 109

slot machines 41, 52, 75, 0-82, 102, 107, 111, 123, 125, 135, 143, 144, 146, 152, 153, 156

Smith, Garry: *see* Campbell, Colin

smoking: *see* anti-smoking

"snow snake" 31, 33, 40

social assistance 64, 117, 145

social issues related to casinos 16, 17, 18, 19, 21, 45, 53, 72, 89, 98, 102, 108, 116, 137, 158, 170

social programs 13, 15, 20, 37, 47, 58, 103, 129, 133, 135, 144, 146, 157, 166, 167, 171

socio-economic: benefits 18, 22, 24; conditions on reserves 55, 57, 63, 84, 88, 106, 114

South Beach Casino 119-21

sovereignty, Aboriginal 58, 87, 93, 126, 164-65, 166, 168, 171; US tribal 71-75, 77, 78-79, 80, 82, 103, 162

Special Joint Parliamentary Committee (SJC) 57, 62

sports versus games, historically 34-40

statistics 15, 18, 101, 171: employment 16, 64-65, 81, 97, 106, 133; gaming 19-21, 68, 71, 81-82, 91-92, 101-2, 109, 123, 138-39, 170; income 17, 64-65, 106; population 63-64, 119

Starnet Communications International Inc (SCI) 163-64